If These WALLS *Could* TALK:

COLORADO ROCKIES

Stories from the Colorado Rockies Dugout, Locker Room, and Press Box

Drew Goodman and Benjamin Hochman

30 YEARS

TRIUMPH
B O O K S

Library of Congress Cataloging-in-Publication Data
Names: Goodman, Drew, author. | Hochman, Benjamin, author.
Title: Colorado Rockies : stories from the Colorado Rockies dugout, locker room, and press box / Drew Goodman and Benjamin Hochman.
Description: Chicago, Illinois : Triumph Books, 2019. | Series: If these walls could talk
Identifiers: LCCN 2018046934 | ISBN 9781629376356 (paperback)
Subjects: LCSH: Colorado Rockies (Baseball team)—History. Colorado Rockies (Baseball team)—Anecdotes. | BISAC: SPORTS & RECREATION / Baseball / General. | TRAVEL / United States / West / Mountain (AZ, CO, ID, MT, NM, UT, WY).
Classification: LCC GV875.C78 G65 2019 | DDC 796.357/640978883—dc23
LC record available at https://lccn.loc.gov/2018046934

This book is available in quantity at special discounts for your group or organization. For further information, contact:
    Triumph Books LLC
    814 North Franklin Street
    Chicago, Illinois 60610
    (312) 337–0747
    www.triumphbooks.com

Printed in U.S.A.

ISBN: 978-1-62937-635-6

Design by Sue Knopf

Photos courtesy of AP Images unless otherwise indicated

Drew's Diary photo courtesy of AT&T SportsNet

CONTENTS

FOREWORD

The Colorado Rockies are a true regional franchise, and that's pretty cool stuff. It's a wide-ranging fanbase—and it's a beautiful part of the country, which goes without saying. The fans are extremely loyal. You can tell from Opening Day, which means so much to Colorado baseball fans. And in 2007 I was the manager of the San Diego Padres during that playoff push, and what I saw from the Rockies fans was awesome.

And the ballpark! Wow, it's been 25 years and it still looks like a fresh, new facility. Having watched it during the last couple years, I'm really impressed by the work they do to maintain it, the commitment to ballpark operations, and all the engineers and people who work on the stadium on a daily basis. It's a tremendous park that's held up for 25 years, and I suspect it's gonna hold up for another 25 years. I admire the overall commitment and love that people have for this park, this part of the country, and their sports teams.

What made the Rockies job desirable? From the interview process, the passion I felt from owner Dick Monfort and general manager Jeff Bridich and the front office was really impressive to me. It was desirable because of how they felt about the Rockies, about baseball, about winning, and their goals to win. The entire state of the organization from top to bottom made this a great job.

The ownership grew the front office. And what I saw from afar about their direction and philosophy on a number of things stood out, especially where they were headed with their pitching programs and the present group of position players, as well as the state of their farm system.

I love this game. It's wonderful for a number of reasons. What I like is that everybody has played baseball at some point. Whether as a young kid, whether it's at recess at school, whether it's organized, whether it's a picnic out front in the driveway, most every boy, girl, man, and woman has played catch, caught a fly ball, fielded a grounder, swung a bat, hit a ball. That's why I think that everybody can relate to our game.

For me, at this level, I still think that the competitive nature of the hitter versus pitcher is a great battle. And everything that goes into winning baseball—defense, hitting, pitching, base running—is special to me.

Early on as a player, I tried to understand all sides of everybody in this game—from the front office to the media. Everybody has a different perspective and job; it's truly all of us who make up this game. And it's everybody working together that makes this the great game it is.

There are people in this game who love it as much as I do.

Even before I was the Rockies manager, I got to know Drew Goodman from watching Rockies telecasts while channel surfing through games, as all baseball people do. I always liked Drew's style. When I was with the Padres, our teams were in the same division, so even then I grew to appreciate and admire Drew's work as a broadcaster.

I also know that Drew has a job to do. He has to be honest, fair, and concise about the good and the bad. There are listeners out there who want the story, and I get that. But he does it in a fair way—and I hear it from my family—he pumps us up but lets us know when things aren't right. It's a balance and a talent.

I'd get to know Drew at the pressers for the visiting manager and I was very comfortable with his presence, his knowledge, his interaction, and his feel. His understanding of the athlete and the manager and the coach, the total comprehensive feel of what we do, is what stands out. For us in uniform, it's a cool thing. Drew gets it. And for me, there's not much of a bigger compliment that I pay to people.

—*Rockies manager Bud Black*

INTRODUCTION

I feel 18 every day I walk into the ballpark. I walk up the stairs to the dugout, take in the perfectly manicured lawn, the immaculate clay of the infield. There will be a game today, and I get to narrate. No two games are identical, and every day there is a possibility we'll see something we've never seen before. I appreciate your nightly invitation into your homes.

We get to share with you the jubilation of a walk-off win, the amazement in Nolan Arenado taking a would-be double and turning it into a ridiculously improbable out, the wicked and torrid flight of a CarGo "take a good look, you won't see it for long" homer to the third deck. We also feel the same pain as you, when the team suffers a defeat that feels like a kick to the gut. It is difficult to fully describe what the game of baseball has meant to me—and to my family. It encompasses us.

Since racing off the bus as a six-year-old to see the New York Mets in the 1969 World Series, I've always known that I enjoyed the game. It was important to my dad. I was born on Long Island, but we moved to Westchester County, north of the city, when I was seven. Pound Ridge is where I claim that I grew up. I started playing Little League there and eventually graduated from Fox Lane High School in Bedford, New York, where I excelled in football and baseball. But of the two, I felt my future was tied to baseball. I received a number of accolades on the field in high school and even had a couple of workouts for professional teams (the Cincinnati Reds and Seattle Mariners). That led to the delusional thought that I would one day get an opportunity to get paid to play. I went on to play college ball but ultimately found my way to broadcasting this great game.

One of my grandest life joys has been teaching my kids the game of baseball, playing the game with them, and watching them play. I was the crazy dad who—when each of my three boys reached 18 months—took a plastic bat and put it in their hands from the left side of the plate. They all throw righty but were going to have the advantage of hitting lefty.

We threw and hit everywhere we went. When they were really young, my wife, Kristi, would schlep them through airports in matching shirts (in case one strayed from the pack) to come stay with me in whatever city the team was playing. In the mornings we would find a park or a strip of grass somewhere and play catch, field ground balls, or play Wiffle Ball.

When they got older, I would take them in the morning to the clubhouse, and we would hit in the cages on the visiting side before players would arrive. Around the age of nine, they would come out with me and shag balls during early batting practice. That was a big deal. I remember when Jacob caught a long fly off the bat of Matt Holliday. Cool stuff. Unforgettable stuff. We took a trip to Scotland when the boys were six, four, and one. I recall playing Wiffle Ball on a patch of grass adjacent to the harbor in Edinburgh. People were quite a bit curious as to what we were up to.

I was recently sitting on a field in the Buckhead section of Atlanta, sweating in the heat of a mid-August Georgia afternoon. Jacob, my oldest, was with me on this trip, filling in for Doug Marino, our regular stats and research guy. We had just finished having a catch and taking some ground balls. We were just visiting about life, about baseball, about his upcoming semester in Spain. A line from our favorite sports movie, *Remember the Titans*, popped into my head. Our whole family loves it. Jacob knows virtually every line verbatim. The line I was thinking of so accurately portrays the almost spiritual relationship I have with the game of baseball, though it can be for whatever sport stirs inside someone. Coach Boone, played so well by Denzel Washington, is standing in the fully lit but empty high school football stadium the night before a big game. He says to the character Doc: "This is my sanctuary right here… This is always right. It's just a game, Doc, but I love it."

Ask my kids where my favorite place is, or where their favorite spot is, and they will say in unison: "Cooperstown." And Dreams Park is where the best 12-year-olds tournament in the country takes place each week of the summer.

My other favorite spot is sitting on a bucket on the edge of the dugout, coaching. This past year, I was an assistant for the Arapahoe High School varsity. It was one of the most rewarding, emotional, and memorable baseball experiences of my life. My son, Zach, was a senior catcher and captain. The school was ranked 48th in 5A to begin the year...and finished in the final four of the state tournament. I take approximately 10 Rockies games off of the 150 we televise, and they are all strategically done to see as many of my kids' games as possible. To be a small part of Zach's senior spring provided me with immeasurable pleasure. And so, to this day, I get very sentimental while I'm jogging on a Rockies road trip and I pass a spot of grass or a park. The memories of those catches with my boys come racing back.

Jacob was a middle infielder who played at Denison University after a strong career at Arapahoe High. He has since transferred back home to the University of Colorado, where he is a 3.9 GPA student in finance and plays with his middle brother, Zach, on a summer collegiate league team. Zach was named to the Rockies Futures game and also honorable mention All-State. He is headed to Webster University in St. Louis to continue his education and baseball career. Our youngest, Gabe, just finished his freshman year by leading Arapahoe's sophomore team in hitting.

I am obviously proud of their baseball accomplishments but even more so in how they conduct themselves. They are personable, bright kids who look you in the eye when they speak. The vast credit for that lies with Kristi. She has had to wear numerous hats at times when I was traveling. I used to naively say she did about 75 percent. That was selling her short about 24 percent. People will occasionally ask how many games she sees a year, meaning the Rockies games. She will answer: "200 to 250 games a year before the All-Star break. And only a couple are the

Rockies!" She loves the Rockies, but the boys' games take precedent. I could not do what I do without her support and the knowledge that our boys, that our house, that our little world is completely handled.

Our baseball conversations and texts have evolved over the years. Initially when I would call in the middle of the game to see how they were doing, the exchange went something like this:

Me: "What did he do in his at-bat?"

Kris: "He is on second."

Me: "How did he get there?"

Kris: "He hit it."

Me: "Where?"

Kris: "I don't know…Right, I think."

Me: "Single or a double?"

Kris: "Call Hal!" (a good family friend of ours whose son was also on the team)

I have coached them in baseball, basketball, and football from the time they were little. Kris, who was an outstanding teacher, coach, and athlete in her own right, would often counsel me on my sideline demeanor: "Have you ever seen the look on your face at times? You look like you are ready to kill someone. Ease up, tell them what they have done well, and then introduce how they could have done something a little differently." These are great tidbits of advice, which I believe over time I have adopted, though that face she referenced probably does appear on occasion.

I earn a living doing something I have tremendous passion for. I believe I have been able to pass onto my kids the understanding that whatever you decide to do in life, if you have passion for it, that that in itself makes you successful (and hopefully content).

We have spent a ton of time on fields and courts, our basement, and in our barn, fielding, hitting, hooping, tackling, and having fun. Kristi would take them, especially when they were young, all over America so we could be together as a family. What she did and continues to do, in being the omnipresent parent, has been remarkable. My happiness and knowledge that all was well at home begins and ends with my wife. We are both proud beyond words of how special the boys have turned out to be in virtually every way. Of Kristi's many great accomplishments, these are her finest.

Editor's Note: To provide a feel of the Colorado Rockies' thrilling 2018 playoff season, entries from Drew Goodman's actual diary from the season are sprinkled throughout this book.

CHAPTER 1
GAME 163, VERSION 1.0

The Hall of Fame closer in an All-Star season took the mound with a two-run lead, but in the Colorado dugout Troy Tulowitzki screamed to his teammates: "We're going to kick his ass!"

It was the last inning in the last game, a game that wasn't even on the schedule, a tiebreaker squeezed into this improbable season, as if no one wanted it to end.

To this day, you can go to The Chophouse in LoDo or Don's Club Tavern on Cap Hill or the Starbucks at Cherry Hills Marketplace and say "Game 163," and folks know what you're talking about. They'll flash a little smile, you'll smile, an eavesdropping stranger will smile, and soon the whole place is telling stories about where they were for Game 163— because it's the greatest game in Rockies history—yes, even better than "Game 170."

It was October 1, 2007. The first day of Rocktober. The Rockies hadn't been to the playoffs since 1995. Todd Helton, wearing a uniform number that would someday be retired, was in his 11th season—and had never played in the postseason. And on September 15, the Rockies were just 76–72, another ordinary season…until the extraordinary came out of the thin Colorado air.

The Rockies won 13 of their final 14 games, including the final game of the season, to tie the San Diego Padres for the wild-card, thus setting up this tiebreaker—Game 163—perhaps the coolest sporting event to ever occur in Denver, Colorado.

But they were about to blow it! Jorge Julio, a name that otherwise would've become an obscenity in these parts, allowed two runs in the top of the 13th inning. And with a two-run lead, Trevor William Hoffman, the eternal savior of San Diego, emerged from the bullpen. "I remember Tulo," said Ryan Spilborghs, a Rockies outfielder in 2007 and my current broadcast partner for Rockies games. "He's coming off the field in the 13th and screaming that we're going to kick Hoffman's ass. There are times when maybe you get your teeth kicked in, and you come into the dugout, and it's quiet. *We got no shot.* The guys are stunned, they're done, they're punch drunk. But then there are other times when you get punched, and the guys want to counterpunch, they want to hit them back even harder. I just remember Trevor Hoffman coming in, and Tulo, always setting his glove down in the same spot at the end of the dugout, just yelling: 'We got this guy! He's going to get his ass kicked!' And Todd's like, 'Yeah!' And Kaz Matsui is leading off and hits a double. Then Tulo hits a double. It's 8–7 in the 13th! Tulo was a gamer. Nobody looked at him as a rookie. It was just like, 'All right, lead us! Go for it!'"

Tulowitzki came in second in the voting for 2007 Rookie of the Year. He could've won it. And Matt Holliday came in second in the voting for 2007 Most Valuable Player. He should've won it. Jimmy Rollins? Are you kidding me with this? He was a brilliant ballplayer, but the MVP? Holliday won the batting title with a .340 average (while hitting .301 on the road) and he led the league in RBIs with 137. Holliday also swatted 50 doubles and 36 homers. Mash Holliday. He was a game-changer, a season-saver, and finished with a .405 on-base percentage and a .607 slugging percentage. "I remember shaking his hand for the first time," Rockies pitcher Josh Fogg said. "There were muscles in his fingers, his thumb, and his hand that I didn't even know existed on people. I remember asking someone, 'Who is that guy?' They're like, 'Yeah, he's a good baseball player, but he was even better at football.' I could believe it. The guy is a monster."

And here was Holliday in Game 163, bottom of the 13th. With Tulo on second, the right-handed Holliday drove a Hoffman pitch the opposite way to right field. It sailed toward the hand-operated scoreboard. Is this going to be a walk-off home run to make the playoffs? Is Brian Giles going to catch it at the wall?

Splat!

Giles hit the wall with his body sprawled, the ball hitting above his outstretched glove. Tulo scored! Holliday scampered to third with

3

a triple. Game tied. No one out. Holliday and his thumping heart stood on third.

• • •

Manager Clint Hurdle stood in the Rockies' spacious clubhouse and shouted: "I've got good news and bad news!" His Rockies had just won the final game of the regular season. After 162 games—this grinding, grueling journey of 2007—they had an identical record as the San Diego Padres. "The good news is: we get to play in Game 163 tomorrow night! The bad news is: the Padres are starting Jake Peavy, and we've got Fogger!"

"Oh no!" Troy Tulowitzki yelled from his locker. "We're fucked!"

The clubhouse erupted in laughter. Of course, Josh Fogg was a back of the rotation big league starter, who retired two years later with a 62–69 record. But his close-knit teammates had faith in him even against the Padres' Peavy, pitching in his Cy Young season. Tulo's playful joke summed up the Rockies. It didn't matter who was throwing or what was thrown at them—the 2007 Rockies were makers of the impossible. At this point, the Rockies felt invincible, impervious.

And so, in a way it was fitting—in Game 163, the Rockies' starting pitcher would be a dude with a near-5 ERA, yet also called "The Dragon Slayer." Fogg had a penchant for pitching well against aces. In September of 2007, he won a key ballgame against Brandon Webb, the reigning Cy Young winner from the Arizona Diamondbacks. And Fogg won back-to-back starts in June against Curt Schilling and Mike Mussina. A teammate would even decorate the clubhouse with an airbrushed painting of Fogg slaying a dragon with a baseball. They just loved their Fogger. "That was the biggest thing with that group, that they wholeheartedly enjoyed playing baseball together," said Fogg, who was 30 in 2007, his second season with the Rockies, "going to the field, hanging out and going to dinner after. For them to allow me to work my way in there and find my own little niche? It was special. I ran the football pools or the basketball pools or this-and-that or fantasy football. I found my little way to contribute to the group, but they were so solid from the get-go. Sure, they would trade a guy or a guy would get released here and there, but the core group stayed together so long. They'd been in A ball, AA, AAA, ridden the busses together, and they had stories. That feeling doesn't happen very much in baseball anymore because there are so many free agents. The teams that do build from within are going to have that ability to not have as much talent but have the chemistry that could overtake the teams with that talent."

Fogg started 29 games for the 2007 Rockies—second most behind Jeff Francis—and finished 10–9, many of the 10 wins being dragon slays. He was such a great guy, a favorite of everyone from the broadcast booth to the clubhouse. And Fogger had one of the most unusual paths to the big leagues of any Rockies player ever…considering that he was cut from his high school baseball team as a junior.

The high school season prior, he'd played second base for the junior varsity but was so bad at the plate that they used the team's designated hitter for him and not for the pitcher. At junior year tryouts, Fogger threw some bullpen sessions but hoped to still play infield. "Coach puts the list up of who's made the team, and I'm not on it," said Fogg, who is from Fort Lauderdale, Florida. "I didn't really know what to do then. I planned on playing baseball my junior and senior year. I go home and tell my parents. I didn't have any big plans to go anywhere after that, so I was looking for what was next. Maybe I could play another sport? But our coach, Coach Petik, was actually our P.E. coach, and we had P.E. seventh period. Two days later, he said, 'Josh, can I talk to you for a second?' He brings me into his office and shuts the door. I was a very good student so I knew I wasn't in trouble. I wasn't getting yelled at for anything. He said, 'Hey, do you still want to play baseball?' I was like, 'Yeah, I'd love to play baseball.' He's like, 'Well, Ray Retzinger just failed off the team, and you're the next guy in line, but you're going to have to pitch.' I was like 'All right, I'll pitch!' He's like, 'Just so you know, you're not going to [actually] pitch. You're never going to pitch. You'll be the No. 5 guy.' We had four legit guys, I think three of them went to Division-I schools."

But that junior season, Fogg learned to throw a curveball. Fogg didn't throw hard but threw with conviction. "People ask, 'You're kind of small. I thought you'd be bigger?'" Fogg recalled. "And I say, 'When I get on the mound, I was 6'4."' I was sure of it. I come back for my senior year and I'm coming in as the No. 1 starter. End up 9–1, or whatever it was, all these strikeouts, and all of these accolades, All-State, and this-and-that—all because of Ray Retzinger."

Local scouts tried to figure out just how good this Fogg guy was. Late on the scene, sure, but the kid was seemingly getting better by the start. He'd visited Stetson, as well as some junior colleges in the South Florida area. And while it seemed like a dream, he had some communication with the baseball program at the University of Florida. "They were down playing one of the South Florida schools," Fogg recalled. "Coach Andy Lopez had been in contact and said, 'Hey, come out to the game, and we'll talk after.' They get done, and the bus is waiting, and people are getting on. Coach Lopez and I are talking on the field. We're probably out there 45 minutes with my dad talking—and all of these guys are on the bus waiting, waiting, waiting. He's like, 'Listen, we want to have you up to Gainesville. How about you come up this weekend?' My dad couldn't go, so they flew me up by myself. Senior in high school, probably one of the first times away by myself. They pick me up from the airport, they take me straight to the field. I'm there for less than 24 hours. I go to the field and I'm sitting in the stands. I don't even know who they're playing. It ends up being Tennessee. Friday night, I'm like, 'Are they any good?' And someone said, 'Well, they have one pretty good player that's going to start.' About two-and-a-half hours later, the infamous Todd Helton had hit a home run in like the seventh inning to win the game 1–0 all by himself. And then I'm thinking—this guy is the greatest player to ever play the game of baseball! I can't compete with this stuff! Then I get to play with him on my team for a few years later in my life. I told him about it, and he's like, 'I don't even remember that game.' I'm like, 'It was one of the most memorable games for me, and you don't even remember it?' It was probably just an average game for him back then."

Helton, of course, also played football at Tennessee. He was teammates with Peyton Manning. And in the spring of 1995, the Colorado Rockies selected Helton with the eighth overall pick in the MLB draft. The first pick in that draft was Darin Erstad to the California Angels. Kerry Wood went No. 4 to the Chicago Cubs. The pick before Helton was the Texas Rangers. They decided to go with Jonathan Johnson, who pitched in just 42 games in the bigs. Imagine the late-1990s Texas Rangers with Ivan Rodriguez, Juan Gonzalez...and Todd Helton.

Also picked in the '95 first round was Roy Halladay out of Arvada West High School outside of Denver. He went 17th to the Toronto Blue Jays. And the 28th pick in that draft selected by the Montreal Expos was a catcher named Michael Barrett, who was then playing shortstop.

As for Fogg, the future dragon slayer became a Florida Gator. "In high school," Fogg said, "a coach once told me, 'Yeah, you're, at best, a No. 3 guy in JUCO.' And I was like, 'Oh, I'll take that.' I wasn't planning on going anywhere. Then I got to Florida and I'm like, 'Screw that. I'm being No. 1 here!' If you're going to doubt me, I'm just going to go out there and throw the piss out of it until you realize that I am good enough. Coach Lopez liked that I had a quick arm. It was a live arm. At one of my first bullpens at Florida, he said, 'You're going to throw 94 before you leave here.' I was dying laughing. I'm like 'Yeah right! I got no chance!' I threw 84 in high school. Sure enough, my junior year in college, now I'm getting big-time scouts. Guys are coming to see me

7

because I'm closing games and doing a really good job. It was against Miami, and I remember my dad told me. He was in the stands and he's watching how they scout. The guns are up, and I throw a fastball. It's 94. He said you could see people grab their phones and start calling. That was probably when I shot up. I was probably a middle-teen rounder at that time. I got picked in the third round."

When he debuted in the bigs in 2001 for the Chicago White Sox, Fogg was a reliever. The next year he started all 33 of his appearances for his new team, the Pittsburgh Pirates. He finished his career with 194 games started in the big leagues.

One of the questions big league pitchers often get is: are you nervous when you pitch? It's a fair question. You're standing on a circular metaphorical spotlight, performing in front of 40,000, as well as a television audience, your family, friends…and intense teammates, who rely on you to perform with precision. But after his crazy journey, Fogg was confident. He felt he belonged. "I can very vividly remember only three times I was nervous on a major league mound," he said. "My first time appearance ever with the White Sox, starting a game in the World Series…and starting Game 163."

• • •

Only six times prior to 2007 had there ever been a one-game tie-breaker—most famously in 1978—when Bucky Dent, the scrawny New York Yankee, homered over the Green Monster and, in part of New England lore, earned himself the middle initial F for the rest of time.

Win or lose, it would be a historic night at Coors Field, our glorious home venue nestled into downtown Denver. The city was painted purple. The Rockies would make the playoffs again in their future, but no vibe will ever match Rocktober, this mystical twist of an autumn. It was just this feeling that you cannot recreate or replicate. What a time to be in Denver.

In the clubhouse before Game 163, Troy Tulowitzki spotted Tiny. Tiny is Mike Pontarelli, a longtime clubhouse manager "who's given more grief to me than anyone in the history of baseball," Ryan Spilborghs said. "You can find Tiny in Denver minor league team photos from back when he was like six years old. His dad, Dave, is a retired Denver cop and works at the stadium. So Tulo is like, 'Tiiiiiny, what are we having for dinner?' And he was like, 'Maggiano's' or something like that. And Tulo was like: 'Nah man, we got to have steak and lobster, no matter what. Steak and lobster!' So they order Chophouse steak and lobster for the whole frickin' team. And remember, this is after September call-ups, so we have a full house including minor leaguers and minor league coaches."

Coors fizzed. The place was brimming with fans. Attendance that night was 48,404. Emotions swirled in the thin air—and in the stomachs. "It was very similar to the beginning of a horror movie, where nothing has happened quite yet, but I still had an uneasy feeling of not knowing what's going to happen next," explained Phill Kaplan, a Denver native and die-hard Rockies fan, who was in the stands that night. He was with his cousin, Brent. Both guys were 24. "That 2007 team meant everything to me," Kaplan continued. "I was going through some serious personal troubles at the time, and that team was my escape, and it couldn't have happened at a better time for me."

But facing Jake Peavy in the one-game tiebreaker was on paper just a terrible turn of events. The day before, on Sunday, Padres manager Bud Black made a controversial decision. A win against the Milwaukee Brewers and they were in. But they didn't start their ace in Game 162, instead saving him for either Game 1 of the National League Divisional Series at the Philadelphia Phillies…or a Game 163 at Colorado.

The Padres lost Game 162 and flew to Denver that night. Peavy is weaved numerous times into Colorado history. In Todd Helton's final home game—September 25, 2013—Peavy was the starter for the visiting Boston Red Sox. In Helton's first at-bat of his last home game—the faithful capturing one last glimpse of the great goateed gamer—he homered off of Peavy. And in 2007, Peavy had started against the Rockies 10 days prior to Game 163, pitching seven innings of three-hit baseball, allowing a lone run. And then with Peavy out, it took the Rockies an additional seven innings to finally win the thing, famously, on a Brad Hawpe homer in the 14th inning.

So, yeah, heading into Game 163, Peavy was pretty much the worst possible opponent. Here's what he led the league in for the 2007 season: record (19–6), ERA (2.54), strikeouts (240), and WHIP or walks and hits per innings pitched (1.06). Oh, and since July 27, he was 10–1, which made it all the more thrilling and bone-chilling when the Rockies got to him right off the bat.

Kaz Matsui was Colorado's cool customer, who with a cigarette in his mouth on a night off, looked like a Japanese James Dean. Kaz led off with a double. Tulo singled. Matt Holliday walked. And so, bases loaded, and here was Peavy vs. Helton...and Todd drilled a sacrifice fly for Game 163's first run. Garrett Atkins' single made it 2–0. Two first-inning runs off Jake Peavy? Two first-inning runs off Jake Peavy! "I've never been to a sporting event where people never sat down," said Lucas Boyd, who was a student at University of Colorado-Boulder, about a half-hour away from Coors. "Even on the bus to Denver, I knew instantly that that night was going to be amazing. The whole ride down, people were cheering and making noise."

And there was Fogger, putting up two goose eggs in the first two innings. "I definitely was treating that more like a regular start," Fogg said. "Or trying to, anyways."

Yorvit Torrealba homered in the bottom of the second—3–0 Rockies—but Fogg got into a little trouble, starting with a third-inning single from, of all people, Peavy. Soon, the bases were loaded...and soon after, the bases were empty, as Adrian Gonzalez tattooed a ball into the stands for his first career grand slam.

The Padres scored one more in the top of the third to make it 5–3 Padres. And after Helton's solo shot in the bottom of the third, this classic game at Coors had the makings of the epitome of a game at Coors. The score was already 5–4 with six innings to go. It was bonkers. I mean, everyone was hitting off Peavy! Well, except Spilly. "After Game 162, I was hitting .304," Spilborghs explained one night over beers at Punch Bowl Social, the bar built inside the control tower at the old Stapleton Airport. "And so, one of the only players on the Rockies roster who would complain about playing Game 163 was me. I went 0-for-4, so I ended up on the season at .299. But I still argue that I hit .304 in the season! In the standard scheduled 162 games, I hit .300. But the back of the baseball card says .299. So I come out of the game in the seventh inning, so now the game's out of my hands, I'm a fan, which is the worst as a player, because there's not a comfortable way to watch the game when you can't do anything."

• • •

Alan Frosh is a sixth generation Denverite. His father taught him to love baseball, even though they didn't have a baseball team. So many people in Colorado have similar stories. And in 1993 all these people were given the same gift—a major league team—and 80,227 got to unwrap the present the same time at the epic first ever Rockies game at Mile High Stadium. (Sure enough, 80227 is a Denver zip code.) Fathers and sons and mothers and daughters could now experience baseball together in real time. Toddlers were raised with "Todd and the Toddlers." And many of these families were at Coors Field for Game 163. My wife, Kristi, and my sons Jacob, Zach, and Gabe, who at the time were nine, seven, and four, and I were on the field level on the first-base line.

Frosh went with his dad. But first he had to get there. Twenty-three at the time, Frosh worked and lived in Colorado Springs about an hour south of his hometown. "The work day got away from me, and I ended up leaving like an hour later than needed to make the early 5:30 first pitch," Frosh said. "I was weaving in and out of rush hour on Northbound I-25—and I got pulled over for speeding just north of Larkspur. When the officer approached my window, he saw a guy in a purple dress shirt, purple bowtie, and a Rockies hat. He gave me the once-over and said, 'If you can show me your ticket to the game, you can go.' But the tickets were in Denver! So I panicked to stammer out an explanation. The cop put his hand up, stopping my excuses—'The Dragon Slayer is my favorite Rockie,' he said. 'I hope he has your luck today.' He walked away. And I got to the stadium just in time."

Game 163 unspooled. Huge moments were reduced to footnotes. Matt Holliday drove in Troy Tulowitzki to tie it at five in the fifth. Garrett Atkins' homer-that-wasn't was called a double off Jake Peavy in the seventh. Holliday's missteps in left allowed a game-tying double for Brian Giles, the same outfielder who later wouldn't catch Holliday's blasted ball, as Giles splattered into the padding of the wall. Rockies reliever Matt Herges—one of the few pitchers who pitched for all five teams in the National League West—got out of trouble in the 10th…and 11th…and 12th. Herges is a forgotten hero of Game 163.

But this was no longer just a game; it was a quest. As for Josh Fogg, done for the night, he got superstitious. "I was one of the guys that was running up and down and taking shots from [trainer] Scottie Gehret's special stash in the training room," Fogg said. "For every inning from the eighth inning on, we were running up there, taking a shot and coming back down to watch the inning. Then, as soon as the inning would end, it was like a dead sprint, like four or five of us just hauling ass, getting up there, hammer it, come back down. We were convinced that was how we were going to win. I remember we were trying not to puke the whole way back down."

In the stands with his cousin, Phill Kaplan was "literally biting the railing in front of my seat because of how intense the action was." A photographer from the Rocky Mountain News happened to capture the image, and it was in the paper the next day.

I was sitting with my family, hanging on to every moment. It is actually easier to be broadcasting than just watching because, amid the nerves, you have to stay in the moment professionally and do your job. As a fan, it's just overwhelming. By the 13th inning, I had to hustle down to the camera well by the Rockies dugout, so I could have easy access to the field. Game 163—officially called "The National League Wild-Card Tiebreaker"—was televised nationally on TBS. But if the Rockies were to win, my assignment was to meet up with our camera person to record on-field and clubhouse interviews for our regionally aired postgame show.

And in the top of the 13th inning, that's when Jorge Julio allowed those two San Diego Padres runs. Scott Hairston hit a two-run homer. The Padres were up 8–6 in the top of the 13th. And Trevor Hoffman was up again in the pen. Julio? Hairston? *These were going to be the names remembered from Game 163?* "When Hairston hit the ball out," Rockies general manager Dan O'Dowd recalled, "I said: 'I've watched an incredible run, but man, oh man, we have dug ourselves a hole.' So I was thinking about going down and congratulating [Padres GM] Kevin Towers because I had the utmost respect for him."

In the dugout Rockies manager Clint Hurdle turned to coach Jamie Quirk and said: "Wow, this is really going to have to get nuts."

New pitcher Ramon Ortiz got the Rockies out of the inning. Tulo scurried in from shortstop and screamed that the Rockies would kick Hoffman's ass. "You could feel that something was going to happen," Ryan Spilborghs said. "And because of my spot on the bench, I remember looking around the stands. Nobody left."

Alan Cockrell was Todd Helton before Todd Helton. Cockrell went to the University of Tennessee as a star quarterback, played for the Vols but became a baseball legend there, getting picked in the first round of the MLB draft. But Cockrell's professional career went a different direction than Helton's would. Drafted by the San Francisco Giants in 1984, he spent 13 seasons in the minor leagues. His final three were in the Rockies organization. At age 33, they called Cockrell up to the big leagues. He got eight at-bats and tallied two hits, including his first big league hit against Tom Glavine. A sweet story. Beloved for his integrity and grit by the Rockies, Cockrell was hired by the organization to be a minor league coach. By 2007 he was the major league hitting coach for Hurdle's Rockies, the instructor of one of the best offenses of the entire era. And so, in the middle of the 13ᵗʰ inning, Cockrell came up to Hurdle and asked: "Do we take a strike? Or do we get after it?"

Hurdle looked at his trusted coach and said: "We're not backing off now. Hit the first thing you like. Tell them to hit the first thing they like. We're not giving this guy strikes. He's had to warm up multiple times. We are going to go out and be aggressive."

The bottom of the 13ᵗʰ was a blur. Kaz doubled, Tulo doubled, and then—on the first pitch he saw—Holliday wallopped the ball to the wall over Giles' glove for the RBI triple. (This hit, incidentally, secured Holliday as the 2007 NL batting champ.)

It was 8–8 in the bottom of the 13ᵗʰ inning. Game 163 was tied. Denver was deafening.

Holliday was on third with no outs. And Helton was up.

(Can you imagine if they had pitched to him?) Alas, Hoffman intentionally walked Helton…to get to Jamey Carroll.

• • •

A decade after Game 163, Clint Hurdle and I met up at the Winter Meetings. He was the manager of the Pittsburgh Pirates, had been for a while, but we're forever connected because of our time together with the Rockies. He's one of my favorite people to talk baseball with because when he tells stories he takes you into the story. You feel like you're right there with him. And so, that 2017 night, I suddenly felt like I was in the dugout in Game 163. "Jamey Carroll was in for his defense, but here in the 13th, he was up with Holliday on third and Todd at first," Hurdle recalled. "And—for a moment—I go, 'How great would it be if we just squeeze right here and win the game?' And it was all of a sudden. We didn't squeeze [much]. We might have squeezed once all year. But the only time I've ever wanted to use a squeeze bunt was to win a game. It's not for the fifth inning. Rafael Belliard once put one down to win a game. It was a walk-off win. Normally I thought Hoff would take some time, but before I could say it, the pitch is thrown, and it's hit…So I'm thinking, *Oh that's plenty deep to right.* [Brian Giles] catches it flat-footed, but then the ball comes out of his hand, and it's like it keeps coming and coming—and is on target!"

Josh Fogg previously played with Giles in Pittsburgh. "He didn't throw a person out in three years, I don't think," Fogg said. "I didn't think there was any chance he could even get the ball to home plate. I knew he had an accurate arm, but I knew his arm was so weak, so I was like, 'This is over. We got it.' He made the throw, and I was like, 'Oh shit.'"

Matt Holliday locomotive'd toward home. And as we all did some quick physics and geometry in our minds, it appeared that the baseball was going to arrive at the exact same time and—whoosh!—Holliday slid head first…and the ball sailed toward the glove of the catcher. The backstop was Michael Barrett, the old Montreal Expos catcher, drafted in the same 1995 first round that Helton was. Neither he nor Helton had ever made it to the playoffs. One of them would in 2007.

The throw landed about three feet in front of Barrett, strategically crouching in front of home plate. The ball bounced toward his mitt while his outside left leg protected the plate. It all happened so fast. Holliday slid beside the plate and reached out with his left hand, but his hand hit Barrett's cleat. As Holliday essentially belly-flopped, he face-planted, his chin driving into the ground, his helmet sailing off his shaved head. But the baseball was loose, too. It had squirted out of Barrett's glove before the catcher could corral it.

The umpire was Tim McClelland, a fine balls-and-strikes guy, but the slowest umpire mechanics in the history of baseball. "The longest pause ever," Hurdle said.

And then McClelland signaled SAAAAAAFE! "And we don't know what to do!" Ryan Spilborghs said. "We just made it to the playoffs! We just literally made it to the playoffs in Game 163! All this

Matt Holliday scores the game-winning run in the 13th inning, allowing the Rockies to advance to the 2007 playoffs.

stuff happens, and you run to see Holliday, and he's knocked out, and [trainer] Keith Dugger is holding his face, so you're like, 'Well, alright, I'll just go cheer with Jamey Carroll over there by first!'"

Alan Frosh, the fan who avoided the speeding ticket to watch the game with his dad, said they stayed at Coors Field "for like half an hour after the game, trying to come down from the most emotional sports high we had ever experienced. Walking out of the stadium, heading with my dad to get a late bite to eat, I remember so vividly high-fiving every single person who passed us. It was like we had won the World Series."

But had Holliday touched home?

It appeared that Barrett's cleat prevented Holliday's hand from touching the plate. This was before replay became available for umpires during games. Even after examining it countless times, I can't tell if part of a finger grazed the black of the plate. A few seconds after the slide, Barrett collected the ball and did tag Holliday. But it didn't matter. He was called safe by the umpire, who believed Holliday touched the plate.

But was Holliday okay? His chin took quite a beating. There was a gross splotch of blood. He was dazed and delirious, but at that moment, who wasn't? "He wasn't quite sure exactly where he was," Dugger said. "I'm not going to say he was concussed, but I'm going to say, was he affected? You can look at the pictures and look at his eyes. Of course he was. He hit his chin, bit his tongue, he was gassed, worn out from the moment. He wasn't quite sure if he was safe or out. Body parts hurt all over."

But the Rockies were in the playoffs, and Holliday wouldn't miss a game. To this day though, I still don't understand why Holliday didn't just drill Barrett. We're talking about a dude that is 6'4", 245 pounds with a football background, and you could hit the catcher then. He could've hit him and knocked him into the third row! And then we wouldn't be debating for the next decade whether or not he touched

17

Drew's Diary

August 25, 2018:
St. Louis Cardinals at Colorado Rockies

In a 0–0 game in the seventh inning with the Rockies limited to two hits against John Gant of the St. Louis Cardinals, Matt Holliday steps up for the Rockies as a pinch-hitter. He was called up on Thursday, started, and went 0–3 in a win vs. the San Diego Padres that wasn't televised. This time he walks to the plate in front of a sellout crowd of just shy of 48,000, a fair amount wearing Cardinals red, as is always the case in Denver and many other cities. Both purple and red-clad fans stood in joint appreciation for a guy who made a huge mark on both organizations. He takes it all in, doffing his helmet a couple of times, and then stands in. We remain silent until he swings and misses by seemingly three feet on a curveball that's well off the plate. I said, "As many times as Matt has taken a big league at bat, the nerves here have to be a little more profound."

Then the next pitch (another curveball) is on its way to the plate, and just as he has done so many times a decade earlier, he mashes the ball on a line 448 feet deep into the left field seats. "Holliday has done it," I said, "a goose-bumps moment if there ever was one." I would later tweet out that for me that was a top 10 all-time Rockies moment. Big Daddy returns and breaks up a scoreless game with a prodigious home run against his other former team. Both fanbases stand for a full minute cheering. If Hollywood has the script, it would have ended 1–0 Colorado, but the Cards tie it in the top of the eighth inning, and then the Rockies put together their best inning of the year, scoring eight in the bottom of the eighth inning. They have 10 hits and a club-tying five doubles in the inning. The final score is 9–1, but what Holliday did will linger in the memory banks for a long time.

home plate. Years later, I asked him that, and he said his instincts at that moment had him dive toward an open section of the plate.

But in a way, it just adds to the mystique of the whole thing, this whole bizarre run that had the Rockies somewhere they hadn't been since 1995: Rocktober. "It was disbelief," Helton said. "I didn't know what to do, I'd never celebrated before. I didn't know the champagne stung when it got in your eyes. When they started pouring it all over me, I was like, 'Damn this hurts a little bit.' I didn't know how to celebrate except to hug the guys and jump up and down like a little kid."

To that point, Helton had played 1,578 regular-season games. He was heading to his first postseason game—the first for many in the Rockies family. "It was really kind of neat because all the Rockies front-office people lined the stairs on the way into the clubhouse," Spilborghs said. "It felt like they were a part of it, too. So we have this celebration, and we don't know what the hell we're doing. We're being told we have to take our cleats off. We don't understand how to celebrate, we've never celebrated before! We get hats and these shirts. So we have this party—I swear, the Coors Field clubhouse still has this faint smell from it even today. We let loose. So we're drinking every champagne bottle. I'm still curious how many bottles we went through. After the celebration family members are getting let in, and a lot of us are pretty hammered. And I'll never forget, Tulo and I are the last two to come in to eat after taking pictures with family members and everybody, and we go in looking for, yep, the steak and lobster. And all the steak and lobster is *gone*. And Tulo was the one who wanted it! So there's essentially this container where the lobster was, and Tulo's in there with his grubby little paws, scraping out the bits and pieces. It's basically just butter! And Josh Fogg, the Dragon Slayer, one of the best characters I've ever been around, he cannot stop laughing. He's watching Tulo in his underwear, eating whatever is left in the container while Tulo's yelling at Tiny to go order more lobster."

The 2007 National League wild-card team was the Colorado Rockies with the rare record of 90–73. The boys partied into the morning and then flew on a red-eye to Philadelphia. No one slept on the plane. They just played cards and partied hard. They arrived to Philly as the sun came up, and the players asked the coaches if they could have the day off instead of going through a workout, batting practice, and a media session. Hurdle was cool with it. "The one guy I felt bad for was Jeff Francis," Spilborghs said. "He had to go to the national press conference because he was pitching Game 1!"

I caught up with Dan O'Dowd in 2017. He was the architect, the man who put together the 2007 Rockies. I had to ask: as Game 163 was unfolding—with all of its chapters—were you an emotional wreck? "Yeah, I was," he said. "And I would go back and do that all over again."

CHAPTER 2

NOLAN ARENADO AND CHARLIE BLACKMON

It's hard to imagine Nolan Arenado as vulnerable, but here he was, 18 in a strange town, a Casper Ghost suddenly a ghost of his former self. Earlier that same year, Arenado was a second-round draft pick, being paid $625,000 for simply signing a contract to do his favorite thing: play a bunch of baseball.

But after his first month in rookie ball in this tiny Wyoming town, Arenado was hitting .228. He called his father, Fernando, after every single game. And one night: "I remember calling my dad crying and saying, 'I think I want to go home.'" Arenado told me. "And he was like, 'Well if you want to go home, you've got to get on a flight tomorrow, but I think you should stick it out.'"

Could you imagine if Arenado had gone home? Initially, he had trouble adapting to a wood bat. "In the beginning, it was kind of tough for me to adjust to that right away because guys are throwing hard. I just wasn't ready for that," said Arenado, now an elite slugger and perennial All-Star for the Colorado Rockies. "Being on the road for 10-hour bus rides, 12-hour bus rides, and you're 18 years old, and everyone is 20-something, and you don't get to hang out with any of them, and they don't want to hang out with you because they think you're the 'bonus baby' and all those little things. And I couldn't hang out with them because they wanted to go have drinks and hang out and I couldn't have drinks. So just little things like that, it sucked. You felt alone at times, but I guess once I started hitting and once I started having success, the confidence started building, and I started having fun, and you get to know guys. I had some veterans that really took me in. But…it was a long adjustment."

Stories like these remind us that even for those destined for the bigs, they don't just show up there. It takes perseverance, it takes mental toughness. And Arenado—and those close to him —admit he had to transition from high school "in shape" to professional "in shape." And the guy who hit 42 homers in 2015 had only hit five in high school

Nolan Arenado readies to hit in 2017, a year he led the national leagues in doubles.

his senior year—and in Casper, Wyoming, in 2009, a season that he ended up hitting exactly .300, he hit only two homers in the 54 games he played. "When I first saw him, we drafted him in the second round out of high school, and he shows up with no pop and cankles," said Charlie Blackmon, in reference to the dreaded calf-ankle amalgamation. "Your boy had freaking pudding for feet. He had a really good feel for getting the barrel on the ball and good balance in the box, so I knew that he would be able to hit well. But I didn't think he'd ever develop enough to overcome his defensive liability. I didn't think he'd hit enough home runs to play first base and I just didn't know it was in him to lose that weight and gain quickness and become the third baseman he's become... He's really turned himself into the best third baseman, I think. I don't know how he's done it."

That's one of the most surprising things to people who don't know much about Nolan's past. He wasn't preordained to play third like a certain Oriole. He's a self-made fielder, whose glove turned into gold. A scouting report I remember well said that he would be a defensive liability in the infield and was best suited to play catcher. "I remember watching him his very first spring training," said my broadcast partner, Jeff Huson, a former Major League Baseball infielder. "That was back when Casey Blake was in camp. And he ended up not making it because of an injury. Casey couldn't move great. But watching Casey take ground balls compared to Nolan? Casey was better. I was looking and thinking: *I can see a little bit, but he's got a long way to go.*"

Arenado forced himself to become a harder worker—and a smarter worker. He scooped countless ground balls with the gray-haired sage Jerry Weinstein, a coach in the organization. He embraced the weight room, which he often disliked—if only because it meant less time playing actual baseball. "I knew I needed to [lift heavy weights] to get stronger, but I needed to lose weight to be quicker," Arenado said. "And once I saw how quick I could be, how much faster I was, I was like, 'Wow, I'm a totally different baseball player.' Like my high A season compared to my low-A, you can ask the Rockies. Jeff Bridich was the farm director then. He would tell you: 'He was just so much better. It was a transformation with how quick he was.' How quick twitch my swing was, I was just letting it fly. That's when I realized it was huge for me."

Arenado can't sit still. He is in perpetual motion. In the field he fidgets between pitches. At the plate his feet are continuously moving.

Heck, in the clubhouse he is constantly punching the air in his batting stance with his right or top hand, programming his body to stay direct and inside to the ball. The repetition of movements, this frenetic energy, has helped turn him into a baseball monster.

Bud Black, the current manager, has a theory about him. Just like Dennis Eckersley used to say, he thrives because he's afraid of failure. "He works his ass off so he doesn't fail," said Black, who managed Arenado and the gang that went to the 2017 and 2018 postseason. "The fear of failure for some people is a motivator."

The 2011 Arizona Fall League might sound like a sports version of an urban legend, but the following offensive players were all there at the same time for that same six-team league: Mike Trout, Bryce Harper, DJ LeMahieu, Brandon Crawford, Wil Myers, and the Cardinals' Oscar Taveras, who was the No. 3 prospect in all of baseball in 2014, the year he died in a car accident. "I was like, 'Man, I'm competing with all of them. I got the Fall League MVP,'" said Arenado, who had 33 RBIs in 29 games. "After that I realized I could make it to the big leagues."

From 2015 to 2017 for the Rockies, his home run totals were 42, 41, and 37. The RBI totals in those three years: 130, 133, 130, more than anyone in baseball. And Arenado is a modern Brooks Robinson. Entering 2018, he had played five big league seasons—and won five Gold Gloves. He also nabbed a platinum glove, which is given to the best fielder in the league regardless of position. He delved into being great and developed greatness. Years from now, defensive third base excellence will be compared to Arenado the way today it is to Robinson. "And to see him from then to where he is now," Huson said, "I've watched Scott Rolen play, Mike Schmidt. I've watched a lot of great third basemen play, but Nolan is the best I've ever seen. With Arenado the thrill is: I don't know what he's going to do defensively, I don't know what magical play he's going to make tonight. [There are plays] that I know how difficult they are because I've tried to make them! And he makes them and makes them look easy. It's as if he knows what the play is going to be before the play is a play."

• • •

With wind whipping sporadically off the cove in April of 2015, it was one of those foggy, cooler San Francisco nights, one you'd swear was the setting for some mystical behavior. In the bottom of the eighth inning, the Rockies were up 3–0 with two on and no outs. Gregor Blanco sliced a foul pop-up headed to the third-base-side seats near the bullpen. From third Nolan Arenado started sprinting diagonally, full speed. He couldn't have run faster. And what happened next was a combination of two of the greatest catches ever—the Willie Mays one and the Derek Jeter one.

In stride Arenado caught the ball over his shoulder like Mays basically because his left eye picked the thing out of the sky. That, of course, would have made it an all-time Arenado catch, and that's saying something. But he then collided with the rolled-up tarp and soared into the stands—face first—like Jeter once did. But Nolan's knees were on top of the tarp, so he popped up and threw a dart to third base—*from his knees on top of the tarp*. Tagging from second, the runner was barely safe at third. What awareness! "All I remember was I kept saying, 'Wow! Wow!' I couldn't get anything out!" Jeff Huson said. "Not only that he caught it, not only that he didn't completely disfigure himself, but he also had the wherewithal to throw the ball. From his knees!"

It was the catch of a lifetime.

But he often gets you out of your seat—even myself in the booth. I've seen so many amazing plays, yet Arenado makes the otherworldly seem routine. And he's just a great dude. And what a great name: Arenado. It sounds like a verb, as if it should start with "aero" or "air." Or it sounds like some sort of overwhelming weather phenomenon. (The arenado is expected to make landfall on Thursday.) Or who knows, maybe in another language it even translates to: Errors? None!

And what's refreshing about Arenado is he doesn't get caught up in defensive metrics. "There are ones that bother me, like the defensive runs saved," he said. "I don't understand how that works. Because I make diving plays with a man on second where if I didn't make that play, he's going to score. So I'm like, 'That's a run saved.' So then I ask the analytics guys about a ball that I bare-handed and threw home. That's not a defensive run-saving play. I thought I saved a run there. So those things I don't understand. The [weighted runs created plus] WRC+, I don't know. And then WAR, I don't understand."

He just goes out and makes plays. And highlight reels.

There was this particular series against the San Diego Padres. It was early in 2018. A pitch got away from a Rockies hurler and accidentally injured a Padre. Two more pitches hit hitters. And then Arenado calmly stepped into the batter's box. The first pitch from Luis Perdomo was 96 and behind him.

Arenado threw his helmet to the ground while sprinting at Perdomo, and Perdomo threw his glove at Arenado. The irate Rockie ducked and came at Perdomo like a derailed locomotive. The pitcher juked out of the way as Arenado fiercely threw a punch, which missed. But he recovered and jumped right at Perdomo. That was followed by players from both teams, leaping upon them. Arenado drew a line in the sand. You learned a bit more about his competitiveness and his constitution, but he has room for improvement in one area. "Brandon Crawford texted me," Arenado said of the San Francisco Giants' All-Star. "And he was like, 'Dude, that swing was awful, but your hair is unbelievable.' He thought the punch was terrible. He sent like a play-by-play of it with me swinging, and my head was gone, and he was like, 'You've got to keep your head on top of the ball like when you hit, but your hair is flawless. I never thought I'd tell you that.' That was pretty funny because he's got long hair."

Drew's Diary

April 11, 2018:
San Diego Padres at Colorado Rockies

An early defining moment in the season occurred on a get-away afternoon game between the Rockies and San Diego Padres. It's rare when you know instantly that a game will be long remembered as the season unfolds, but such is the case with this one. The Rockies had gone 1–4 on their first homestand of the year and had lost three in a row amidst an offense that had scored only 14 runs. Last night a pitch, which got away from Rockies pitcher Scott Oberg, hit Manual Margot in the ribs, forcing him to the disabled list. Oberg contacted Margot after the game to apologize and let him know there was no intent. During today's game Padres outfielder Hunter Renfroe was hit on the wrist by German Marquez, and Trevor Story was hit by Padres pitcher Luis Perdomo. In the bottom of the third in a scoreless game, Nolan Arenado led off, and the first pitch sailed shoulder high at 96 behind him. He immediately sprinted out to the mound. Perdomo threw his glove at him, and Arenado chased him to the third-base line, throwing a glancing right hand. A full-out, old-school brawl ensued that took the better part of 20 minutes to restore a semblance of order. In the aftermath Arenado, Gerardo Parra, and Marquez were tossed. Marquez threw a towel at someone in the middle of the melee, and Parra threw a punch at A.J. Ellis. Ellis and Perdomo were ejected for San Diego.

The altercation seemed to galvanize the Rockies, as Ian Desmond, hitting for Arenado, reached on an error and then stole second. Carlos Gonzalez singled him in, and then eventually the bases were loaded for Tony Wolters, who had only two hits entering the game—both of the infield variety. He fell

Continued on next page

Continued from previous page

behind and then worked the count to 2-2 before lining a single to center that was misplayed by Franchy Cordero into three runs with Wolters ending up at third. Pat Valaika, who also struggled coming in, fired a base hit to left, and the Rockies had a five-spot in the immediate aftermath of the fight. This was a huge win, considering the three-game slide and the fact that the road trip begins with four against the talented Washington Nationals and three at the red hot Pittsburgh Pirates. Will this be a rallying point moment in reflection after what has been a relatively slow start for a team with high expectations? We shall see...

Few players ever are more outwardly intense than Nolan James Arenado. He's like a linebacker. His passion and pride just radiate from his pores. He famously got into a dugout shouting match with teammate Nick Hundley, a catcher, following a disheartening home run the Rockies' battery allowed. "He's an incredible competitor," Charlie Blackmon said. "He doesn't give anything away. He wants every hit, doesn't matter what the score is. There are some things that I would change about Nolan. Sometimes I think he needs to mature with the way that he deals with failure. I think he takes everything so hard because he cares about it so much, sometimes it almost works against him. That's something that's hard to curb. You don't want to tell a guy to care less. How do you deal with making outs better? That kind of stuff becomes counterproductive."

Even as a boy playing ball, Arenado was constantly stomping his cleats at a borderline pitch or slamming his bat in the dugout. Robert Sanchez, the profile writer for Denver's magazine, wrote that: "He treated each failure as if it threatened his very existence, as if it proved he wasn't good enough...A game might be going great, but then Nolan would pop out and fling his bat, prompting Fernando to ground his son on the car ride home. When Nolan was nine or 10, a Little League umpire mailed the Arenados a book on how the Amish trained their horses. The implication was clear: Nolan was a thoroughbred who needed to be broken."

To his credit, Arenado acknowledges his evolution. He specifically looked back at those days in Casper, Wyoming, and the minor leagues and shared: "I took it too serious. I'm an emotional player now as you know, but I was mentally not as strong. But experience is the key. Minor leagues is hard because you want to get to the big leagues, and you have to become selfish in a way, and nobody plays good when you become selfish."

He just wants to win—so badly. You can see it, and that's why fans adore him. "Nolan is a talented player, one of the best I've ever seen," Carlos Gonzalez said. "He's obsessed with baseball, obsessed. I think that's why he's probably going to end up in the Hall of Fame. He wants to get better every day, every year. No matter what you do the day before, he's always the next day hungry. If he hits two home runs the day before, he wants to hit three homers the next day. I think that's what separates him from the rest of us.

"I have one of the best stories with him because when he first came up, he was so hyped. He never rests. He's always catching 300 ground balls before the game, hitting in the cage before batting practice, then batting practice, then after batting practice. Then after the game he's doing dry swings everywhere. So I was like, 'Man, I know you're super young so you don't get tired, but you need to save some energy for the game.' And he started laughing. That was before he became that monster. The very next year, he was like, 'Man, I think I'm doing well because of what you told me.' We're talking about a year later. I'm like, 'What did I tell you?' He's like, 'I'm resting more. I'm saving my energy more. You were right!' He still takes his ground balls, but he doesn't take 300 anymore. He takes 250! He's doing better."

Drew's Diary

May 2, 2018:
Colorado Rockies at Chicago Cubs

Finally! The Rockies swing it as we are accustomed to seeing. Nolan Arenado ambushes Yu Darvish in the first inning for a 440-foot two run homer to center. Colorado added a run in the second and third and then blew it wide open in the later innings. Trevor Story and Chris Iannetta hit solo homers, and Arenado added a three-run jack onto Waveland Avenue in the eighth inning. The damage would total 11 runs on 15 hits and four homers. The offense almost overshadowed another stellar start—this one by Tyler Anderson who went seven innings, allowing three hits and two runs (with solo shots from Anthony Rizzo and Kris Bryant). That's four straight starts of seven innings for the Rockies' rotation. There was a funny start to the day as the vets made Noel Cuevas go to the Starbucks across the street with a 25-drink order. He had to go in full uniform! He pushed a cart back with the entire order for the clubhouse. It only cost $111.55. He was smart, adding that he saved money. If they didn't specify, he bought the drink in a "tall," the smallest size. He did it all with a smile. You gotta love the rite of passage for a rookie in baseball. He came off the bench for two hits late. And with the club busting out, he may be requested to make a Queens Starbucks run on Friday afternoon!

• • •

Charlie Blackmon's beard has gotten so big and thick that he could sneak Gerardo Parra into the movies in that thing. First sprouted in the fall of 2013, Blackmon's beard is now a personality in and of itself. Is Blackmon the beard...or is the beard Blackmon? "I feel like we're a

31

bit of a yin and yang," the center fielder explained. "It suits the baseball player Charlie very well...I don't get caught up in details, I like to play the game tough. I like to have a very aggressive mentality. I don't want to look very friendly...My fiancee, she's never seen me without a beard. I feel like unless I talked to her or we made eye contact, I'm not so sure she would know who I was without it...But I think she would double-take at me because I'm still a pretty good-looking guy."

Charles Cobb Blackmon of Suwanee, Georgia, is a captivating character. He signed a $108-million contract extension but drives a Jeep Grand Cherokee that's as old as Matt Holliday's career. He's witty and goofy and then, suddenly, stoic and intense. He was drafted as a pitcher—twice—and then a third time as an outfielder. In the offseason he's wont to go "off the grid," as he'll say. He loves fishing and once had a mullet. "Chuck is a different case, man," said Carlos Gonzalez, a fellow Rockies All-Star outfielder. "When he first came up, he was one of those quiet guys. We all knew his talent was there, but he had it rough at the beginning with [several injuries]. Then, of course, the beard. He showed up with the beard that year, started raking, and we still miss his face ever since that day. We don't know how his face looks anymore. I haven't seen it in a while. His personality...he's a unique person. He's such a nice guy, has a great heart, cares about others, cares about his teammates, always trying to improve as a family man. But when it comes to baseball, I don't know who that guy is. He doesn't talk, doesn't listen. He just wants to kill people." CarGo laughed while offering this description to me in the summer of 2018.

An All-Star in 2014, the hairy terminator had even better years in 2015 and 2016. Blackmon then returned to the Midsummer Classic in 2017, posting one of the best statistical seasons Colorado has ever seen. Consider that Blackmon led the whole damn league in batting average (.331) and plate appearances (725), as well as hits (213) and runs (137). He also mashed 37 homers, and his 104 RBIs is the most ever by a lead-off hitter. His OPS (on-base plus slugging percentage) was exactly 1.000. And he finished fifth in the MVP voting—just behind Nolan Arenado, who finished fourth. "A big goal of mine is always to do better than you did the year before; keep getting better," Blackmon said. "Very broad, linear goals like that make sense…I just feel like this is my chance and I need to squeeze out every bit of productivity I can or every bit of success because it's totally up to me. If I end up coming up short that night, when I go 1–4 and don't drive in those runs, I wonder, is there something else I could have done to make sure that that didn't happen? Generally, the answer is yes. There is something I could have done. At the same time, you've got to keep your sanity. You've got to not be afraid to fail. You've got to stay on a routine that you can sustain."

Friends also help you sustain. Friends are there for helping you out when your 2004 Jeep Grand Cherokee runs out of gas on the side of the road. And friends are for then posting a photo of you stranded on the side of the road on the Internet.

This happened to Blackmon back in January of 2016. Both he and DJ LeMahieu were living in Atlanta during the offseason, when Blackmon got cocky and ran on empty. It made for a funny and humanizing moment shared with fans—ballplayers can run out of gas, too—and it also captured the friendship of the star second baseman and center fielder. "DJ's my favorite, for a lot of reasons," Blackmon shared. "He's kind of like my baseball compass. When I don't know how to react to certain situations or how to feel, he's just like my compass for all that stuff. I'm always asking him, 'What do you have on this, what do you have on that?' My second favorite thing is that he shuts up and plays baseball. He's not wasting time running his mouth or doing fluff that doesn't matter. He's just there to play ball. He brings it every day. He's such a solid player across the board. Personally, he's a great guy, and I like his family. He's a great basketball player. We play video games together. We used to work out in the offseason together before he got tired of me. I really hope he has a great experience in free agency. I'm really jealous of the team that gets him. I hope he somehow finds his way back to the Rockies. I think he's that guy who is easy to undervalue. He's the epitome of synergy. The sum of the parts is equal to the whole, or something like that, I don't know. Having him be there is worth a lot more than his numbers would suggest."

Gonzalez has been Blackmon's teammate since the latter cracked the big leagues in 2011. "Chuck Nazty" patrols center with "CarGo" either to his left or right. Their relationship is hilarious. "CarGo is just so entertaining," Blackmon said. "He's got funny voices, he's always making up songs, he does great…CarGo and I have played next to each other for a long time. He does this thing that really gets on my nerves. When there's a ball hit in the gap and it's going toward the gap, usually it's really hard to break your focus off the ball and call it. So at this point I kind of know what I should get to and what he should get to. Usually, I can just glance quickly at him, and he does the same. I know when he's going to catch the ball, and he doesn't have to say much. The worst is when there's a ball in the gap and usually when you do the glancing, you're kind of expecting the other guy to get to it. The worst is when we glance at each other at the same time. It's like, 'Are you going to go get that?' We both have that look on our face."

Blackmon brought this up independently during our chats. And sure enough, Gonzalez himself brought up his own perspective, which makes it even funnier. They're like an old married couple. "He doesn't talk!" Gonzalez said. "If I say, 'Hey, Charlie, did you hear me calling that ball?' He would shake his head and go back to center field, nothing verbal. If he says something, it's going to be good but the hard way. Like this year, I think this was Pittsburgh. I like going to fly balls. He knows that. We've been playing with each other for so many years that we know each other so well. I don't have to call fly balls. He knows I will go under the ball. If I don't hear anybody, then I will catch the ball. Because I don't like getting in between the 'I got it. I got it' thing, and then oh, it drops. So I'm like, 'You're in charge. You're the center fielder.' I'm going to try to get to every ball. If I hear you say, 'I got it,' I'm out. It's your responsibility. You're the boss. So we're playing in Pittsburgh. It's super cold. There's a shallow fly ball, and I'm coming in hard. I end up catching the ball. But DJ, he doesn't hear me coming so he's trying to catch the ball. I end up catching the ball and barely touch DJ. DJ goes flipping out, like four flips on the ground. It didn't look too pretty, but no one got hurt. When I went back to right field, I hear this big man yelling at me like I'm a five-year-old: 'You gotta call the ball! Come on CarGo, you're better than that!' And I turn around, and it's Charlie Blackmon. Charlie Blackmon is super angry at me because DJ almost got hurt, and I didn't call the ball. And I say, 'Sorry sir. It won't happen again.' Then he just turned around in center, like an angry dog. That's who Charlie Blackmon is. He's a different person when he's playing baseball.

"I really want to make sure he says something during the game and I think it bothers him. He knows that I'm just trying to hear his voice because normally whatever comes out of his mouth during the middle of the game is mean. Because I know who he is, it's funny. I go to center field, like during a pitching change, or we're getting our ass kicked, or the pitcher made a mistake and took the lead or whatever, I think that's when I take advantage and start asking him questions. 'Hey, where was that pitch?' or 'Hey, Charlie, what did you see on that pitch?' I just want to hear his voice. He doesn't want to say anything, and after five minutes, before I go to right field, I keep asking, and he goes super mean like, 'That was an awful pitch!' But I want to hear him because he's a different person when he's playing. I just want to hear his voice because he's super angry and doesn't want to talk to me. But he always responds."

There's this video of a little boy in a high chair, watching the bearded one during the MLB All-Star introductions. "Leading off, playing center field, from the Colorado Rockies—Charlie Blackmon."

A fan favorite, Charlie Blackmon has been growing his prodigious beard since 2013.

And suddenly the boy's eyes bulge and he points to the screen and screams: *"It's Charlie Blackmon! Yeah, he's here! Charlie Blackmoooooon!"* It was wildly adorable. Naturally, the video went viral on social media. Around town, Denverites would jokingly scream: *"It's Charlie Blackmoooooon!"*

So the ballclub invited the family down to Coors Field. It was a cool little moment. Charlie walked into a room to meet them, and the boy,

Tommy, was still-faced, walking tentatively toward the ballplayer. "He was a little timid," Blackmon said. "I'm probably scarier in person than I am on TV."

Blackmon has become a fan favorite in Denver, going from cult hero to just hero, an All-Star stud who plays hard and loves the fans. In August of 2018, the Rockies had "Charlie Blackmon Beard Night," giving out fake beards to all fans, making for ridiculous images of fans in the stands, notably the bearded women.

The beard has grown as Blackmon's name and game have grown. They're forever entangled. "Even my parents are on board now," he said of his beard. "At first, they were a little hesitant about it. Grandma hated it for sure. I think Dad really likes it now. Since I've had it, he's kind of messed around and grown his out, too. He's experimenting with his facial hair. And my mom loves me no matter what."

CHAPTER 3
TODD HELTON

"This," Jim Tracy said, "is one of the fuckin' classics that happened to 'The Tracer' in 11 years of managing in the big leagues."

When Tracy tells a story, it's a saddle ride of comedy, curse words, high-pitched punch lines, and even higher-pitched howls. "So I see 17 looming over there," Tracy said, "and I know he's coming."

Before he managed the Rockies, Tracy managed the Los Angeles Dodgers. In 2004 Tracy's Dodgers made the playoffs, but the very next year, L.A. was in disarray. His club was 40–44 heading into the game at Colorado's Coors Field on July 7, 2005. The Dodgers, wouldn't you know, took a 5–0 lead into the fifth inning. By the bottom of the seventh, the game was 5–5 with two Rockies on.

And No. 17 is looming over there. "If you look it up, Kelly Wunsch had some success facing him, in retiring Big 17," Tracy said. "That's what we called him when I managed him. So anyway, we got a situation. We got a couple guys throwing out there, and our club that year is not good, so I tell [pitching coach] Jim Colborn to get Kelly ready for Todd Helton."

Indeed, the venerable veteran reliever Wunsch was good against Helton. In fact, the lefty-swinging Helton was hitless against the sidearm lefty specialist, including a pretty dominating strikeout in L.A. "So I start walking toward the mound and I'm making the change," Tracy said. "If 17 is going to beat us, he's going to beat Kelly Wunsch. And I hear the word 'Trace,' and it sounds like it's coming from fucking right behind me, but that can't be right, so I keep walking and take two or three more steps—and 'Trace!' So, I wheel around and I'm like: 'Fuck, what?' Colby is standing right in front of my face, and he said, 'Kelly just sprained his ankle coming down the steps from the bullpen. His ankle's all blown up. They're sending the cart down there right now to go get him.' That's exactly right. He fell all the way down the steps. He's laying there in a pile of shit. And that's when Colby started running to me."

Wunsch was the lone lefty in the bullpen. So Tracy had to go to the bullpen. "And who's left standing there?" Tracy said. "Old Smiley, I used to call him. He's the guy next to Kelly in case the game gets out of hand and Helton does some damage. The kid's going to come in and finish it off. Franquelis Osoria. To have this fucking kid come in to face Todd Helton, that's like David vs. Goliath, do you hear me? What a mismatch. I looked at Franquelis coming in and I looked at Colby and I was like, 'I'd like to kill you right now! You've got to be fucking kidding me.' But we had no choice. I said 'Fuck it, bring Osoria's ass out here.' So here he comes and he has no idea that there's a fucking mountain lion standing at home plate with his mouth wide open ready to swallow him. I hand him the ball and I said, '*Buenos suerte*, kid.'

"And as I walk into the dugout, I take my lineup card out and I hand it to [bench coach] Jim Lett and said, 'I'm not fucking watching this.' Because 17 got up every morning just to take these kind of at-bats. I went down that little hallway down there—and I owe Dick [Monfort] a garbage can—because I absolutely tore that garbage can to hell and back. So now I know he's warmed up, and they're ready. Next thing I hear, it sounded like one of those perfect swings with the golf club where you compress it right into the grass. That's what that noise sounded like with the ball coming off of Helton's bat. I heard the crowd simultaneously go 'Ohhhh!' So I went, 'Fuck!' I knew it was going to happen! I picked up the can and threw it three or four more times. Then I asked the horse's ass bench coach, I said, 'Homer, huh, hit it far?' So, I'm getting ready to walk away, not thinking I was going to get an actual answer, and this fucker says to me, 'It hit the back wall of the bullpen, out in right center.' Then I scream back up at him: 'Did you have to be so fucking specific about it?'"

The Helton homer put the Rockies up 8–5, which would be the final score. The headline in the *Los Angeles Daily News* read: "IF ANYTHING CAN GO WRONG, IT WILL FOR DODGERS." And the headline in the *San Gabriel Valley Tribune* read: "Things get

Wunsch worse." Tracy was fired at the end of the year, and Helton finished the year hitting .320 with a .445 on-base percentage—best in the National League.

• • •

Todd Helton, among other things, is the best quarterback in Rockies history. A schoolboy legend for Knoxville Central High, Helton stayed in town to play both sports for the Volunteers. As a quarterback in 1993 and 1994, Helton started three games, threw for 484 yards and four touchdowns (and three picks) before injuring his knee. His replacement was Peyton Manning, who turned out to be pretty good.

Helton never got his job back, though he and Manning became lifelong friends. Both share a dry wit. After that injury Helton focused on baseball, his first love. Over the years he would make self-deprecating jokes to me about his quarterbacking days, but the reality is: he was a talented starting quarterback in the SEC. One wonders what path his career would've gone if he continued with football? And how would that have affected the history of the Colorado Rockies? And the career of Peyton Manning?

Sometimes, during a long football practice, Helton would sneak away to get in some swings in the batting cage. "Most times I'd be down there by myself," he said. "That's where I wanted to be."

Jerry Helton, a former minor leaguer, had taught his son a passion for practice. Todd said that next to the boat in the Helton garage, "Dad made a tee out of a washing machine hose. He was pretty resourceful. We had a fishing net up that wasn't that big. We had a VCR and we taped Rod Carew on *This Week in Baseball*, and he was talking about hitting the other way. That was sort of my bible. I probably watched it five or six hundred times. That's what we did; we hit the ball the other way. We would hit the ball that was away the other way and we'd hit the ball that was [inside] the other way, too. If I hit the boat, which was on the pull side, I'd get a whipping. So that didn't happen too often...I always considered myself a doubles hitter, gap to gap. I never cared about home runs, even when I was hitting them. I enjoyed a ball in the gap far more than anything else."

The Rockies chose Todd out of UT with the eighth pick in the 1995 draft. His first summer, though, he hit .254 with just one homer in 54 games in A ball. There were so many ground-outs to second that Clint Hurdle would later refer to it as "The Summer of 4-to-3." But Todd was understandably fatigued from fall football, the injury recovery, and then the spring baseball season, which went all the way into the College World Series in June.

But in the next summer, 1996, he torched poor pitchers who thought they could sneak one by him. While hitting at a .336 clip in 1997, he got the call on August 2, 1997—18 days before he turned 24. Todd Lynn Helton became the 14,726th player in major league history and would become the No. 1 player in one team's history. "I love Todd; he was the epitome of the Rockies," team owner Dick Monfort said. "I mean, he was sort of a grouchy guy during his career, but he was the most dependable guy for all those years. Every time he came up, you thought you had a chance."

At the time of his retirement in 2013, Helton held Rockies career records for games played (2,247), hits (2,519), doubles (592), home runs (369), RBIs (1,406), and walks (1,335). By the end of the 2018 season, his 592 doubles still stood as the 19th most by any player ever. And his .953 OPS (on-base plus slugging percentage) is 19th, too.

Asked what came to mind when he thinks of Helton, Larry Walker said: "The franchise, I guess. I think everybody saw it coming. He came in with high expectations and he didn't let anybody down. The guy played the game hard and was good at it when he played it, and he's going to go down as the No. 1 player in that franchise's history. It was all good from the get-go. A lot of guys, you can tell how good they're going to be from what they do in batting practice. His batting practice approach, how he hit the ball, the spin off his ball, the left field-to-right field coverage he had during batting practice—for me as a hitter told me that, wow, *this guy has got the strike zone figured out*; he knows how to swing a bat."

Helton wasn't much of a talker or a rah-rah guy. He was a Tennessee boy who became a Colorado man. He was a pro's pro who inspired prose for the press box scribes. He was this larger-than-life athlete who just blistered baseballs. His teammates revered him. In 2006 the Rockies were at Shea Stadium in New York. Some Mets fan was hollering at Helton. A young Ryan Spilborghs stood up for his teammate and shouted back: "Look at his stats! He's one of the best players in baseball."

The guy looked down at Spilborghs, whose last name had as many letters as his uniform number, and queried back in his New York accent: "Who the fuck are you, Spillagus? Just go get on the bus, don't even shower!"

The nickname stuck. At least I use it on occasion to substitute for "Spilly." Helton's was a little cooler. They called him "The Toddfather."

For his career, from 1997 to 2013, Helton hit .316 with a .414 on-base percentage and a .539 slugging percentage. He made the All-Star team five times and had numerous cartoon-like seasons, but none more absurdly astounding than the year 2000. He led the league in hits (216), doubles (59), RBIs (147), batting average (.372), on-base percentage (.463), slugging percentage (.698), and, of course, OPS (1.162). He hit 42 home runs. He produced 100-plus extra base hits in both 2000 and 2001. For context, that has happened exactly 15 times in the history of the game. Helton, Lou Gehrig, and Chuck Klein are the only players to accomplish the feat twice. And somehow he was *fifth* in the MVP voting! (First place went to Jeff Kent followed by Barry Bonds, Mike Piazza, and Jim Edmonds). Inevitably, some writers probably whined about Todd hitting at Coors Field, but here are his home/road splits:

Home in 2000: .391/.484/.758

Road in 2000: .353/.441/.633

Here are the splits of MVP winner Jeff Kent.

Home in 2000: .335/.419/.567

Road in 2000: .333/.429/.624

So yeah, even away from Coors, Helton had better numbers than the dude who actually won MVP. Colorado fans unfortunately have become all too familiar with the national bias. Often voters never take into consideration how hard it is on the body to constantly be going from sea level to altitude and back, as well as the change in ball movement. It is an injustice that I address numerous times throughout a season.

Over the years Helton displayed an incredible ability to fluidly swing and produce, but some of his most-important at-bats had his body contorted in a strange way. He had an amazing knack for fouling pitches off to stay alive in an at-bat. His hand-eye coordination was remarkable. When Jim Leyland managed the Rockies, Clint Hurdle was the hitting coach. Early in the year, Helton fouled off a particularly dirty pitch off the plate. Leyland said to Hurdle: "Does he do that a lot?"

And Hurdle said: "That's nothin.' Wait 'til he leaves his feet!"

In 2018 Hurdle called Helton's ability as "Cirque du Soleil-ish."

Over the years, as he prepared for games, Helton's dedication in the cage was contagious. "When Matt Holliday made it to the major leagues, it was probably '04-ish, he gravitated to Todd Helton," trainer Scott Gehret said. "He watched Todd work, and you've seen Todd work. I think he emulated that. Matty never had a bad work ethic, but he went from a work ethic to a Todd-like work ethic. He went from being a big, strong young man to a tough son of a bitch. You could not get him out of the lineup, and I think he got that from Todd because Todd was not coming out. Period. There would be days when Clint would try to get him a day off, and Todd would say, 'No, that's not an option.'"

Helton was the thread that laced together two eras of Rockies baseball. At first, there was this spry kid from Tennessee who looked like he had never shaved, let alone had the capacity to grow a goatee as thick as a southern accent. Before the hair, he was the heir, the phenom who would take over for the graying Andres Galarraga at first base. In his first years, his famous teammates included Walker and Dante Bichette and Vinny Castilla. Into the new century, Helton's best years were wasted by lean years from the club. But into the middle of the new decade around 2005, some of the young players began to blossom, be it a Holliday, Garrett Atkins, or Brad Hawpe, like Helton, a former SEC slugger.

Hawper had a fascinating role as Helton's teammate. "He could calm Todd down," trainer Keith Dugger said. "Todd was getting at the end of his career a little bit and Todd's very intense when he plays. He was his check and balance. Brad was very good for Todd. Sometimes the superstar players need the checks and balances more than the other guys. They actually will respect you if you talk to them that way and be a true friend and a true teammate. Whether that's things you do off the field, on the field, or the way you play the game. Who's going to tell Todd Helton he did something wrong? Not too many people. Not too many coaches, trainers, wives, whatever. Mothers. There's not too many people that are in that inner circle that he would listen to anyway. Hawpe was one of those dear friends that would treat him as a buddy. Todd respected him."

And, of course, Helton became an iconic Rockie in 2007, when he helped lead the team to its first World Series. People in Denver still talk about that homer against the Los Angeles Dodgers. And Helton, outrageously superstitious, shared this with me about that September run: "I was swinging the bat very well. I got two speeding tickets in a row in the same place in consecutive days and I wasn't mad at all. I tried to get another one, but he wasn't there the third day. I'm not crazy. I know that it probably had nothing to do with it. But if it gave me the confidence that I was going to do well that day, that was enough for me. It's a tough job to go out there and fail seven out of 10 times and have a happy face. So I looked for any edge I could find. If it was just a stupid superstition, so be it. I stole a lot of stuff from lockers—from pants to batting gloves to shoes. If a guy was hot, I was getting their stuff and getting hot, too."

But one of the most fun moments of Helton's 2007 run was his first ever postseason at-bat, which took place against the Philadelphia Phillies in Game 1 of the National League Division Series in Philadelphia. Helton said that a day prior he'd decided he was going to swing at the first pitch because: "Cole Hamels always tried to get ahead in the count, so I wasn't going to wait around for anything. I should have hit that ball out."

Helton retired with 9,453 plate appearances in the major leagues, and only 37 of those resulted in triples. Yet in his first-ever postseason at bat? "I was in the bullpen; I pitched in the bullpen in that series," Josh Fogg said. "I remember we were out there, and he hit it. We were like, 'Oh…he hit it pretty good.' He's rounding second, and everybody gets quiet, like, 'Uh. He can't get hurt. Jog in for a double, Todd! You don't need to be sprinting for third and sliding.' I think it was kind of a collective hold-your-breath. Let's make sure he stands up after he slides here so that we don't lose our best player going forward, even in this series. Who cares about the next one? We need him to win this one."

Helton's triple ended up being his only hit in the NLDS, which Colorado swept. He tallied three more hits in the National League Championship Series, which Colorado swept. But his best postseason series was actually the World Series, which Colorado was swept in. Helton went 5-for-15 with two doubles and two walks, finishing his lone Fall Classic with an on-base percentage of .412.

It was fitting—or, at least, fascinating—that Colorado's opponent in the 2007 World Series was Boston because Helton was almost on that Red Sox team. "That Thanksgiving of 2006, a deal was basically agreed to," former general manager Dan O'Dowd shared, "that Todd was going to Boston for Mike Lowell. Now think about the irony of that because Lowell was the MVP of the World Series against us. And we were probably going to put Mike Lowell at first base, not third base. And at the end of the day, Todd didn't really want to go. And I am so happy that it turned out that he didn't. Because for the Rockies franchise having a [legendary] player that started his career there and ended his career there? That means more than prospects. I see that now; I didn't really see that then."

The 2006 season had been the Rockies sixth straight under .500. And he had six years left on a nine-year deal that paid $141.5 million. "It was to get out of the long-term commitment, and he had expressed to me that he was done," O'Dowd said. "He didn't think we were going to win there. He sat with me in my office and said, 'Dan, buddy, you know as well as I do. There is no way we can win. And I am getting older in my career, and I want to go somewhere else now.' And I got it. And I said, 'Okay, walk 100 yards down the hallway and knock on the door and say that same thing to the person who is ultimately going to make that decision.'"

The trade didn't happen that November but picked up steam before spring training in 2007. Colorado asked for Lowell, reliever Julian Tavarez, and another pitching prospect—Manny Delcarmen or Craig Hansen. But the Boston front office became too wary of trading a prospect—Jacoby Ellsbury was another name that surfaced—so Helton remained a Rockie for 2007. "Keli McGregor and Dick Monfort came down, and I thought they were going to tell me I was traded because my agent said the deal was done," Helton said. "But they sat me down, and we had a great talk. They both said they really wanted me there and they thought we were going to have a special year. And boy, were they right. Looking back on it, Boston won the World Series that year. They obviously beat us, so I'd have been in the World Series either way. But I'm happy that I got to spend my whole career in Colorado. It worked out for the best."

That same winter before 2007, there was a rumor he would go to the Los Angeles Angels of Anaheim. The Angels offered catcher Jeff Mathis, shortstop Erick Aybar, and first baseman Casey Kotchman for Helton. But Helton had a no-trade clause and had to sign off on any deal. "But I never approached Todd with that deal because that never got far enough down the road to do anything," O'Dowd said. "But it was close."

• • •

Todd Helton once told me this story. He arrived to Coors Field the day after a quality performance, but as he pulled into the lot, he remembered the previous day's drive. He had stopped at a fast food restaurant and picked up some food. So, he literally drove all the way back to his home in Brighton and began the drive to work again—this time stopping at the same fast food spot.

He was a superstitious superstar, suffering through OCD for the sake of his OBP. "He started taking pees between innings," the trainer, Keith Dugger said. "He took a piss, hits a double. Next thing you know, every inning he's pissing—whether he has to or not. Sometimes he just went and stood in there because he got a hit the day before. So he'd get a knock the next day and do it again. Todd would sometimes change his whole uniform in the middle of the game. I'm not kidding you. And while I can't be sure, I'm not convinced he didn't have two different shoes on at times…He'd go through lockers to find stuff to use. The one thing I didn't see him steal was bats. He had his bats. Guys would try to steal his bats. Neifi Perez would try to do that every single time…didn't matter if it was a size 36 or 31. If you got a hit, you'd better watch your bats. Neifi was going to grab the bat. I never saw Todd grab bats, but he'd grab stuff all the time."

I recall one night began with Helton sporting a full beard. He didn't get on base the first at-bat. So when we saw him come up for at-bat No. 2, he was sporting a goatee. That didn't help; he was now 0–2. For his third at-bat, he strolled to the plate with a Tom Selleck mustache…still no luck. And, yep, in his fourth at-bat, a clean-shaven Helton didn't reach base. One can only wonder what would've happened if that game went to extra innings.

Another time, back in the day, we were in Montreal to face the Expos. Helton was batting in the indoor cage, and our video coordinator at the time, Mike Hamilton, was throwing him some batting practice. I watched for a quick minute, as Helton gave him some grief for his poor pitches. Hamilton, theatrically, dropped the baseballs, pointed to me, and said, "You throw to him." I chuckled, but I knew Todd's quirks. So I took my jacket off, loosened my tie, and went behind the L-screen. I threw Helton a full bucket of balls. After about 10 minutes, Helton thanked me, and Hamilton deadpanned, "You better hope he doesn't get three hits tonight!" While that would've been cool, it would've meant throwing BP every day for weeks, cutting into my pregame research time.

Around the club and the clubhouse, his crazy superstitions became part of the culture. One year at spring training, I did a long interview with Helton at his rented home in Tucson, Arizona. He shared that as much as he loved the game—when the season ended, it gave him tremendous relief because he could let go of all the superstitions and live normally.

In 2005 Helton did a rehab assignment in Colorado Springs, about an hour south of Denver, where the Triple A team played. Ryan Spilborghs was on that team for a while. Spilly didn't really know Helton too well; no one really knew Todd too well. But Helton asked Spilly to dinner, "And we sat and talked baseball with him in Colorado Springs for four hours," Spilly recalled. "He was the big money guy. If there was ever one person in the clubhouse you'd say, 'Oh leave that guy alone,' it's Todd. But Todd was kind of perceived the wrong way. He took me out to dinner with my future wife that night for dinner. He was quiet and to himself, but those years when it was 'Todd and the Toddlers,' he was kind of on an island on his own. There wasn't this supporting cast yet."

Helton was a fascinating and hard-to-pin personality. Still is. He was funny, but not a jokester. He was smart, but not a nerd. He was quiet, but not lacking in confidence. I'd sometimes rib him for being such a particularly bad interview, but the reality was he hated talking about himself publicly. He was great if you asked him about a teammate.

And he could and would rib, well, anyone. "My favorite was when we'd bring these young doctors down here," Dugger said. "He'd drill them just like they were young players. 'Hey, Doc, where you from? How old are you? You up to 13 years old? What kind of F---ing college did you go to? Where'd you take your boards at?' He said, 'I went to Knoxville Chiropractic College. They've got an online chiropractic degree.' He really liked putting a scare into these young orthos. They finally get to come down here, work for a big league team a little bit, and here's Helton: 'Are you worth a shit, doc?' 'What's you're go-to provocative test?' The young docs would be scared shitless. If a guy was nervous, he'd put his arm around them…and take a little pot shot."

He could rib you, or even playfully hit you in the ribs, but he would also care for you, even if you weren't a star teammate—or even a teammate at all. He was notoriously playful. He'd sneak up behind you and plant a kiss on your head. When my oldest, Jacob, was around nine, Jacob was in the clubhouse on a Sunday morning and wearing a youth Ryan Spilborghs jersey. Helton called him over and took his own game jersey out of his locker and had him put it on: "Wear mine instead of Spilly's." Later, when we were getting ready to leave the clubhouse, I told

Jacob to give the jersey back to Helton. He wouldn't take it and wore a different one that day instead. What a gesture by Helton. "I would be remiss if I didn't mention Todd Helton in all of this. Todd and Christy Helton took me in like I was family," said Mike "Tiny" Pontarelli, the longtime Coors Field clubhouse manager. "I had Thanksgiving with them numerous times, I've been over there for Christmas day. Todd's a very private person as everyone knows. But he's one of the most generous down to earth people—once he opens up.

"I've got a lot of good Helton stories. He wanted a ranch. He bought a ranch in Kersey in 2012. I'm casually working the ballpark one day in the fall that year. He goes, 'Hey, Tiny, you want to go to Vegas tomorrow?' And I'm like, uh, sure, yeah and I said that sounds reasonable. What's the event? 'The cattle that come over to ranch are getting shipped to Vegas for the world championships.' They flew Todd and I down there in their small plane, and we sat in the very first row of the opening night of the NFR [National Finals Rodeo] world championships of the NFR opening night. So, they got Todd on the big screen, and he's pumped up. I watched the movie *8 Seconds* about Lane Frost, so I knew about [Rodeo Hall of Famer] Tuff Hedeman, and Tuff Hedeman comes over and wants to hang out! For me my relationship with Todd, he was like a big brother to me, and I could talk to him about girls or whatever it was, or whatever you would talk to your big brother with. I'm so fortunate to see him have a storied career. It gives me chills."

In the days leading up to Helton's 2013 retirement, the media tried to put Helton's longevity into perspective. Perhaps there was no better way than to look at Jack Woodhull. Then a high school sophomore at Kent Denver School, Jack was born on August 2, 1997, the day of Helton's major league debut. "The entire time I've been living," Woodhull said at the time, "one guy's been playing for one team. I went from an infant to a high school student and I've had so much change in my life. Whereas Todd Helton, over that entire time span, he's been doing the same thing with the same team. You must have major love for the sport to do that for that long."

The day Woodhull was born at Avista Adventist Hospital, another baby face came into our world. That August day against the Pirates in Pittsburgh, the rookie Helton singled and then walloped a homer over the right-field wall, a mirrored image of his masterstroke a decade later against the Los Angeles Dodgers, the walk-off amid the magic of the autumn of 2007.

Seventeen seasons for No. 17. But really, it's been a blur of doubles and dingers, raucous Rocktober, and sputtering Septembers. And suddenly, your hero is 40. "It just doesn't seem fair that it goes by so fast," said Jack's father, John Woodhull, at the time. "And it's so quickly over."

Parenting seems to be the same way. It makes us want to not lose days, to clutch onto moments, to cherish the present before it becomes the faded past. "It's amazing how fast it goes by," Jack's father said. "You think about when they're little kids and you're raising them and watching little events go by in your life, the good events, sports events, like when the Rockies went to the World Series and all the great things Todd has done over that period of time, just being a total clutch player and leader on that team."

In Helton's final home game, they gave him a horse. And Helton homered. It was his 369th homer, which by the end of 2018, was still the 80th most in baseball history. That was tied with Ralph Kiner, three more than Lance Berkman, and 10 fewer than Hall of Famers Tony Perez and Orlando Cepeda. I still can't believe he homered in his first at-bat of his final home game. It's like something out of a movie. "That was probably my favorite home run," Helton said. "I just remember driving to the ballpark that day and I had a bunch of people there, so I'm thinking to myself, *There's no chance I play well tonight.* I'm thinking the worst, like I'm going to strike out three times. So to hit a homer in my first at-bat was pretty amazing. I hit a double that I thought was going to be a homer to left-center. It was a great night, it was a fitting end to be a good career."

The following season, on August 17, the Rockies retired Helton's No. 17 to honor his 17 seasons with Colorado. To this day my sons still have Helton posters on their bedroom walls.

CHAPTER 4
CARGO, TULO, AND UBALDO

What he was doing while sick was—as my sons would say—sick. Carlos Gonzalez had gone 4-for-8 in the previous two games with two homers. But when he arrived to Coors Field that next day— July 30, 2010—he told manager Jim Tracy that "I felt awful," Gonzalez recalled. "I'd had a fever all night. I felt really bad and didn't think I could play that day."

Tracy was understanding, sure, but the guy had hit two bombs in two days anyways. Oh, and that day's opponent, the Chicago Cubs were starting a righty, and CarGo, as all of Colorado called him, was, of course, a lethal lefty. "Play today," Tracy said, "And I'll give you a day tomorrow because their pitcher is a lefty."

CarGo played. He singled, doubled, and homered, and the Rockies beat the Cubs 17–2. "So after the game," Gonzalez recalled, "Tracy's like, 'How do you feel?' I was like, 'I feel better. It's gone now. I feel a lot better.' He was like, 'I'm glad you're feeling better, but even if you were in a coma, you were going to play tomorrow!' I started laughing."

That next night was July 31, 2010. CarGo singled, then tripled, the rare hit he needed the day before for a cycle. Then he doubled. "I was like, 'I'm going to hit for the cycle today.'" CarGo said. "I'm 3-for-3, I'm missing the homer and I get another opportunity. I hit a really hard ball to center field, but it was caught for a sac fly. It should have been a home run, but I hit a low line drive to center. So I was like, 'Well, today's another day in a row I fell short of the cycle.' So I go play defense, and we blew the save. Derrek Lee hit a home run to center field to tie the game in the eighth. So I was like, 'Well…I'm going to have another opportunity.' So, in my mind I'd already seen every pitch. Everything was down and away, breaking balls, fastballs away, I was hitting everything everywhere. So I was like the only thing I haven't seen is a fastball in. They had Sean Marshall in, and he was a tough lefty and he had a good fastball. So I said, 'If he throws me a fastball first pitch, I'm going to pull it.'"

Holy shit, did he pull it. One of the hardest hit balls I've ever seen. It went to the third deck in right field. A walk-off home run...to complete the cycle, too. "Man, that was a movie story," Gonzalez said. "It's one of those stories where people don't realize what happens behind the scenes...And that night I hit for the cycle, I was not supposed to play!"

The homer went 462 feet to the first row of the third deck. And it landed perfectly into the hands of a seated fan...in a Cubs jersey. "The look on his face was *priceless*," recalled Jeff Huson, my broadcast partner.

"After the game," CarGo said, "I get to the clubhouse, and everybody's hugging me, and I just remember sitting in my locker, trying to soak it in, trying to realize what I just did, and I was like, 'Man, I can't explain what the hell happened.' But I was really happy, really thankful. And I ended up getting the ball, too."

Carlos Eduardo Gonzalez, of Maracaibo, Venezuela, is my all-time favorite Rockie. Of course, this is not a slight on anyone else. It's just that Carlos has been this perfect Colorado confluence of skill, personality, and heart. He is a warm guy, transcendent in the clubhouse. He possesses a quick wit and cracks up his teammates with spot-on impersonations of their idiosyncrasies. He is just a beautiful person, and you see the best of Carlos when things are actually going the worst for him. Consider that in 2017, as his batting average plummeted, he was often spotted encouraging the young players. His arm would be around the shoulder of Trevor Story or Tony Wolters. He truly is the consummate team player. "Carlos is one of the finest human beings you'll ever meet," trainer Scott Gehret said. "He's caring, he's loving, he's the guy that you want to be around because when you're around him you're happy. He gives you that smile, and it doesn't matter if you're having a miserable day. When you see 'Cinco,' he lights up a room, and it's all genuine. He's incredibly smart. He catches on to things like that. He's another guy that we taught football. He loves watching ball. When

I compare Carlos Gonzalez—perhaps my favorite Rockies player—to Gumby because he stretches so far before he uncoils during his swing.

Colorado State doesn't do well, he gets mad at me and threatens to switch over to being a Colorado Buffs fan. At the end of the day, he's the guy you want to be your brother, your son, who you want to marry your daughter. He's just that kind of guy."

• • •

Carlos Gonzalez is an artist. "You go through the history of guys I've seen in the Rockies uniform," Jeff Huson said, "and by far he's got the prettiest swing."

His swing generates such incredible bat speed. It produces effortless violence when it collides with the baseball. He is tremendously strong and twists his body like Gumby—and combined with a leg lift—that creates ridiculous torque. With a handful of the true power hitters in baseball, you will hear players speak of a different sound when they hit the ball. When CarGo hits the ball, it clearly makes a different sound. He was the 2010 National League batting champion, a two-time Silver Slugger award winner, and a three-time Gold Glover. "He's a freak show!" My favorite of CarGo hits—as fun as it is to see him hit it five miles—are the five to six times a year he hits the ol' 1 iron to center field. And the center fielder thinks he's going to come in and field it, and it goes over his head to the wall or flat over everything. Madison Bumgarner, who CarGo has taken deep five times in his career, once told me that his favorite swing to watch of any player was CarGo's. "I was down at BP one time, and CarGo was hitting," owner Dick Monfort said. "And Todd Helton was standing there next to me. Todd said, 'I haven't seen a talent like this since Larry [Walker] left.'"

Or maybe Matt Holliday, Helton's teammate in the mid-2000s. So when the Rockies dealt Matt Holliday to the Oakland A's, most people figured the Rockies would never have a player that productive again in the outfield. Not only would they have another, but they also got him in the Holliday trade itself. On November 10, 2008, the Athletics traded Carlos Gonzalez, Greg Smith, and closer Huston Street to the Rockies for Matt Holliday. "So when Holliday gets traded, I get an opportunity to play," said Ryan Spilborghs, one of my current broadcast partners. "I'm heading into 2009 as my first year as a left fielder. We just traded our best player, though. So we get to camp in 2009 and see CarGo. Even in spring training, I don't remember anything about CarGo standing out. Who was impressive was Dexter Fowler; he ended up making the team out of camp. Ian Stewart was impressive. But Carlos Gonzalez? He played in the minors. We get through the first month. We're underperforming. I'm doing well, but the team isn't. Clint Hurdle gets fired on May 29th, and for that group, Hurdle's firing meant a lot because we got our manager, the guy we went to the World Series with less than two years before, fired. We underperformed. We failed him. Hurdle always said, 'When the team does well, I give you the credit. When the team does bad, I fall on the sword.' Hurdle's in a suit, addressing the team. He had no reason to do that, but he did. He said, 'I fell on the sword, but I know you're better than this. I know you're a better team than this.' That was the message he left us, and he was right.

"We had complacency, and Hurdle was that shock to the system for that group in 2009. And what coincided with that was they called up Ian Stewart and Carlos Gonzalez. So CarGo starts in place of me, and he's pressing. He's not doing well. And Jim Tracy would not take him out of the lineup. And eventually I go to the clubhouse and talk to Tracy. I go, 'Hey, I'm a starting outfielder with a lot of doubles, even though I've been moved to different spots. How did I lose my job?' He said, 'I'll use you in a position that allows you to succeed'...So I detracted from the team. Coming to work was really difficult. And while I'm watching CarGo play, I'm cheering him, but CarGo was trying to hit a home run every single time. I'm fed up with the Rockies at this point because I feel like I'm not being treated fairly. And I come up to CarGo and I told him: 'If I'm going to watch you play and I'm feeling bad about myself, can you at least be good? Can you at least have fun? Just relax.' There's no denying that his talent was elite. The way the ball came off his bat, the way he played defense. No matter how bad he was hitting, his defense was always unbelievable."

But the offense was offensive. Spilly was right. By July 4 CarGo was hitting .194 (13-for-67) with just one home run. But the team had been rejuvenated under the new skipper Tracy, whose Rockies squad was 42–38 overall on July 4 and was continually pestered with questions from the media about Gonzalez. "They were hounding me about CarGo!" Tracy said. "Here's the reason why: I'm taking over the club, and Carlos Gonzalez has shown up in the big leagues. And, hey, let's face it, he struggled. He had a batting average that looked like a bingo number. But we had an 11-game winning streak until Joe Maddon and the Tampa Bay Rays broke it up. Then we won the next two and swept the next series to win 17 out of 18. When we get back in town, I'm getting a few questions here and there bombing away with, 'Hey how much longer can you keep playing Carlos Gonzalez?' We've gone from last place, basically 10 or 12 games under .500, to becoming completely relevant in the playoff hunt now. And they're asking how're you going to be able to continue playing this guy? And I had heard enough of it from the point now I'm getting a little pissed because I'm going to protect my players. And this kid here is trying really hard—and I knew how really good he was—and I finally looked at a writer and said: 'Hey, look, here's how long he's going to play. When I walk in this clubhouse every day, and I say to Mike Pontarelli, 'Is Gonzalez here,' and if he says, yes, then I'm writing his name on the lineup card.' He was brought here to the big leagues for a reason. He has to have some time to figure it out."

On the Fourth of July, CarGo went hitless. The Rockies are known for putting on a splendid fireworks show, so after the game, the players gathered in the tunnel into the dugout to watch the fireworks with their families. "And I," CarGo said, "was hitting in the cage. Next thing I know, I hear this call from Jim to come into his office, so the first thing that comes to mind is that I'm going to get sent down. That's when he gave me the biggest words. It could have been easier to hear, 'You'd better start hitting,' or whatever, but it was a great conversation. It was so positive. He gave me everything that I needed. He gave me all the confidence because he said: no matter what I do, I was going to be his every day left fielder because I was playing tremendous defense. When it comes to hitting, it's easier for people to notice when you're hitting or not. But they don't realize you could be helping your team in other ways, like a small walk, or scoring from first base on a ball to the gap, or avoiding a guy, taking an extra base on a single. He was one of those managers that pay close attention to that, and that's why he won a bunch of ballgames that year. After that conversation I felt much better, and that's when I started putting up better numbers. I had a strong second half, we clinched the postseason, and that was when my career took off... It all goes back to that July 4."

The Rockies had 82 games remaining, and CarGo's performances were so nice, so needed. In those games he hit .313 with a .381 on-base percentage and a whopping .592 slugging percentage. He hit a dozen homers and stole a dozen bases. "CarGo is the best player that nobody knows about," former Dodgers star Orel Hershiser, a former World Series MVP, told *The Denver Post*. "When I see a Rockies game on TV, I have to stop and watch when he's up to bat. I just love seeing him hit."

Tracy became just the second manager to replace a fired manager midseason and win the National League Manager of the Year award. (Jack McKeon won it with the Florida Marlins in 2003). Tracy's Rockies were 74–42. "Boy, when CarGo started to go, I mean, to tell you, we became one dangerous ass ballclub when this kid figured it out," Tracy said, "there's no doubt about it. We were firing on all cylinders. No doubt about it."

In the 2009 National League Division Series, they'd face the defending NL champs, the Philadelphia Phillies, the cocky squad that in 2007 said was "the team to beat" but then got swept by the Rockies in the NLDS. Two years later, a rematch of sorts took place.

The series was tied after two games. In the third game, which was at raucous Coors Field, the game was tied in the ninth. Street, the son of legendary University of Texas quarterback James Street, had also thrived in his first season in Colorado, saving 35 games. But a pair of ground-ball singles, a bunt, and a sac fly gave Philadelphia the lead for good. In Game 4, also at Coors, the Rockies jumped to a 4–2 lead, and CarGo had reached base three times. The ninth just seemed ceremonial. Street would close it down, and these two new postseason rivals, who had nearly identical regular-season records, would battle it out in a decisive Game 5 in Philly. My bags were packed in my car, anticipating a late-night flight back east. "That loss was heartbreaking, from the point of view of we could see it coming," Spilborghs said. "Jim Tracy rode Huston Street really hard. And he was out of gas. You could see it in the first batter. Jim Tracy had that old-school mentality to leave it on these guys but to their detriment, too. He should've seen it because we saw it. We're like, 'Get our friend out of there! Ivan Drago is about to kill Apollo Creed!'"

Single, walk, double, single. It was suddenly 5–4 Philly.

The Rockies actually had a chance to tie it up—thanks to CarGo. He singled, unflappably, in the bottom of the ninth. So did Helton. But with two on and two out, Troy Tulowtizki struck out. The pitcher who K'd Tulo was Brad Lidge, a Denver native. "That 2009 team was the better talent [than 2007]," Spilborghs said. "You felt shell-shocked after 2009…But Carlos Gonzalez's postseason in 2009 was his coming-out party. He was 10-for-17. He was batting leadoff then, too. And then in 2010 he was third in the MVP and won the batting title and truly became an elite player in the game."

You read that right: he was 10-for-17 and he had two walks, too. And, of course, there was his sterling fielding in the outfield. "Everything clicked," recalled CarGo, who was 23 during that particular season. "Not only did I have a great series, but I won the confidence from my manager, the front office, my teammates, the fans and I knew that I was at the place I always wanted to be: an everyday player establishing my career. At that point, I was like, I'm not going back. I'm not going back to that position where everyone was having doubts about me like, *Is he an everyday player or not? Why are we going to keep playing this guy?* In the minor leagues and even when I was in Little League, I was always the type of player who put up big numbers offensively and still went out there and kicked some butt defensively. I was finally getting to start doing that in the big leagues and I knew I was going in the right direction. So I just kept working and I knew with the confidence I have playing the game and the understanding of how I was able to do it, at any level. I was like, 'Here we go.'"

On May 30, 2018, I wanted to ask CarGo about May 30, 2008. That was his big league debut, the culmination of his journey from Venezuela to Missoula through the minors to the majors. He said in his first at-bat that night, playing for Oakland, he hit a line-drive double down the left-field line. The pitcher for the Texas Rangers that night was Kevin Millwood, the former All-Star. "My mother has the ball," he said.

She keeps most of his memorabilia and trophies. She also has the home-run ball for the cycle, acquired by the club from the fan of the Chicago Cubs. He's won three Gold Gloves, but he said his most rewarding honors are his two Silver Sluggers. "Those are hard to earn, you have to be the best at your position in the whole league," he said. "I'm not that guy that collects all the things that I do on the field. My mom is the master. She wants to have it all. If you go to my house, you don't think a baseball player lives there. I've got pictures of my kids, family stuff. I try to make sure home is home."

CarGo thrived under Tracy and had a good experience with Walt Weiss, too. But he was particularly excited when he got a phone call, in November of 2016, from Bud Black. "I was in Orlando, Florida, and I think I was one of the first players that he called," Gonzalez said of the new skipper. "He was extremely happy, but I was even more happy because I know what type of manager he is. He was Manager of the Year in that 2010 season that was really special for me. I remember he was the manager because we faced him a lot when he was a Padre. Pain in the ass, always bringing the right pitcher to face you. He still does. He's a great manager when it comes to pitching. Always trying to make sure he gives you the best opportunity to succeed. He's a different person, too. You always see his eyes when it comes to baseball. When he's on your side, he's a funny man, joking around, making sure everyone is loose in the clubhouse."

But the 2017 season, a year after making yet another All-Star team, CarGo's play was unfamiliar. He entered the year with a career average of .291—and in 2017 he hit .262.

And entering September that season, his batting average was .239.

But he epitomized the word "teammate" that summer. His hitting wasn't contagious, but his smile was. And then September came, and there were flashes of the familiar CarGo. The resurgence was unexpected, exciting, and integral to the Rockies' push for the postseason; Colorado hadn't been in since 2009, CarGo's breakout October. "You could tell the players were happy for him," Huson said. "They knew how hard he struggled."

In the final month of 2017, CarGo hit .377 and swatted two homers in a key game to beat division rival Arizona Diamondbacks. He also led the Rockies to a huge sweep of the Dodgers in Los Angeles while going 6-for-13 with a pair of homers. "The thing that made me most proud of Carlos," trainer Scott Gehret said, "is when we clinched and made the playoffs, and he hadn't been in the playoffs since '09, there was not a happier man in the clubhouse than Carlos Gonzalez, smiling ear-to-ear, passing out hugs. That guy was genuinely thrilled to be back in the postseason and to succeed as a Colorado Rockie."

CarGo homered in the final game of the regular season. The game was at Coors Field. Colorado would only return if it won the wild-card game played at, of all places, Arizona. "We had that special day where we go around the stadium, shake hands, give fans gifts, and sometimes they get to hug you," CarGo said. "It's an every year thing. It's like, 'Okay, this is the last home game.' But last year was different for me because I was going to be a free agent. I didn't realize how people were kind of affected because I was going to be a free agent. They didn't know what the future was for me. I saw people crying and stuff, and it's like what's going on? People saying, 'Hey, come back. Please don't leave us,' and stuff like that. That's when I realized, maybe this might be my last opportunity to put on this uniform. Time flies. I'm here now for 10 seasons with the Rockies. So you think this is going to be forever, and things don't last forever. When you see fans react in that way, I felt very humble. They don't get to know you as a person, but watching you every day and listening to your interviews, they get a sense of who you are. These kids, all they know is the Rockies."

In the wild-card game, CarGo had two hits, including an RBI single in the ninth, as the Rockies tried to mount a comeback. But they lost 11–8, a score fitting for old Mile High Stadium. And in one of the most-surprising twists, after all the years and tears and good–byes, CarGo ended up signing with the Rockies for one more run in 2018 for another year of the sweetest stroke I'll ever see in the batter's box.

• • •

His presence led to resonance, his name pronounced in a variety of manners or even mannerisms. There's the Rockies' public-address announcer, Reed Saunders, who would bellow: "Now batting: Troy! Tuuuu-looooow-itzki!" Or those around Denver who would sing the old Hammer song with a twist: "Tu-lo git, Tu-lo git to quit!" And, of course: "Clap-clap, clap-clap-clap, clap-clap-clap-clap, TU-LO!" (It'll be the year 2073, and someone will hear that clap cadence and shout: "TU-LO!")

Shortstop Troy Tulowitzki was a bona-fide star for a while there, one of the best talents to ever play for Colorado. His legacy will always include injury. He's a first-ballot "what if" player. Even with the hundreds of missed games over his career, Tulowitzki had some resplendent seasons, in fact, four with a wins above replacement (WAR) of over six. At the time in 2014, only eight active players had done that. "For me, as a former infielder, to watch someone as big as he is move as well as he does?" My broadcast partner Jeff Huson said. "Cal Ripken was just as big but didn't have the range. To watch Troy make that jump-throw in the hole like he did or the spin up the middle, it was amazing because those were tough plays for even guys like Omar Vizquel's size. That was fun to watch."

Tulo is one of those guys who just loved being a ballplayer—and not even necessarily for the celebrity of it—but for the competition of it. As a kid he had his walls decorated with photos of shortstops. He was the seventh pick in the draft in 2005, was a Rockie by 2006, and a Rocktober hero by 2007. "My first impressions of him was: young, dumb, just full of energy," veteran pitcher Josh Fogg said. "Man, he could do anything he wanted out there. You knew he was going to screw up two or three times, doing something full boar 100 percent and mess up, but he was also going to do two or three amazing things. As he cleaned up those screwups, he was pretty special to watch."

He was 6'3", about 210 but looked even bigger and stronger than those numbers imply. He became the fans' favorite player and even played to the fans with playful walk-ups songs, such as those by Justin Bieber or Katy Perry. He finished his Denver days with five All-Star nods, two Gold Gloves, and two Silver Sluggers. Sure enough, the two seasons he made it to 150-plus games, the Rockies made the playoffs (2007 and 2009). His best season—and this is saying something, considering he only played 122 games—was 2010, when he slashed .315/.381/.568, while finishing fifth in the MVP voting.

Though, it's sure fun to daydream about the ultimate "what if": Tulo's 2014 season. Ben Reiter of *Sports Illustrated* pointed out that at the "quarter pole" of that season, Tulo was on pace for the greatest season of any player ever. Tulowitzki was hitting .375 with 14 homers with stellar defense. "By Baseball Reference's numbers, Tulowitzki's current WAR of 4.6—the statistic factors in his fielding—projects to a seasonal WAR of 14.9," Reiter said at the time. "Barry Bonds' best WAR was 11.9, which he produced in his 73-homer 2001. The WAR record for a position player is Babe Ruth's from 1923. It was 14.1."

Troy Tulowitzki celebrates after hitting the game-winning single in the 10th inning of a 2009 game against the Los Angeles Dodgers.

Alas, the shortstop got banged up again. Tulo played only 91 games, hitting 21 homers, finishing with a slash line of .340/.432/.603.

Tulo was famously moody, though some chalked it up to passion. During his official rookie season of 2007, No. 2 played like No. 2 in a particular game. But the Rockies won. After the game the kid was stewing. Trainer Scott Gehret recalled Tulo coming into the trainer's room after the game. The veteran Fogg tried to lighten the mood—and lighten him up. Troy said something along the lines of "nothing went right" on the night. Fogg verbally pushed him: *"Nothing, Tulo?"*

"Nothing went fucking right!"

So, the veteran Fogg chewed out the rookie and chewed up the rookie, telling him that the team was more important than any individual accomplishments or failures. Tulo stormed out. Fogg turned to Gehret and said: "Hmm, I think I taught him well."

"I think that resonated with Troy," Gehret said. "He may or may not admit it, but I think he remembered it because he's a very happy-go-lucky guy 90 percent of the time in those days. Fast forward to the playoffs. Now Troy, as you know, became a superstar that year. He drove in 99 runs, hit 24 home runs, and really was becoming the face of the Colorado Rockies. We had that miracle run, made the playoffs, fly all night to Philadelphia. No one went to work that next day because we were all exhausted, but we show up in the morning for a 3:00 game to open the playoffs against the Phillies. Clint had named his three starters for the short series. It was Jeff Francis, Frankie Morales, and Ubaldo Jimenez. That offended Josh Fogg because he had made 60 starts over the previous two years. That morning Josh is in the training room and he was kind of bullshitting with us, but he was pissed. Troy walked in. Josh is offended that he wasn't named a starter and is going on this rant about he had taken the ball every five days for two years. He said, 'I'm never coming back here [as a free agent]. I can't believe Clint wouldn't start me!' This, that, and the other thing. Troy overheard this and he turned around and said: 'Hey Fogger,' in a very stern voice. 'It took more than 30 of us to get here, and if we're going where we want to go, it's going to take all 25 of us in this fucking clubhouse. That fucking means you, so get ready to fucking pitch.' Well, we won Game 1 going

69

away. But Game 2, Clint pinch-hit for Frankie Morales early in the game. It ended up being the same inning that Kaz [Matsui] hit the home run that put the game out of reach, but Josh came in and threw two-and-one-third innings of shutout baseball and got the win that day. After the game those two had a pretty touching embrace in the training room. Tulo came in and jumped on Josh and said, 'I fucking told you!' It was pretty neat."

• • •

Ubaldo Jimenez was the starting pitcher for the National League in the 2010 All-Star Game. He threw the first no-hitter in Colorado history. But his greatest contribution to Rockies lore was his cameo in the team's commercial for fake products, when he held up an Aerosol spray can and gleefully said: "If Ubaldo, try Hair-Be-There!"

The lanky righty was one of the best pitchers to ever wear the purple pinstripes. And you could make the argument that he had one of the best first halves of a year by any pitcher ever. After the playoff season in 2009, Jimenez's 2010 was glorious. The sinkerballer scorched the catchers' mitts. The flamethrower was absolutely filthy for three-plus months. I anticipated his starts like I remember anticipating the starts of Tom Seaver and Dwight Gooden when I was younger. When he arrived in Anaheim for the All-Star Game, his record was 15–1, and, of course, many of his starts were at altitude in Denver. As late as June 17th, his ERA was 1.15. By the break he was at 2.20, and his opponents' batting average was .198.

I often tell my broadcast partner Jeff Huson that when my broadcasting days are over I'll go to scout school because I just love watching and talking baseball from every aspect. At spring training I'll saunter to the back fields to eyeball the prospects and I'll never forget this duo in the spring of 2006—one righty, one lefty, these two power arms. It was Jimenez and Frankie Morales.

But Jimenez's journey to the majors was detoured in Single A. He suffered a stress fracture in his right shoulder. But even teammates thought he was faking the injury. So to prove to them he was hurt, he actually pitched in a game with the injury. "Some of my teammates didn't even believe me," he told *The Denver Post*. "I will never forget going out on the mound and throwing 58 miles per hour on the first pitch and 60 miles per hour on the second pitch. It was obvious something was really wrong."

He was 20 at the time, that summer of 2004. But he recovered and rediscovered his stuff. By 2006, at age 22, this kid with the strange delivery and the strange name was called up to the Colorado Rockies. Dan O'Dowd used to excitedly say: "Wait til you guys see this guy Ubaldo!'" He had this 98 mile-per-hour two-seamer.

In his first matchup against the division rival Arizona Diamondbacks, Jimenez faced Orlando Hudson, this engaging personality nicknamed "The O-Dog." Jimenez unleashed two heaters and then complemented them with a knee-buckling breaking ball. Hudson's smile was as flashy as his play, but this thing lit up his face as if to say: "You've gotta be kidding me!" He walked back to the dugout, wearing that incredulous grin.

Later that inning Jimenez faced former Rockies outfielder Eric Byrnes. The kid's 98 mph sinker splintered Byrnes' bat into a thousand pieces. Byrnes shook his hands from the vibration after the slow roller became a ground-out. The next day I went to see him in the Arizona clubhouse. "Who the fuck is that guy?" Byrnes said. "And where the fuck did he come from?"

Jimenez had this presence to him and also a nice smile—a warm smile. I remember one time we were on the West Coast and I was over at an LA Fitness by the hotel in Anaheim, lifting weights, and Jimenez comes in. Mid-morning, there he was—one of the best young pitchers in the sport, showing up at a public gym to sneak in an extra workout. He

Drew's Diary

May 15, 2018:
Colorado Rockies at San Diego Padres

You show up at the park and, as the saying goes, "You never know what you may see." How about Jordan Lyles plucked from the San Diego Padres' pen for one start and getting a follow-up start against his former club, throwing a near perfect game? Going into the eighth inning, he had 72 pitches with nine strikeouts and two balls out of the infield. He struck out Carlos Gonzalez to begin the eighth inning and then gave up an end-of-bat line drive to left by Trevor Story for the only Rockies hit of the day. It was the longest perfect game ever against Colorado. This from a guy, who once told reporters after another sub-par performance with the Rockies, "That's the situation with Jordan Lyles. You never know what you are going to get." He said that, referring to himself in the third person to describe his roller-coaster performances. After that comment, which was devoid of self-confidence, I remember thinking that he couldn't be long for the Rockies. He was let go not long after.

So far this year, Lyles has used a four-seam fastball and power curve coupled with new found aggressiveness to pitch very well. My Twitter account lit up with many frustrated Rockies fans basically writing, "Jordan Lyles! Are you kidding me?" The loss snapped a six-game road winning streak. The most poignant stat of the day: since the start of 2017, the Rockies remarkably have a better road record than home record. That is a span of more than 200 games. I was shocked and mentioned that when I ducked into Bud Black's office at Petco Park in the late morning. He looked at me, removed his cheaters for a moment to

Continued on next page

Continued from previous page

fully digest my statement, and thought for a moment. "I never would have guessed that," he said. He added that he has never mentioned a different approach or mind-set between home and road. He has gone to great lengths to instill in his team that it's about how they play day-to-day, how they play to their standard, and never mentioning altitude. I have long thought this was the absolute right approach to playing and sustaining winning baseball in Denver.

and watch history? I remember watching the whole game, waiting for the catch Dexter Fowler made to keep it alive. In Afghanistan it's a connection to home. You can read about the Rockies or watch Ubaldo's no-hitter and you take your mind away and imagine you're watching it on the couch in Denver."

My view was from the comfortable confines of the broadcast booth. But you're always nervous during no-nos. Your job is to call the game and you want to use an economy of words. Let the pitcher and pitches tell the story. Let the moment resonate. So when Brian McCann hit the ground ball to Clint Barnes, I said emphatically: "Ubaldo Jimenez has no-hit the Atlanta Braves!" You're now attached to it. It was truly a moment of goose bumps. Sports is truly the last bastion of reality television. You don't know what you're going to see. That's the beauty of baseball. And that night in Atlanta, we saw something never done in Rockies history.

That night, back at the team hotel, Jimenez couldn't sleep. He said he was groggy, trying to process it all. "It was like a wonderful dream I was having," he said the next day. "If it was reality or a dream, it was wonderful."

So, finally, he just got up at 6:00 AM, went outside, and started jogging on the streets of Atlanta's Buckhead. He went six miles, still glowing from the history he made.

Jimenez finished third in Cy Young voting behind winner Roy Halladay and Adam Wainwright, though Jimenez had a better WAR than Wainwright. In 2010 Jimenez finished 19–8 with the best winning percentage in the National League (.704). He struck out 214 batters in 221⅔ innings. And his ERA was a remarkable 2.88, including a 3.19 mark at home (nine wins) and 2.63 on the road (10 wins).

And his success got him in yet another commercial. This one was made by MLB. He was in a full uniform in a gift shop, looking at those mini license plates with first names on them. He's meticulously looking at all the names, trying to find one with UBALDO. Teammate Jorge De La Rosa comes into the shop and tells Jimenez the bus is waiting for him. "Uno minuto," he pleads to De La Rosa, then looks at the cashier and says: "Do you have any more in the back?"

CHAPTER 5
ROCKTOBER

The Dodger was a giant. Relief pitcher Jonathan Broxton stood 6'4" and weighed, give or take a pound, a metric ton. It was as if he put his whole body into his fastball, this searing, sizzling Rawlings fired at 100 miles per hour. And he was just the set-up guy!

As their closer, the 2007 Los Angeles Dodgers had Takashi Saito, who had faced 14 Rockies batters that season, not allowing a single hit.

It was a laborious day in Denver—September 18, 2007—since the boys had to play two that Tuesday. In the previous game, the Rockies avoided a home sweep of the perennially lowly Florida Marlins, but even that win in front of a scattered Coors crowd of 19,161, put the Rockies at just 77–72. It was going to be another one of those middling seasons in the middle of a seemingly lost decade for the franchise.

The Rockies stole the first game of the twinbill. But here they were in the eighth inning of the second game and they trailed 8–5…seemingly sent to the plate ceremoniously to face the indomitable Broxton and Saito.

Ryan Spilborghs, the lovable Rockie, often garnered grief from his buddies in the clubhouse for his incapacity to hit fastballs, let alone one like Broxton's triple-digit deliveries. But with teammate Garrett Atkins on first, Spilly belted a Broxton pitch. "A two-run shot!" Spilly recalled. "I come running in the dugout, and we're all pumped up. And I'm excited because I couldn't hit Broxton, and he was really good and threw 100. And I was like, 'I got him, see? I don't have slow bat speed!' And all the guys are like: 'Nice homer, but that was off the slider!' We're still talking trash to each other, keeping each other grounded…It didn't feel like a big league team. It just felt like you and your buddies. It was a frat house. So you get into September, and we knew our backs were against the wall, but we also knew we had plenty of talent."

But the one guy who was a little aloof was Todd Helton, the 34-year-old reserved and revered veteran. His college was Tennessee, but his "school" was old. He was still hitting balls hard in 2007, and thanks to Spilly's homer, there was a chance Helton would get one more at-bat in this ballgame.

But there was Saito. I'd seldom seen anyone dominate Colorado the way this guy did. He was surgical. And with an 8–7 lead in the ninth, the Dodgers seemed destined to split the doubleheader, essentially canceling out a day's work, losing a day on the calendar that was running out of them.

But with two outs, Matt Holliday drilled a ball the opposite way. It was like a boxer getting cut; Saito had actually allowed a hit to the Rockies. With two outs Helton got down two strikes, including a paltry foul ball as he stumbled in the batter's box. I watched from my perch in the broadcast booth when I exclaimed: "Todd drives one high and deep, right field! Get up and get out!...Helton has done it! The Rockies win it, Todd Helton a walk-off two-run shot!"

And as he rounded third, Helton showed Colorado a Helton never seen before. Raw emotion. And think about this: he'd been in the bigs for a decade. He heaved his helmet off his head. His hair seemed to shoot up, as his jaw dropped and his eyes popped. He jumped into his teammates like it was a mosh pit at the plate. "When Todd beat Saito with that walk-off, that's my favorite baseball memory ever," Spilly said, "at any level. Watching Todd and that team was my favorite memory. I know the other guys would talk about that memory, too, because Todd meant so much to us, because Todd was always on the outside...We always had this tight-knit group, but when he comes around the bases it felt like: come on over, we're all in it together! That's the guy we admire the most, and he just jumped in the pool with the rest of the group. And the rest is history."

With the doubleheader wins, the Rockies were 79–72. In the winning clubhouse, the Rockies players waited for Helton to finish his on-field interviews—so they could give him a standing ovation. That type of thing just doesn't happen in big league clubhouses.

Todd Helton shows rare emotion following his walk-off home run against the Los Angeles Dodgers in September of 2007, a victory that spurred the Rockies' momentum down the stretch.

With the doubleheader losses, the Dodgers were also 79–72. The Dodgers' manager, Grady Little, said from the losing clubhouse: "We gave the ball to probably the two most dependable people in the league, and it just didn't happen. We've got to run the table now and still depend on other people. That's not a good feeling."

But for the Rockies, it was a different kind of feeling. Daunting, sure, but after winning both those games—and the way they won the second—it was like they cherished the feeling of outside doubt.

The next day general manager Dan O'Dowd pulled into his parking spot at the stadium when his cell phone rang. It was Keli McGregor, his boss. What a man, a man's man. He was a Colorado kid, a football star at Colorado State, drafted by the Denver Broncos. And then, after getting his master's degree and a stint as the associate athletic director at the University of Arkansas, he became an executive for the Colorado Rockies. He worked his way up to team president at just age 38. That was in 2001. He passed away, unexpectedly, in 2010 due to a rare virus in his heart. He had this magnetic ability to just connect with people— from a room full of owners, to the clubhouse, to the ushers that worked the ballpark.

McGregor was 6'6½", extremely handsome, and still looked like he could play a few downs at tight end. Every year McGregor and I would go on a ski trip with Greg Feasel (the chief operating officer of the Rockies) and Tim Griggs (the Fox Sports Rocky Mountains GM). On one such trip, I recall sitting and having a beer after a long ski day. We talked about winning a championship. McGregor shared with me that he badly wanted to see the day, but he yearned that it be done a certain way. He didn't want some mercenaries on the team with little connection to one another. Sure, they'd pour champagne in celebration, but it wouldn't have the same meaning as it would for homegrown teammates with a bond. I've always remembered that conversation.

And so, on that 2007 day after the Helton walk-off win, O'Dowd received a call from McGregor: "Buckle up, Dan," he said. "We are about to go on the ride of your lifetime."

• • •

Entering the 2007 season, the last time the Rockies had been in the playoffs, Troy Tulowitzki was 10. Colorado hadn't even had a winning season since 2000. "But 2007 was one of the first times ever that I was around a group of guys where I realized it wasn't just 25 guys on a big league team," said Ryan Spilborghs, who had a very respectable .848 OPS (on-base plus slugging percentage) that year in 300 plate appearances. "Because the years prior, 2005, Matt Holliday and Garrett Atkins are becoming established, and there are a handful of big leaguers who are, I guess, in transit—Eric Byrnes, Larry Bigbie. There were all these strange names who were on the 2005 Rockies. But there was starting to be the mix of a core. You start seeing the likes of Brad Hawpe and Jeff Francis, kind of getting this group together.

"And then you get into 2006, and Holliday starts going to another level. I remember we're in Anaheim. And [Rockies coach] Mike Gallego is good friends with Mark McGwire. Gallego and McGwire, of course, played together in Oakland. [Gallego used to always tease that his workout with McGwire after a game was putting weight on the racks for McGwire.] So Gallego gets McGwire to come and have a private hitting lesson with Holliday...These guys are turning into pretty good major leaguers, and Matt Holliday is getting a personal hitting lesson with Big Mac? Holliday gets a little tweak to his swing, and the second half, he takes off to another level. And Garrett Atkins finishes that year with 120 RBIs. So you're kind of going into 2007 thinking, *Our guys aren't that bad!* We were sort of earning our stripes in the baseball community. You start hearing from other players that your guys aren't that bad. Homegrown talent. So that big league team didn't feel like you were joining a major league team, where you really have to be quiet. You could have personalities. And it went a long way. The characters were allowed to be who they are, and it changed our dynamic; it was comfortable. And whenever you start playing comfortably, it carries over to the field because the guys, who hold you accountable, are your friends."

But April stunk. Ten wins. And then May and June were just about .500. By the July All-Star break, the 2007 Rockies were 44–44. "That season was such vanilla," manager Clint Hurdle said of the prelude to late September.

The National League West was pretty stacked that year, though. Some people forget that. Every team except the San Francisco Giants was battling for the division or wild-card. But when the Rockies did lead late in those early months, they had a Takashi Saito of their own, Brian Fuentes, who went by "Tito" or "T-Rex." The Colorado closer had been in the All-Star Game in 2005 and 2006. Fuentes was on pace for the All-Star Game again in 2007. But then he blew a save on June 22. And June 25. And June 28. And June 29. "He's shaving his head in the bathroom in the clubhouse in Houston—and he's crying," Spilborghs recalled. "It was really heartbreaking. The next day he shows up to the field, and it's a day game, and Hurdle's called him into the office. And Fuentes said it was the best/worst feeling he ever had because he got announced as an All-Star but lost his closer job."

The Rockies went 1–9 on that June road swing. The Griswolds had a smoother ride to Wally World than these guys. Hurdle made 24-year-old Manny Corpas the closer, replacing the All-Star Fuentes. "That road trip would have just ripped the heart out of just about most teams," Dan O'Dowd said. "I thought we were done. And then Corpas, oh my God, is he filthy. And then that just made our bullpen so much deeper. Tito moved back to an earlier role in the eighth, and now we have a lefty earlier in the game, which allowed so much more flexibility for Clint to deploy his weapons. But we had a deep pen. We had LaTroy Hawkins in there, Matt Herges in there, and he complemented because he had that incredible change-up. Hawk had that rising fastball. And then Tito came from here, and Jeremy Affeldt was more of a hard slider or three-quarters guy—and could ride his fastball…Some people don't realize it was the formation of this bullpenning concept that exists today [in 2018]. We won with our bullpen in '07. I don't think we could have won that way all year, but pretty much from September through October, we won games with our bullpen. Now, Jeff Francis had some big games and some things in there. But for the most part, that bullpen was just freakin' lockdown."

Fuentes' integrity was integral. Hurdle called his performances a "closer meltdown" but also pointed to his "heart and guts" to accept that set-up role, to own up to his mistakes, and to just own his new responsibility. And that also allowed Corpas to evolve. And even when he got back to pitching crisply, Fuentes never needled Hurdle about being the closer again. And sure enough, Fuentes earned his first win of the year on August 24 in one of the most implausible comebacks…until you realize who the Rockies had on their side.

Two years prior Hurdle was at the grocery store when he got a tap on his shoulder. The Rockies manager met Joanna Blakeman and her son, Kyle. The teenage boy had cancer.

He and Hurdle struck up a conversation—and soon a friendship. They would chat numerous times throughout the coming years. Hurdle gave Kyle strength, and Kyle gave Hurdle strength.

An avid Rockies fan, Kyle had played baseball and football at ThunderRidge High School in suburban Denver. But Kyle was back in the hospital that August of 2007. He had renal medullary carcinoma, a rare disease. His parents never told him the exact name of it because when you Googled it, it read: "terminal." They wanted their boy to believe in living. He was 15.

Hurdle visited Kyle at the hospital after the August 23rd loss. The Rockies had 64 wins at the time, and that night was the 63rd loss, a particularly ugly one to a poor Pittsburgh Pirates team. Bedside in the hospital, Hurdle told Kyle the Rockies needed some luck. "What's your lucky number?" The manager asked the boy.

"It's 64," Kyle said, explaining that was his football number as an offensive lineman. So the next night, the 64–63 Rockies took on the Washington Nationals at Coors Field. Hurdle wrote Kyle's "64" atop of the Rockies lineup card. But by the ninth with Fuentes in for mop-up duty, the Rockies trailed 5–1. "And then, within five minutes, we win the game," Hurdle recalled.

It was a furious flurry of runs, including a Holliday homer. "So I bring Kyle the scorecard that night and say to him: 'Are you kidding me?' And he says, 'You asked for some good luck, how about that ninth inning? Was that good?'"

Kyle died four days later. And every game in 2007 from then on, Hurdle wrote 64 atop the Rockies' scorecard.

• • •

After the Los Angeles Dodgers' doubleheader on September 18—when Ryan Spilborghs took Jonathan Broxton deep, and Todd Helton walked-off against Takashi Saito—the Rockies were 79–72. Keli McGregor told Dan O'Dowd to buckle up. The Rockies won their next two to sweep the four-game set against Los Angeles.

Colorado was suddenly 81–72. "We look at September, we basically have to win every game and we're in it," Spilborghs said of both the division and wild-card races. "And we're like, 'Okay, we'll just have to do that.'"

So, before the 13-inning classic against the San Diego Padres, there was the 14-inning one. To get to Game 163, the Rockies needed to first win Game 154. It was Friday, September 21, the first of three at San Diego and, indisputably, the biggest Rockies series of the century—to that point.

Jake Peavy got the start for San Diego (85–67) and allowed one run in his seven innings. But that one run was going to get the job done. The Rockies led in the bottom of the ninth…until Manny Corpas blew just his third save of the season, allowing a game-tying solo homer to Adrian Gonzalez. As the game crept into the unknown of uncharted extra innings, it was complemented by a murky maritime fog in San Diego that cool night. It was a heavy air, where fly balls don't fly. Joe Thatcher, a rookie in 2007, was a gnarly, nasty lefty. With two outs in the 14th inning—*the 14th*—the lefty faced lefty hitter Brad Hawpe. "I'll never forget it," trainer Scott Gehret said. "This son of a bitch went left-center about as far back as you can go."

Opposite field homer. Oh, and that season, Hawpe hit just .214 against lefties. And here he hits a no-doubter, lefty on lefty ball. Helton shared with me in 2018: "It was a holy shit moment. For him to hit that ball out of center field, it was amazing…Thatcher was a thorn in my side, I couldn't get a hit off the guy."

Sometimes in the booth, you get a premonition a guy may go yard—but honestly, not there, not in that environment. Hawpe did it nonetheless. "The sound even on the TV off the bat was something else," O'Dowd said. "It was just like this explosion of the ball off the bat, and honestly Hawpe knew right away. It shows you how strong he was… In the heavy air, in that time of year, that just doesn't happen. It was like really freakish…The other thing about that club that people don't know: we had tough players. Brad Hawpe is a tough guy. Garrett Atkins might not have said two words, but Garrett Atkins was tough. We didn't have many soft guys on that team. They were competitive men. It wasn't this beautiful No. 1s and 2s in the draft. This was a mixture of guys from all over the place mixed in with some really good players."

The slugger we called "Hawper" was an 11th-round pick out of LSU, who became a formidable bat, driving in 116 runs in 2007, none more important than the run he scored himself that foggy night in San Diego.

The thing I always loved about Hawpe was his unflappable demeanor. You could skip the game, go into the postgame clubhouse, talk to Hawpe, and not know if he went 4-for-5 or 0-for-5. Even-keel. Team-first. A ballplayer's ballplayer. "The beauty of our club," Clint Hurdle said, "was the guys had almost gotten calloused to any negativity. 'We are gonna score this inning. Okay, so now we are just gonna score this inning.' And when that ball went out, that was just another moment you thought guys were going to turn around and start hitting their heads on the dugout [while going crazy]. It was just like we were six years old again. It always kept going back to when we were six again. It was like Little League."

The 2–1 win came on Friday night, spilling into Saturday. The Rockies won the next two, sweeping San Diego. That made for eight straight. The club headed a little north from there to Los Angeles. The Rockies scored 21 runs in that three-game sweep of the Dodgers, but the play that stands out wasn't even a hit. It was a throw of throws, a Colorado cannon that saved the day, maybe the season.

Sully and Spilly. This spry partnership of Cory Sullivan and Ryan Spilborghs would split duty in center, and it was Sully this night in L.A. The Rockies were on the ropes. Ubaldo Jimenez had just been chased after allowing a three-run homer, and the Rockies trailed 5–4 in the fifth inning. Jeff Kent, who hit .339 in his never-ending career against Colorado, walloped a ground-rule double. He advanced to third and tagged on a potential sac fly to Sully in center. "What I remember about it fundamentally," O'Dowd said, "was it was picture perfect."

"People will ask," Gehret recalled, "about when did I know that team was really, really good? Everybody talks about that Helton home run to beat Saito. Then I thought that had a chance to turn into some momentum. But when I really knew, I remember the moment that I knew, *Alright, it's on now.* We went into L.A., who traditionally kicks our ass, no matter how good they are. It was kind of a back-and-forth game, and Cory threw out Kent at the plate. As good a throw as you'll ever see. Yorvit applied the tag, and I thought, *Okay, here we go*. At that point, I knew something was going on."

The day after Sullivan's throw, Dodgers slayer Josh Fogg didn't allow a run in his six-and-two-thirds innings, and the Rockies won again. "Everybody talks Holliday, Helton, Tulo, the main guys," Gehret said. "In my personal opinion, there were four guys that drove that team. It was Josh Fogg, Yorvit Torrealba, LaTroy Hawkins, and Jamey Carroll. Fogg was in charge of the starters, LaTroy Hawkins was in charge of the bullpen, Jamey Carroll was in charge of all of the non-starters, and catcher Yorvit Torrealba was kind of in charge of everybody else. That included everybody. He kind of gravitated toward the Latin speaking guys, but he made sure everybody was in unity in that clubhouse. Jamey, having been kind of a lifetime utility player, understood his role and understood what it takes to do that role, which is very, very difficult. When we were making our run, he had T-shirts made. They were all black T-shirts and they said, 'The Resistance.' The R on the resistance was the Rockies' R. Resistance. He gave those shirts out to five, and only five, guys. The guys who got those shirts were himself, Spilly, Chris Iannetta, Sully, and Jeff Baker. They were: The Resistance...He said, 'What we're instilling in these guys is we're The Resistance. We're the last stop, the last line of defense that they have to get through if they want to beat the Colorado Rockies. I want the other team in that dugout to know that if you're going to win a game tonight, you gotta get through The Resistance.'

"He instilled a lot of pride in those guys. In fact, you know how it goes, of course, fourth inning rolls around, and those guys not in the game start getting ready to pinch hit, play defense, whatever. If we were tied or losing in the fifth, Jamey Carroll would whistle. He would say, 'Resistance, let's go. We got to bail these fucks out again.' He'd head up the tunnel, and those four guys would follow him like the Pied Piper."

The Rockies and The Resistance swept L.A. in L.A. When the Dodgers had arrived to Denver earlier in the month, they were thinking playoffs. But by September 27, the swept Dodgers were 80–79. They were cooked. The Rockies were 87–72, winners of 11 straight games —with three to play. Prior to the run, I remember my oldest, Jacob, asking me, "What are we going to have to do to make the playoffs?" Not wanting to kill the spirit of a baseball-obsessed nine-year-old, I told him, "Buddy, it's not impossible, but it will be very difficult. They probably have to win the rest of their games." Damn, if they almost did.

Entering the final weekend of the season, Colorado trailed San Diego by one game in the West—and the Arizona Diamondbacks by two. Meanwhile, atop the National League East, the New York Mets and Philadelphia Phillies had the identical record of 87–72, same as the Rockies. So you had five teams playing for three playoff spots with three games to play.

The Rockies returned to Denver for the final series against first-place Diamondbacks. The Mile High City was Rockie high. At the first game of the winning streak, 19,161 fans were at Coors Field. Eleven wins later, 48,190 were there for Friday night's Game 160—Colorado's Jeff Francis versus Arizona's Brandon Webb. The Rockies' best in 2007 against the Diamondbacks ace.

• • •

In our minds, it's like the sun doesn't fully set over Salt River Fields at Talking Stick; it's a permanent brushstroke of oranges and yellows and purples, hovering above the outfield. Fantasy Camp is a fantastical, mystical baseball experience. You're in Scottsdale, Arizona, just playing a bunch of baseball as if you're a Colorado Rockie at spring training… and you're surrounded by actual Colorado Rockies: Larry Walker. Dante Bichette. And, of course, the dreammakers from the 2007 team. I called my wife once after a couple days there, and she said: "I can hear the smile on your face."

The campers get to create memories, while the Rockies rekindle the old ones. In 2017, a decade after the 2007 season, pitchers Jeff Francis and Josh Fogg reunited at Fantasy Camp. "Can you believe some little soft lefty had one really good year," Francis said, "and I got to play for 11 years?"

"Jeff," Fogg said, "you had a lot of really good years."

"Yeah," Francis replied, "but I had one really good year and I was rolling really good at the end."

In 2007 Francis ended up on the cover of *Sports Illustrated*. He finished ninth in the Cy Young voting—even more of a feat considering he pitched half his games in the pinball machine that is Coors Field. And in the final nine starts, he tallied a 3.66 overall ERA marred really by one eight-run game. During the final months, he threw a shutout at the San Francisco Giants and won two vital games during the 11-game win streak.

And on Friday, September 27, 2007—Game 160—he kept the Rockies in it against the Arizona Diamondbacks, allowing four total runs through six innings at Coors Field. He could've done better, but it wouldn't really have mattered anyway. Brandon Webb allowed just two runs through seven. Besides Kevin Brown, he had the best sinker I'd ever seen, and that night in a 4–2 loss, the Rockies hit 19 ground balls.

The Rockies were now 87–73, and the Diamondbacks had clinched a spot in the playoffs. As Arizona celebrated on the infield at Coors Field, my broadcast partner George Frazier said on air: "This should ignite you, what you're watching. That should get you going for tomorrow's ballgame."

At his locker Ryan Spilborghs recalled all the media talking about "a hell of a run" and "What does it feel like now that the season is over?'" He said. "And we're like: there are two games left…We had a heartbeat."

On Saturday the Rockies were two out of the wild-card with two games to play.

The San Diego Padres had two games at the Milwaukee Brewers. If San Diego won either game, the Rockies would be mathematically eliminated. Padres-Brewers was in the afternoon. Diamondbacks-Rockies was that night.

Buckle up.

After the Rockies took batting practice, they watched Padres-Brewers from the clubhouse. Reporters and cameras were in there too, lingering like vultures around the Rockies. The Padres led 3–2 in the ninth inning, so they brought in Trevor Hoffman for the formality. And with two outs and a runner on, the Brewers' batter was, of all people, Tony Gwynn Jr.

The son of the San Diego legend, he idolized Hoffman as a young boy. Gwynn Jr. was 16 when the Padres went to the World Series in 1998. So here was the most famous name in Padres history facing the most famous pitcher in Padres history. And Gwynn Jr. ruined it for the Padres. Down to his final strike, he tripled in the tying run. "And so," Spilly said, "The biggest triple in Rockies history was by Tony Gwynn Jr."

And then in the 11th inning, a fellow named Vinny Rottino knocked in the game-winning run for the Brewers. The Padres pitcher was Joe Thatcher, the same seemingly surefire lefty who blew the game to Brad Hawpe and the Rockies in the 14th inning, earlier that September.

The Rockies indeed had a heartbeat. "I was hitting in the cage during that. I just couldn't watch it," Todd Helton said. "I'm a pessimist. I walked back up and I saw everybody celebrating. That was one of the happiest moments of my life."

That Saturday night they devoured Arizona, winning 11–1, setting up the final day of the regular season. With a game to play, the Philadelphia Phillies and New York Mets were both 88–73. One would win the National League East. The Padres were 89–72, and the Rockies were 88–73. They both had Sunday afternoon games. All the Padres had to do was win, and they were in the playoffs.

This was 2007 before iPhones, so this was one of the last times this happened in sports history: fans at a stadium watched the in-house, hand-operated scoreboard for updates on an important game. In the booth we had both games on TV, so I spent the afternoon cheering silently for the Brewers while broadcasting the Rockies. I literally was turned toward the TV of their game, keeping my head on a swivel, so I could call the Rockies game.

Perhaps the coolest moment in Coors Field—and the coolest image—was during the sixth inning of the Padres-Brewers game. The Brewers already led 6–4 when Milwaukee's Gabe Gross hit, if you will, the second biggest triple in Rockies history. He cleared the bases. And at Coors, instead of replacing the No. 6 with the No. 9 on the scoreboard, the person twisted the No. 6 upside down for all to see. I got goose bumps.

To force a tiebreaker game with the Padres, Colorado still had to win Sunday. Up 4–3 in the ninth inning, closer Manny Corpas fielded a cue-shot swing barehanded, chucked the thing over to Helton at first to nab the runner. It was happening. Colorado won and would host the wild-card tiebreaker game against San Diego—because the Phillies won and the Mets lost, meaning Philly was the East winners.

The Rockies had won 13 of their final 14 games. "I knew we had the talent on that team, but I hadn't won [before]," Helton said. "Previously, I'd only finished above .500 maybe one time in whatever year that was. Did I think we were going to do it? No. To be honest with you, I'm a pessimist and I was always waiting for something bad to happen, and it just never did. We just kept winning ballgames. And the fun part about winning all those ballgames is everybody contributed."

The Rockies and the Padres were both 89–73. Monday night would be Game 163. And with that win, the team granted luck by the late Kyle Blakeman—and his No. 64—would advance to Game 164.

Drew's Diary

2018 National League Wild-Card
October 2, 2018:
Colorado Rockies at Chicago Cubs

Resiliency and the phrase: "nothing is going to be easy" came out of my mouth with great regularity in the final month of 2018. After Game 163 against the Los Angeles Dodgers, which Colorado would lose 5-2 despite home runs from Nolan Arenado and Trevor Story, the Rockies left in the middle of the night to take on the Cubs at Chicago's Wrigley Field in the National League wild-card game. It was a night of very little offense but gorgeous pitching from Kyle Freeland. Neither nine innings nor 10, 11, 12 could decide anything. In the top of the 13th inning with two outs, the Rockies finally got a key hit, and it would come from one of the least likely sources. Tony Wolters, hitting below .180 and saddled with two strikes, knocked a hard ground ball to center to give the Rockies a 2-1 lead. Scott Oberg closed it out, and the Rockies celebrated in the tiny and antiquated Wrigley Field visitors' clubhouse. After showering off the champagne and beer, they headed on busses north to Milwaukee to begin a best-of-five National League Division Series against the Brewers.

• • •

The Philadelphia Phillies, according to the Philadelphia Phillies, were "the team to beat." That was the Philadelphia mantra all 2007 after Jimmy Rollins famously said before the season: "The Mets had a chance to win the World Series last year. Last year is over. I think we are the team to beat in the NL East finally. But that's just on paper."

Said Ryan Spilborghs: "I ran my mouth all the time, but so did Rollins. I thought it was comical. So my response was: 'But we're the better team. They're the team to beat, but we're the better team.'"

The 2007 National League Division Series started in Philadelphia, and that city had this haughtiness to it. Even though the teams had the same amount of losses in the regular season—and even though Colorado had the best batting average and the best fielding percentage in the league—the Philly fans and media swept aside the notion that the Rockies could win. In the end, of course, it was the Rockies who did the sweeping.

Rollins, who beat out Matt Holliday for the 2007 MVP, was the first Phillies hitter of the series. The *Sports Illustrated* cover boy Jeff Francis started out 3–0 on Rollins. The crafty lefty seemed understandably nervous. Rollins took a pitch for a strike and then fouled one off. Full count. Francis had been humming fastballs. It made sense to try to locate one here. But catcher Yorvit Torrealba called for a change-up. The audacity! Francis followed Torrealba's order, and Rollins swung through the pitch.

Torrealba was the embodiment of the 2007 Rockies squeezed into that stout catcher's body. He was, if I may so eloquently say, a "fuck you guy." He wouldn't back down to anyone. That includes intimidating slugger Matt Kemp later on in the decade in a famous on-field interaction. Torrealba gave the young Rockies swagger and daily energy. He was revered by all in the clubhouse. "Yorvit was a bullfighter, he was a matador," Clint Hurdle said. "He liked the attention to some point. Think about his at-bats. There was always a little drama. Nobody stepped out more than him hitting. He didn't mind the camera. He didn't mind being in the moment. How about the job Torrealba did? He caught every game for the whole stretch—even in the playoffs. He found a pitching staff that actually believed in him and he believed back in them. And it became dynamic."

Twenty-nine at the time, the Venezuelan backstop had an infectious personality and a penchant for the clutch. "Yorvit took control of everything behind the plate," trainer Scott Gehret said. "I'll tell you another thing. In September and October, if the game's on the line, I want that son of a bitch hitting."

Indeed, he had two hits and an RBI in Game 1 at Philadelphia, which the Rockies won, 4–2. And he loved being part of Colorado. He even adopted Colorado State University—the green and gold—as his own. That was the alma mater of Gehret and team president Keli McGregor. "Yorvit convinced himself that he went to CSU and would tell local people that," Gehret shared with a laugh. "He would come to me and say, 'Hey, I was at the bar last night and I had my CSU gear on. I told some girl that I went to CSU, and she wanted to know what I studied—and I didn't know what to tell her. So what am I supposed to tell her?' 'In the future, it's an agricultural school.' He was like, 'What does that mean.' I said, 'You're a farmer!' His personality was very contagious. He could turn a dugout like that. When things got tight, when guys were pressing or whatever, he would march up and down the dugout and he'd say, 'No tight *kulo* tonight. No tight *kulo*.' [Kulo is Spanish for, um, backside.] That was his thing. 'No tight *kulo* boys. No tight *kulo*.' He played with passion, he played with fire and he played with a smile on his face."

Torrealba tallied two more RBIs in Game 2, but the unlikely offensive hero that afternoon was a man who hit only four homers all year.

Back in Denver, Chris O'Dowd was in class at Regis Jesuit High School. "And I had earphones in," said O'Dowd, the son of the Rockies general manager. "And I had this little radio receiver tucked up in my sleeve and was leaning up against my desk strategically all day, listening. All of my buddies knew I was listening to it. I went out to football practice and ran the same wire all the way up through my helmet."

In the fourth inning, the Rockies trailed 3–2. The Philadelphia fans incessantly waved their little white towels when, with the bases loaded,

Kaz Matsui golf clubbed a pitch for a grand slam. *Kaz Matsui.* He even flipped the bat upon running to first. "I regret not bringing my son with me because of stupid football," Dan O'Dowd said. "That was an awful decision on my part. That was all on me."

Since the game was televised nationally, my job during the NLDS was to be a fan and then conduct interviews after the game for our postgame show. I sat in O'Dowd's box in Philly, along with executive producer Ken Miller, and I remember high-fiving Miller after the Matsui slam.

No player had ever hit for the cycle in the postseason. But in Game 2 of the 2007 NLDS, the Rockies' Matsui doubled, tripled, and hit a homer (a grand slam, as we know). He finished 3-for-5 but without a single. "When Kaz hit the grand slam, I was in the bullpen warming up because I was coming in the game," Josh Fogg said. "He killed it. I was actually standing in the bullpen when he hit it. It was just chaos in the bullpen, not so much with the fans. It was just chaos down there. I'm continuing to get ready to pitch in my first playoff game ever and I'm just so excited. I don't even know what the score is at this point, but I know we're winning now. Adrenaline starts taking it up to the nth degree at that point. It was already as high as it could go and it just doubled at that point. I came into that game feeling pretty good about myself. And I actually stole the win that day because I came in for the fifth and the sixth."

Up 2–0 the Rockies returned to a raucous Coors. Ubaldo Jimenez pitched his butt off. Jeff Baker, one of the Rockies' members of The Resistance, drove in a run in the eighth inning, to take a 2–1 lead. Brian Fuentes, pitching the eighth, got the win. Manny Corpas, pitching the ninth, got the save, his third of the series. The "team to beat" had been beaten. The Rockies won their first playoff series in franchise history and were now a series win away from the World Series.

• • •

"The Diamondbacks were in a similar situation as the Rockies in 2007; they didn't realize how good they were," Ryan Spilborghs said of the Rockies' opponent in the National League Championship Series. "We saw them in the same light, a lot of homegrown talent. So it wasn't lack of respect, it was just—we see you all the time, and you're not that good! I've seen Conor Jackson his whole career! Eric Byrnes, I've been around you! That was the mentality for us looking at them, but I'd have to imagine, they looked at us and thought: *Brad Hawpe? Jeff Francis is their ace? Ryan Spilborghs is playing?* From our perspective as broadcasters now, you look at the Kansas City Royals: they're terrible for years and then they get and win a World Series, and you're like, *How did those clowns end up winning a World Series?* You look at a group that comes up through the ranks, they take their licks, and then it's like: I guess they were better than we thought."

Entering the NLCS, the Rockies had won 17 of their past 18 games. That's absurd. That sounds like something from a University of Kentucky basketball team or maybe an elite New England Patriots team, but not an MLB team, especially one that hovered around .500 for the first five months of the season. But the Rockies were blossoming. Five years and five months under Clint Hurdle had culminated in this confluence of confidence.

So what was Hurdle doing by starting Willy Taveras in center? He'd been injured in early September and was just a spectator for the magic run. A healthy Taveras, though, could run. In 97 games that season, he stole 33 bases, while hitting .320. And Taveras was healthy again for the Arizona series. "We talked [internally] about facing Brandon Webb in Game 1," Hurdle said. "We are going to move up in the batter's box and try to do some things. The hardest decision to make was with Tavaras coming back. And you want to talk about being torn in the middle! Because I have two players—Spilly and Sully—pouring their hearts into this thing at center field to get us to this point. And then you're thinking about Arizona's ballpark. That outfield is huge. We've got the most elite fielding center fielder that there is, and he's healthy. I just got the point where Dan had his vote. I asked a few other people what they thought. I don't think it was unanimous. And I called a couple of the leaders in before I posted the lineup just to let them know. I can remember Todd saying: 'You're doing what?'"

Todd Helton had a point. The Rockies were 17 of 18 without Taveras. "And Todd said, 'Well, I only have one thing to say: this better damn work.' And he walked out."

But there went Taveras, singling off Webb in the third in a 1–1 game. There went Taveras, stealing second. There went Taveras, scoring from second on a Kaz Matsui single. They won Game 1. And then in Game 2, Taveras made the two biggest plays. Phoenix fingernails were disappearing by the inning that night. The game was airtight. The visiting Rockies led 2–1 in the seventh, but Arizona's Tony Clark (the future head of the players association) already had two hits on the day and then he hit this one even better than those. He just drilled it into right center. But Taveras—in a dead sprint, extended dive—reached and snagged it. He was the only person on the Rockies who could've made this catch. It was one of the best catches, considering time and place, in playoff history.

Manny Corpas blew it in the ninth, but in the 11th, Taveras came up with the bases loaded against Arizona's closer, Jose Valverde. Four-pitch walk. It turned out to be the game-winning RBI.

The Rockies headed back to Colorado for three games. If they won two of them, they'd win the pennant. "I remember we had a huge meeting before Game 3," Dan O'Dowd said. "I felt like we were fortunate to win Game 2 there, really fortunate. We had momentum. But the weather was pouring rain. And they didn't like water. I remember talking to Keli [McGregor] because at that point we didn't control any decision-making. It was an MLB issue. But for us, I am such a believer of momentum, I don't want to give these guys [anything]. And at that point in time, the Indians were up on the Red Sox three games to one. And for me it was very personal because I had spent most of my years in that Cleveland organization and had an incredible run over 10 years. I just remember vividly saying: 'We got to play, we've got these guys. We have to keep this momentum.'"

The league gave the go-ahead for Game 3. And Josh Fogg, the Dragon Slayer and Dodger Slayer, became the Diamondback Slayer. Fogg pitched the game of his life on that soggy night, six innings of one-run ball, and the Rockies won Game 3. One win away from the World Series? The whole thing was surreal, inexplicable, as if someone from above was stirring this up.

• • •

Kyle Blakeman's younger sister, Macie, was 13. As the family grieved throughout the fall, they used baseball as an escape. And the Rockies asked Macie to throw out the first pitch of Game 4. She wore Clint Hurdle's white pinstriped jersey, tucked into her blue jeans. She wore a pink Rockies ballcap with her hair in pigtails. And when she pushed out a smile, you could see her braces.

She threw a strike. The pitch was—and still is—bone-chilling.

Hurdle, as he always did, wrote Kyle's lucky No. 64 on the top of the lineup card. In the bottom of the fourth, Hurdle gambled and pinch hit for starter Franklin Morales, who had allowed just one run. Morales' pitch total was 64.

The pinch hitter, Seth Smith, who I dubbed "Mr. Late Night" for the rookie's penchant for producing huge hits off the bench in the late innings, drilled a double, driving in two to take the lead. When the fourth inning was over, the Rockies had scored six times. Six in four.

The Rockies relievers allowed three runs, so as closer Manny Corpas got the third out in the ninth, the final score of the game was 6–4. "That kind of stuff," Hurdle said, "you can't make up."

The final out created an iconic image. The batter was Eric Byrnes, the former Rockies and 2007 Diamondbacks player who played with his hair on fire and wasn't fearful of speaking his mind. He made the mistake, though, after Game 2, to say that Arizona was better than Colorado. As it was, Byrnes was the final batter of the National League Championship Series.

His checked swing made contact with the pitch, producing a paltry grounder between third and short. Troy Tulowitzki gracefully scooped it up and rifled an off-balanced throw to first. As Byrnes slid headfirst into the base, Todd Helton caught the low throw for the 27th out. The greatest Rockie—with his left foot still pressed into first base—punched both arms straight up into the sky. His left hand was in a fist, while his right hand, nestled in his oversize black glove, squeezed the final out. He screamed toward the heavens, and his thick black goatee circled his mouth. Byrnes was sprawled face-first just past first, defeated. "That photo is hanging up in my office," Helton said in 2018. "That was just pure emotion. I didn't know what to do. I really didn't care how I looked. I was just so happy and so excited. That was 10 years of frustration let out right there."

The Colorado Rockies were going to the World Series. "That last out could have been a fly ball to center field, it could have been a strikeout," Hurdle said. "But for Helton to be the guy?"

The Rockies had just won 21 of their past 22 games. It truly was unbelievable. Unfortunately, they wouldn't win another one. "We played a really good team that was hot. Tip your hat to them," Hurdle said of the Boston Red Sox. "But talk about taking the steam out of an unstoppable force. With nine days off, we couldn't replicate or regain our momentum."

Nine days. The Rockies waited as Cleveland, Dan O'Dowd's old organization, fumbled away a 3–1 lead, severing dreams in Game 7.

The Rockies celebrate after sweeping the Arizona Diamondbacks in the National League Championship Series to advance to the 2007 World Series.

You never forget your first time at Fenway. I was a college intern in the 1980s, working at the CBS affiliate in Boston. You climb just a couple flights of stairs and, whoa, you're already at the top of the stadium. It's a little bandbox placed right in the middle of a neighborhood. It's preserved nostalgia. If the Green Monster could talk? The stories, the lore. And here was Colorado, this expansion franchise and first-time pennant winner, trying to keep this candle lit in the windy autumn of New England.

The Red Sox won the first two games of the World Series in Boston. Josh Fogg started Game 3 in Colorado. "I remember standing out there and I kind of looked around at the masses of people," Fogg said. "The city was just alive. That was the main thing going on, not only in Denver, but in the country at that time. That kind of sunk in a little bit where it was like, yeah, this is kind of the pinnacle of where you want to be if you're going to play baseball."

Until the Red Sox scored six in the third off him to make it 3–0 in the series. One night later—October 28, 2007—the Red Sox won 4–3 and thus won the World Series. After sweeping the NLDS and NLCS, the Rockies were swept in the World Series.

To this day in Colorado, on barstools and mountain hikes, baseball fans wonder what would've happened if the Rockies didn't have that nine-day break before the World Series. "Seven games," Dan O'Dowd said. "I am not saying that we would have won. They had one great team. But our mojo, we exhaled. I sensed it, I knew it. Trying to think of a million different ways to replicate a game environment. Simulated work. But there is just no way to replicate what we had experienced. And once we caught our breath, it was going to be impossible. And I knew that. I was really upset at the Indians, more than anything. You could tell, even by just watching us take batting practice. It wasn't the same, wasn't the same team. And good for the Red Sox, they were an incredibly talented team. It's just that would not have been a four-game sweep."

It's been more than a decade now. Octobers were no longer Rocktobers. Most everyone from the 2007 Rockies has moved on or left us. But man, Keli McGregor was right: O'Dowd and all the fans buckled up for the ride of their lifetime. It's hard to believe any team will ever win 21 of 22 like that. There have been hundreds of pennant winners, but the 2007 Rockies are unique.

In 2018 Hurdle still managed the Pittsburgh Pirates. About once a year, he'd pop in the documentary called *21 Days*, which captured the stories of that elite run. "It invigorates me," Hurdle said. "It just gives me passion."

CHAPTER 6

LARRY WALKER

The 1986 Burlington Expos weren't even all Expos. It was a co-op Single A minor league team, so half of the Expos were actually Royals. At their home games in Burlington, a small river town in southeast Iowa, the team would wear Expos uniforms, but on the road, the players would wear Royals' royal blue. And so, when Burlington would play in these other Midwest towns, I bet there were at least a few fans thinking they'd spotted the next George Brett…unaware that Larry Walker was just a fastball-smacking facade.

That 1986 season Montreal prospect Walker hit 29 homers…in just 95 games. He was only 19 years old. The '86 Burlington season was Jeff Huson's first in pro ball. Long before his big league career— and then his career as one of my Rockies broadcast partners—Huson was a Burlington infielder, along with another infielder, this mustached Canadian who was brutally raw…but had raw brute strength. "Larry actually started out playing third base for us in Burlington," Huson recalled. "But after he nearly killed like the first five people in the front row with his wild throws, they decided he'd be best in right field."

Walker didn't play much baseball as a kid or teen—he was a hockey goalie in British Columbia—but his athleticism got him signed professionally and off to Utica, New York, in 1985. The next summer in Burlington, Huson heard a story about Walker's first pro baseball season in Utica. "It was on a hit-and-run, and he took off to second base, rounded toward third, but they caught the ball," Huson said. "So instead of going back to second, tagging it, and going to first, he beelines right over the top of the mound to first base! And he beats the throw and is like, 'Yeah!'" When they tagged him standing on the bag and the umpire called him out, he didn't understand why. But that embarrassing moment fueled his learning of base running in the future.

In many ways the story of Walker's rise is inexplicable. How could someone pick up baseball so late in life—but then pick up baseball better than most who ever played the game?

"He was one of the top five players that I ever played with," said Huson, who played in the majors from 1988 to 2000. "He and Roberto Alomar and Ken Griffey Jr.—they could do whatever they wanted whenever they wanted to—and with ease."

Walker made his big league debut in 1989 at 22. He came to Colorado for the 1995 season, spearheaded the playoff run that year, and played with the Rockies until 2004, when he was traded to the St. Louis Cardinals and made his second career playoff appearance (hitting six home runs in three rounds for the Cards).

But Walker is most associated with the Rockies—he'd be a Mount Rushmore Rockie if they ever made one—and his 1997 season is part of Rockies lore. Even baseball lore. Walker hit .366 with 49 homers and 130 RBIs. He stole 33 bases. He won a Gold Glove and the MVP. His on-base percentage was .452 and slugging percentage was .720—both best in the league—and his OPS (on-base plus slugging percentage) was 1.172.

How good is a 1.172 OPS for a season? It's literally the 32nd best season ever. Walker's 1997 OPS is 32nd on the list just behind Babe Ruth's 1928 and Lou Gehrig's 1934 seasons. And right away, I'm sure some of you might say: "But he played at Coors Field before the humidor!" And sure, yes, that's true…but consider this: in 1997 on the road, Walker hit more home runs (29) than he did at Coors (20)! And he had a higher road OPS (1.176) than at home (1.169). "That 1997 season, we had so much fun," recalled pitcher Jerry Dipoto, now the general manager of the Seattle Mariners. "We got off to a subpar start, but by the time we got to the middle of July, so many characters on the team, we were about four games out of first place and right in the thick of the wild-card race. We were waiting to see what that extra boost was going to be. We didn't add to the team, which may have been prophetic because we came up short, but we went on a roll. We hopped on Larry's back…It was about as crazy a year as you'll ever see. The loudest contact that you'll ever hear night after night, it sounded like rockets coming off of his bat. He roughly carried us into September with a chance to knock into the postseason. We fell short in the end, we stumbled on the end of that trip, and ultimately finished three or four games back, but it was a fun ride with an awesome group of guys. It was probably the most talented team I ever played with in Colorado.

"Larry Walker is the most efficient and polished outfielder you'll ever watch; he was unbelievable in his heyday. The throwing, the accuracy, the routes, the range. For him to do what he was doing in that ballpark at that time, it was phenomenal. He was the best ballplayer I ever played with, pure and simple. The things he could do on a field were outrageous. It felt like there was nothing he couldn't do, and in the moment, when he wanted to flip the switch, he could do things no one else could do. In my baseball life, I probably spent more time as a teammate of Larry Walker than any other player I played with. He was funny, he was engaging. When Larry was your friend, you had a friend. He was there for you, which I always appreciated about him. You could be a star and you could be the 25th guy on the team. If he invested in you, you were his friend."

Walker had one of the game's most infectious personalities. He was a fun-loving guy but truly a loving guy. And Walker was wonderfully wacky and quirky. Remember when he put his helmet on backward while batting against Randy Johnson in the All-Star Game? There's a notion that Walker tried to avoid Johnson's starts during his career. But Walker had 28 at-bats and hit .393, slugged .571, and had an OPS of 1.056 against "The Big Unit."

Walker was refreshing and after all he was "The Accidental Ballplayer," as a 1997 *Sports Illustrated* article called him, while sharing this tidbit: "Among his quirks is an obsession with the No. 3. He wears uniform No. 33, takes three practice swings before stepping into the batter's box, and sets his alarm clock for three minutes past the hour. He

Larry Walker singles during 1997, the year he won the MVP award.

got married on Nov. 3 at 3:33 P.M. "And three years later, I got divorced, and it cost me $3 million," he said.

• • •

The cool thing about the 1990s Rockies is they altered a city's identity and lifestyles. Kids finally had a team, a team they could share with each other. As a passion for baseball organically grew in Denver, a generation of kids grew up wanting to be like Larry Walker.

107

But when he was a kid, Larry Walker didn't have a Larry Walker. "Hockey is what you grow up following as a kid in Canada. I think in my mind I was convinced I was a better hockey player," Walker said. "You get woken up early in the morning and you throw your hockey uniform on over your pajamas and you go practice before school. That's what we did, and I think I had the ability in hockey perhaps. I did well for what equipment I had. I was using hand-me-down equipment from my brother that was falling apart. I remember trying out for a team and I was playing for one of their exhibition games, junior A hockey team, and I remember my goal crease was covered in horse fur because that's what's stuffed inside the goalie pads because there's holes in the bottom of them. It'd fall off, and I'd be sliding all over the crease like, 'Oh lord, I have bad equipment.' The other goalie's got these big gloves; I've got one from 20 years earlier that was a tiny little thing. I didn't have the…I guess the money or the equipment to really fit in up there. But I think if I had pushed hockey a little bit more, I think, possibly in my mind at least, I would've had a chance to make it."

He picked up baseball, joining a youth team in Vancouver. They played a few dozen games, and Walker just seemed to have this knack for hitting the crap out of the ball. Sure enough, in 1984 he made a national junior team representing British Columbia. They headed up to Saskatchewan to play, a peculiar experience, considering he'd hoped to play hockey for a team in Saskatchewan. It was after getting cut in his tryout that he'd shifted to baseball in the first place.

An Expos scout saw him on the junior national team, decided to gamble some loonies and toonies, and offered Walker $1,500 to sign. In the months between the '84 season and '85 season, the new professional ballplayer returned home to Maple Ridge, British Columbia. He actually joined a local team playing "windmill softball, like the ladies play in college that you watch on TV, stuff like that in a men's league," Walker said. "We were in my little hometown of Maple Ridge. I played in that when I was 16 with my dad on the team, and my brothers Barry, Carey, and Gary. [I] played for the Maple Ridge Lanes, the bowling alley. I won the MVP of the league at 16 years old in the men's league."

Again, it's just bonkers to think about the stops on Walker's peculiar journey—from the goalie crease, to giving baseball a shot, to getting signed by the Expos and from the windmill softball league, to pro baseball in Utica, to running from third back to first by going over the pitcher's mound, to exploding offensively in Burlington, and becoming a legit big league prospect.

But it happened. "If I didn't make it in baseball, what would've happened after that, I don't know," he said. "I worked at the bowling alley for many years where my mom worked. Across the street my dad worked at a lumber yard. Maybe something in that could've happened. I really don't know the answer. That's why not a day goes by where I don't knock on wood and say thank you because I'm fortunate for what happened in my life and how baseball found me basically—not me finding it. I was a fortunate one that I had athletic ability and I was able to use it, and it worked out good for me."

Of course, he'd dreamed of playing professionally for Montreal, but it would just end up being the Expos, not the Canadiens. "A chance to play in the big leagues, it really never entered my mind until Double A when I made it to Jacksonville," he said. "I was a top prospect by *Baseball America*. I think I was maybe the No. 1 prospect in the Expos organization, I guess. All that stuff was new to me. I was just playing the game because I got asked to play and they gave me 1,500 bucks to do it. And whatever it was, 500 bucks a month after that, to play and live with five other guys in a house, that was just fun. I enjoyed it, never thought there was any seriousness to it, that playing in the big leagues was a possibility."

Before he was part of Rockies history, well, Larry Walker was actually sort of part of Rockies history. First called up in 1989, Walker was on the Montreal Expos in 1993, who played in Colorado for the first ever home Rockies games. And when Eric Young homered in the first ever home Rockies at-bat, "It was like—holy crap, this is awesome," Walker said, even though he was on the visiting Expos. "You're just like, oh my Lord, this is good stuff right here. We struggled in Montreal to fill the seats. And then you step into Mile High, and there's 83,000 people, whatever the heck it was. As a performer, those are the highs that we live for, and if you're putting on that uniform, you're going to go out there and perform in front of everybody. You want people to be there to watch you. Whether you fail or succeed, it's still…it's that adrenaline pump and rush that you get taking the field. That was a big motivation for me [to sign in 1995, the first year of Coors Field]. There's that sense of 'new.' This is new, man. This is like brand new. It's just a package that just got opened up, and we're all giddy little kids—at least for me coming to Colorado."

Few towns had a better run in sports than Denver from 1995 to 1999. The Rockies made their first postseason, the Avalanche arrived and won a Stanley Cup, the University of Colorado won a bowl game annually, Sonny Lubick had the Rams rolling every fall in Fort Collins, and the Broncos won two Super Bowls. What a fun time to be in this exploding city. Everything was new and fresh: the teams, the revitalized downtown, the architecture, the vibe. Denver became a destination—and not just to visit.

The 1995 Rockies, an expansion team in its third year playing in its new stadium, fittingly won the first ever National League wild-card. Before that team the soonest an expansion team had made the playoffs was eight years in (the 1969 New York Mets and the 1976 Kansas City Royals).

And for the first time since the 1977 Dodgers, a team had four hitters with 30-plus homers. Walker hit 36 for the 1995 Rockies. There was also Andres Galarraga (31 homers). "If the guy wanted to, he could probably beat you to a pulp," Walker said. "But there's not a mean bone in the guy's body." Vinny Castilla (32 homers)—"You can't sneak the cheese past the rat; there wasn't a pitcher in the league that was going to throw a fastball by him inside." Dante Bichette (40 homers)—"Stuff that was tried to be written about us was completely false. I 100 percent don't think Dante had a problem with me and vice versa, I had zero problem with him." And Ellis Burks (14 homers in 103 games)—"We were like brothers of a different mother."

To win the wild-card, the Rockies had to win the final game of the season on October 1, 1995—12 years to the day before the famous Game 163. The Rockies starter was actually Bret Saberhagen in his lone Rockies season. The Royals legend was 31 at the time and was traded over from the Mets at midseason. And Coors Field without the humidor was about as nightmarish for Saberhagen as Saberhagen was for the 1985 Cardinals in the World Series. And so he lasted just two innings in the final game of 1995, allowing six earned runs. The Rockies trailed 8–2 in the third. But Walker homered in the bottom of the inning, as did Eric Young, and by the end of the fifth, the Rockies led 10–8.

The zany but reliable reliever Curtis Leskanic, who pitched a league high 76 times in '95, came in for the save. And Walker finished the biggest game of his life 3-for-4 with three RBIs. "You would think we won the dang World Series, the way we were celebrating," Walker said. "Everybody was going crazy outside the ballpark and in the stadium still. Dante and I took the elevator up to the top level and overlooked the front entrance there on the top level and we were up there screaming with champagne and spraying it, just going nuts. And then other players started coming up, and I remember just thousands of people started getting below us, and we started throwing souvenirs and stuff. Unfortunately during this, it stopped when I think it was a woman who got trampled. And paramedics had to help her, and that was the bittersweet part of it. The funny part of it was, I remember throwing my uniform pants over. Like, 'Here you go!' And in the back pocket was my athletic supporter, so it was like, *oh shit, there goes my pants with my jock in it.* I wonder who got that?"

Alas, Colorado faced eventual National League champ Atlanta Braves in the first round. The Rockies lost the games started by Greg Maddux and Tom Glavine—stole Game 3—but lost to Maddux again, and the season came to an end.

• • •

At the baseball winter meetings, trade winds can stir up nostalgia. I had dinner with Dan O'Dowd at the 2017 winter meetings. He was general manager of the Rockies from 1999 to 2014. He made dozens of transactions over the years but few more complicated and emotional than the 2004 trade of Larry Walker.

In 10 seasons for Colorado, some marred by injuries, Walker hit 258 home runs. And his slash line while in a Rockies uniform was something out of a video game my sons might play: .334 batting average, .426 on-base percentage, and .618 slugging percentage. So for 10 seasons, Walker had an OPS (on-base plus slugging percentage) of 1.044. These days the media makes huge deals about a player with an OPS over 1.000 for just one season. Walker averaged it for a decade!

But the Rockies kept losing. From 1996 to 2003, every year the win total was between 72 and 83. In 2002 Walker wanted out but wouldn't just accept a trade anywhere. That 2017 night at dinner with O'Dowd, the biggest news in baseball was Giancarlo Stanton's trade demands. The reigning MVP for the Miami Marlins wanted out but wouldn't just accept a trade anywhere. "Yeah, so what [Marlins executive] Michael Hill is going through now with Stanton, I went through the exact same thing. Well, I went through it first with Mike Hampton and then with Larry Walker," O'Dowd recalled that night. "And then the Larry situation is what basically held me hostage. You know, I got it... It was Larry Walker to the Diamondbacks for Matt Williams. I flew to

Arizona and ate with Matt Williams. It was David Dellucci. Remember the guy Erubiel Durazo? The guy who hit all of the home runs. So we were gonna take him. Dellucci, we felt like really would have played well in our ballpark. Matt Williams would have been our third baseman. But you know what, when you give guys a no-trade clause…"

That deal was nixed. And for the next two seasons, O'Dowd carefully considered trading the popular player. In 2004 the Rockies were having their worst season since the Mile High Stadium days. "The Texas one was true," Walker said of 2004 trade rumors that involved him. "And I literally took a good day and a half or two days to contemplate that one. I had numerous people from Texas that I talked to. I had numerous people close to me that I talked to. And everyone of those people said: take the deal. The only one that didn't take the deal was me. I made that decision solely on my own. Why, I don't know, but I just remember sitting at the house, thinking about it for days and just something didn't feel right, I guess, for me. Some of the phone calls I had with the Texas personnel—almost everything they said ended up being incorrect or lies—and so something, maybe the tone of voice, didn't seem right to me. I'm glad that I didn't take that one. There were a couple other ones I was told, but nothing really that I had to make a decision on."

O'Dowd said that deal with the Rangers would've nabbed the Rockies a prospect that had hit .402 in 60 games of A ball that year (and then hit .300 in 71 games in Double A that same year). It was Ian Kinsler, who went on to become a four-time All-Star. "And then the St. Louis one came along," Walker said. "And for me, that was a no-brainer."

Why a no-brainer? "I think they were [nine-and-a-half] games in first place at the time. That's a big reason," said Walker, who had a .424 on-base percentage with Colorado at age 37, when he was traded in August of 2004. "I'm like, oh my God, I get to play in the playoffs again. This is great. And yeah, the birds on the bat, that's one of those uniforms that are in the league that have such a rich history and all the World Series championships and the amazing players that have gone through that clubhouse. It really made it easy, and once again, another ballpark you go to where the fans fill every seat—and make it exciting to play every day."

"He said, 'I'll go to St. Louis,' and they knew that, and it was the only place that he was going to go," O'Dowd said. "And I got back whatever I could get back, which wasn't real good." After the second greatest Rockies career ever, Walker was dealt to the eventual league champion Cardinals for Jason Burch, Luis Martinez, and Chris Narveson. None ever played for Colorado, though Narveson was part of a trade that got the Rockies pitcher Byung-Hyun Kim. Also and not incidentally, with the $975,000 saved in pro-rated salary, the Rockies were able to offer that to recent 14th-round draft pick—Dexter Fowler— and convince him to forgo college to sign with the Rockies.

Walker forever appreciated the trade. You could hear it in his voice, as he explained the difference between personal accomplishments and team accomplishments. "I have an office at my house in Florida now and I have put my stuff up in there. Some of it is not in very good shape; even the MVP award's got a big crack on it," said Walker at age 51 in 2018. "Those are things that come with the game, but the most fun I've had is in '95 and '04–05 when there's champagne flying around the clubhouse and you're hugging your teammates and coaching staff and celebrating a victory either making it to the playoffs or winning a round in the playoffs. Those are the best times for me playing. All the other stuff—don't get me wrong, I'm happy that all that happened; it means I had something good to contribute to the team and us winning, so it does mean a lot to me—but I think you can ask any athlete; winning, that's the top of the heap right there, doesn't get better than that."

So, should Walker be in the Baseball Hall of Fame? It's a borderline case, but when you look at the whole body of work—hitting, power, base running (improved from his wayward minor league days), defense—and consider his dominance of his era and the respect of his peers, I think he's a Hall of Famer. As of 2018, Walker wasn't in.

You could make the case that he's one of the most underrated players in history. Even though WAR (wins above replacement) is one of these more modern stats, which weren't on the backs of baseball cards when we were kids, it's a telling stat and an all-encompassing stat. Well, Walker's career WAR from baseball-reference.com is 72.7—good for 86th and just above Derek Jeter. So only 85 players are arguably "better" than Walker if you are a devotee of WAR. And Walker's WAR is better than numerous people in Cooperstown, including fellow outfielders Dave Winfield, Willie McCovey, Billy Williams, and Andre Dawson, as well as enshrined position players such as Ryne Sandberg, Barry Larkin, Alan Trammell, and Gary Carter.

The brilliant baseball writer Jay Jaffe wrote *The Cooperstown Casebook* in 2017. Jaffe created a fascinating stat called JAWS, which is like WAR but for Hall of Fame worthiness. It also weighs ballparks played at. Jaffe's intricate system lists Walker as the 11th best right fielder ever. Walker compares favorably to Vladimir Guerrero, who is now immortalized in Cooperstown. I'm selective in how I view WAR, but clearly there is no denying his greatness and the impact he had during his prime. And, honestly, you can even forget WAR or other recent analytics; I defer to the players and their view of another player. Superstar players glowingly speak about the talents of Walker. He's revered by his contemporaries.

Asked about what he's most proud of in his career, Walker said: "Making it. Getting that phone call in '89 that you're going up to big leagues, like *holy crap, really*? I sent Tyler O'Neill a text the other day, a kid that just got called up to St. Louis [in 2018]. He's from the Maple

Ridge area where I grew up. And in that text I said, you know what, I really set one goal that stands out from when I first got called up to the big leagues, and that goal was to never get sent back down. I said make that a goal of yours; now you've made it—do everything you can to stay. That was probably one thing I was proud of…I tried to set a goal to stay healthy, but, unfortunately, I got injured a lot. I played hurt a ton. There was a big difference between the two for me, but to make it to the big leagues and to not be sent back down because you suck basically was an accomplishment for me. I hope the same for him. "I woke up some days and couldn't even move. And it's like, oh my God, does that hurt so bad. You do everything you can to get ready for the game, whatever it takes, and sometimes it just didn't work. You just can't go, and I play the game—or I played the game or I tried to play the game—at a different level. And my different level was I was going to go all out to catch the ball that was hit to me; I was gonna go all out to try to steal a base, whatever it takes. I try not to play it at anything other than 100 percent. I couldn't do that a lot of the times and I paid the price. Coors Field is the biggest outfield in Major League Baseball. There's a lot of land to cover out there, and the last thing I wanted to do was be out there compromised. And some people disagree. They'll tell you at 60 percent is better than someone else at 100 percent. Balls getting by me or balls that I should catch, I don't want my pitcher looking at it like: what the hell are you doing? I think I played the game hard. I wasn't afraid to run into walls and make sliding, diving catches, steal bases, first to home, second, first to third. Whatever it took to win I would try to do, so there was a lot more to my game than some players."

CHAPTER 7
THE SKIPPERS

His boss was coming to his house to fire him. "But," Clint Hurdle recalled, "at least he is going to do me the favor of tellin' me at my home and not at the ballpark." While waiting for Dan O'Dowd to arrive that day, Hurdle called his own father. "'Dad, I think I'm going to be fired,'" Hurdle said. "And he goes, 'Really?' We had been talking for two months [about the possibility]. Our team wasn't good."

O'Dowd arrived at Hurdle's Colorado home. The general manager locked eyes with Hurdle and said: "I am making a managerial change… And I have you as the guy to step in and help us move on. What are your thoughts?"

Hurdle was the Rockies hitting coach in 2002, but instead of being fired along with manager Buddy Bell, Hurdle was promoted that day to replace Bell. This was a pivotal moment in Rockies history. "I don't think I said anything for a good 30 seconds, which felt like five minutes," Hurdle said. "Because I didn't see this coming, I had everything the other way. Then my mind starts rolling, and I go: 'Oh my gosh.'"

On April 26, 2002—that day at Hurdle's home—O'Dowd hired Hurdle as Rockies manager. On May 29, 2009, O'Dowd fired Hurdle as Rockies manager. In between was a Rockies roller-coaster ride, including the thrill of thrills—a trip to the World Series. Forever tanned and forever fun-loving, Hurdle is forever remembered as the manager who led the Rockies into Rocktober and to their first ever National League pennant.

Of that day O'Dowd hired him as a manager, Hurdle said: "I had to calm myself down, gather my thoughts because this was going to be a big deal. It wasn't about me just being so happy, I was getting asked to manage [and do this important job]. I needed, however long it was, to give it some cerebral thought on what was happening. Okay, I thought I was getting fired. A baseball man is getting let go and a man that entrusted me to do a job [of hitting coach] that we didn't do very well. So there were no pom poms, no balloons going up. This was really bittersweet, probably more bitter than sweet. However, at the same time, Dan lays out a landscape: 'This is going to be hard, this is what we need, this is what I've seen from you.' I was fortunate enough to have enough experience managing in the minor leagues. I had a guy pour into me— Darrell Johnson, the former Red Sox manager. He had talked about a lot of different experiences, and one of them was: if you were going to be a guy that came in during the middle of the season, make sure that your first order of business is honor the man that left. Because too many times, a new manager comes in saying we are going to do this or we are going to do that, but you really don't think the previous guy was trying to do all of that? You don't think this guy wasn't waking up in the middle of the night, trying to figure out ways to make the ballclub play better, hit better, field better, whatever it was? And there are all the other coaches, too. Just be careful. Tread lightly. And then just focus on the staples of the game, fundamental demands of the game. As time goes on through observation with eyes and ears, you can develop your own gameplan. The personality is already set. A lot of the time [a promoted coach to manager] comes in and tries to be somebody different than the guy that you have been. The players are going to know, just like that. They are gonna know just like that. So that was all great advice that he had shared with me."

The 2002 Rockies began 6–16 under Bell, and then went 67–73 with Hurdle. "It was like drinking from a fire hose the first year," Hurdle said. "And I remember partway through the year, it felt like duct tape and chicken wire, just to hold it together."

• • •

"That shortstop," Eric Young said from the visiting clubhouse that 2005 day. "How do you pronounce it?" It was Clint Barmes. No, not Cliff Barnes from the TV show *Dallas*. Clint Barmes, pronounced Bar-miss. He had the same first name as his manager and a similar grit, too. It was Opening Day of 2005, Clint Hurdle's third season managing

Colorado, and Hurdle's team—and tenure—would be defined by some of these Rockies rookies.

In the bottom of the ninth, the Rockies trailed 10–8. And the San Diego Padres closer was, of course, Trevor Hoffman. But with two outs, youngster Cory Sullivan doubled in a run. Then youngster Aaron Miles singled to tie the game. And then—how do you pronounce it?—Barmes came to bat, and Hoffman didn't miss his bat. "The memory of this game gives me goose bumps," Hurdle said, more than a dozen years later. "Because for me it gave the players a belief for the first time that we can win big games against big people. It's a packed house, we are down big, they have the best closer on the planet coming in."

Two years before Hurdle's Rockies beat Hoffman in the final game of the regular season, they beat Hoffman in the first game on a drilled walk-off homer by the rookie Barmes. The kid from Vincennes, Indiana, didn't even get a Division I scholarship offer out of high school, so he went to Olney Central College in Illinois (to play basketball and baseball), and then back to Indiana State University.

On the morning of Opening Day of 2005, Barmes arrived five hours before game time. He stared at his jersey for an extra moment before putting it on. "I'm still shaking," he told reporters in the postgame clubhouse before taking the jersey off. "That's the biggest rush I've ever felt."

Young had made Rockies' home-opener history on their literal home opener with his 1993 leadoff homer against the Montreal Expos and now he was an opponent, playing for the touted Padres, picked to win the National League West in '05. "Out of the chute, they came out swinging, acting like they belong," Young said from the visiting clubhouse of the young, scrappy, and hungry Rockies. "That shortstop, he got some big hits for them. Miles got big hits. I think their first two guys set the tone. Whenever you get those little guys on base at the top of the order—that used to be our trademark back in the day—things are going to happen."

As I said in my broadcast call of the home run that day, "I don't know what the rest of 2005 holds, but I won't soon forget Game No. 1."

And we don't. Neither Clint does. But it was just a glimmer, a glimpse because 2005, as Hurdle said, was hard. It hardened the team. And then, "[In] '06 we got on a playground and then got punched, then we got beat up," Hurdle said. "And you either go home and tell your dad you got beat up or you find a way to get bigger, stronger, faster and get back on the playground."

And you look back to the 2005 Clint Barmes Game, numerous young participants were part of Rocktober of 2007—Matt Holliday (known for the slide), Sullivan (known for the throw), Brad Hawpe (known for the San Diego homer), not to mention Todd Helton and Hurdle.

• • •

Clint Hurdle, the manager—and Clint Hurdle, the man—were forever works-in-progress. He endured alcoholism, two failed marriages, and a career that began like a comet—and success that ended as fast as one.

Raised in Merritt Island, Florida, he was a phenom in the area. As recalled in a *Pittsburgh Post-Gazette* story, a young Hurdle would be on a ballfield while his buddies were at the beach. In the outfield were his mother, Louise; his two sisters; and the family dog, Pooh Bear the black poodle, running across the outfield, shagging flies for the boy. "He was the planet," friend Peter Kerasotis told the paper, "and they were all satellites."

A football and baseball star, Hurdle was heavily recruited—even by Harvard. "I was fortunate to have options. I had good grades all through school," Hurdle told me. "The only B I had was in drivers' education. One of the funniest stories I tell people: I didn't win—what do you call it?—the valedictorian. I was second in my class. With one B, I was 3.96.

The B I got was with the football conditioning coach and track coach. That's when I decided I wasn't going to go out for football—and to focus on baseball. Drivers' ed—so you get to the part where you take the actual driving exam. So we drive to Coco Beach and I am on A1A [a famous Florida State Road, immortalized in both a Jimmy Buffett song called 'A1A,' as well as in Vanilla Ice's 'Ice Ice Baby']. He is in the front seat, and there are two kids in the back. We all took turns driving. And I can remember going to the light, and all of a sudden, the light turns yellow, and he goes, 'Gun it! Go.' So I gun it and peel through the light. And he yells, 'Pull this car over!' It was a test. He goes, 'You're telling me that this is the first Friday night you're out, and this is what is going to happen?' And then he goes, 'F. You get an F on the driving test.' I ended up getting a B in the class because I aced everything else. That was how I got my B. But how smart was that? Truthfully, he made his point. I didn't run a red light for probably 30 years!"

Numerous schools came after Hurdle, who might've been a good college quarterback—if the drivers' ed teacher wasn't such a jerk—had he stuck with football. Florida, Florida State, Miami, Georgia, as well as Virginia, Ivy League schools, and even the Naval Academy showed interest in this intriguing football prospect.

But it became clear that schools needed Hurdle more than Hurdle needed schools. As the famous story goes, a Florida-based Royals scout, Bill Fischer, had the director of the Kansas City Royals' scouting department fly down. Fischer threw Hurdle batting practice, and Hurdle launched balls over the wall. "I've seen enough," the director said.

"Don't you want to see him run and throw?"

"If he can hit like that, I don't care if he can run or throw."

Hurdle was 17 when the Royals drafted him ninth overall in 1975. His draft class would become infamous in baseball as one of the weakest ever. Not one first rounder became an All-Star, whereas in 1974, 1976, 1977, each first round produced six All-Stars. The Royals gave Hurdle a $50,000 signing bonus. "It was a ton of money," he said. "It was more money than my dad could make in a couple years of work."

At the age of 20 years and 50 days, he made his big league debut. It was September 18, 1977. Sure enough, Hurdle homered in his first game. And he played nine games that month, finishing with two homers and a .308 average. The kid looked good. "So, I can count how many times I had a photographer take a picture of me in the minor leagues—five," Hurdle said. "Back then you would get your picture taken with your team and in one picture you're holding a bat. So I got to spring training [in 1978], and someone comes up and says they want to shoot a couple of *rolls* of film on you, a *Sports Illustrated* thing. And I'm like 'What?'

"'Yeah, we need you down here at seven in the morning. I have to keep shooting and find that sweet spot and after that I am going to shoot some more. I've got to look for the three or four good pictures, and it's going to take us an hour to do it.' They had me running, hitting, throwing. It was very uncomfortable. It was all about the attention, it was all about me. But young teammate Willie Wilson also had his picture taken. I'm 20. And you hear SI and the SI jinx, and they don't ever tell you who's going to be on the cover. This was going to be the rookie section.

"So it had been a few days, and nothing happened. I pretty much wasn't even waiting for the article to come out. I can remember getting out of my car in the morning, going to 7-11 like I did every morning. I'd get a quart of milk and I'd get a honeybun. And more often than not, it's the same guy behind the counter. So I get the honeybun, I get the milk. And this is back in the day when there are three magazines on the counter—*Time*, *Newsweek*, and *Sports Illustrated*. We are in Fort Myers, and I look down and see the *Sports Illustrated*. And it is me. It's me on the cover. I'm like 'Whoa!' And the guy goes 'What was that?' And I go 'Ahh.' And he looks at me, and I am still staring. He looks at the picture and goes, 'What the…' And he looks back at me, and I just walk out. I don't purchase anything. I just walk out. I get in my car and I sit down. I was numb. I can't call anybody, I don't have a phone. And then I get to the park, and they've got these things all over the place. They've got them on the walls, in the toilet… And I just got torched."

It was the cover of the March 20, 1978, issue of *Sports Illustrated*. There was Hurdle, "Royals" streaking across his chest, and a smile streaking across his face. And this was back when they didn't promote like five different articles on a cluttered cover. It was just Hurdle and the headline: "THIS YEAR'S PHENOM."

Well, that year's phenom went on to hit only .264 with seven homers. The following year was rough, too; the cover boy hit .240.

But 1980 would prove to be a rewarding season for Hurdle—but who would've thought it would be his only rewarding season? For the American League champs, Hurdle hit .294 in 130 games…and .417 in the World Series.

But a combination of booze, injuries, and the 1981 strike deflated any remaining hype. Hurdle bounced to the Cincinnati Reds, New York Mets, and St. Louis Cardinals (and Mets again). The Mets organization, though, liked him enough to hire him as a minor league manager down there in Florida, near where it all began. Hurdle worked his way up and was Buddy Bell's hitting coach for the Rockies, in 2002, when the team started off poorly. "Dan O'Dowd believed in me at a time in my life where I don't think anyone else said, 'You need to be our guy,'" Hurdle said in a quiet moment to me. "'We are gonna do some hard work for awhile and you're going to be the guy.' He empowered me…But Keli McGregor? That was a godsend to me, personally."

McGregor was one of those humans who was too good to be true. Strapping and confident and warm-hearted and faith-based, the son of a football coach and a Colorado native, he was truly a late bloomer. McGregor went to Colorado State around 6'6" and 180 pounds after a good high school career. He wasn't even playing football initially. A coach saw him in the weight room and convinced him to come out. By his senior college season, he was 6'6" and an All-American. His career led him eventually to the Colorado State Hall of Fame and the NFL draft. After a brief pro stint, he became a rising star as a sports administrator at the University of Arkansas. He joined his hometown Rockies in their inaugural season of 1993. And by 2001, at age 38, he was named president of the Colorado Rockies. "He was the right man, in the right spot, at the right time for that organization," Hurdle said. "He grew people up, wherever he would go. He grew boys into men and men into leaders. He was able to instill a pride within that organization that wasn't there. I remember we started wearing purple, like, 'What, are we wearing purple in public?' 'Yeah, we are wearing purple.' Everything he touched, he touched. He impacted things. He dug in with you. He cared about the person. He cared about the product. He cared about everybody. Everybody that was working there, every fan that would come in. I mean he did put a heartbeat to it.

"He was the first man that shared the idea of love with me— unconditional love and what it meant for a man. And I embraced it. And I can remember for years, him telling me that he loves me. And I can remember telling him that I loved him back. But he was probably the first man that I ever told that I loved him. And I can remember going home to my dad, telling my dad 'I love you.' And he goes, 'Yeah, me too.' He transformed people along those lines. We would go on walks in Denver. He loved the city. We would walk to Starbucks. My God, did we drink a lot of coffee. He would pick up trash along the way. I remember the first time he did it. I was with another guy, Rod Olson. And Rod was like 'What're you doing?' And he goes, 'This is my city. I love my city. I'm gonna walk by the trash? No.'"

Even the 2009 day that McGregor, O'Dowd, and the Rockies fired Hurdle, both Hurdle and McGregor privately spent time together and prayed together. "At the end of the day, I might still have some people in my life that have some anger on how it went down," Hurdle said of his firing. "But I don't. There were too many good things to happen, and I felt it was so important to transition out positively. I told the Rockies players: 'I am taking a walk, and it is probably the best thing that could happen to you guys because some of you here are still playing for your manager and not to get fired. You know who you are. And I don't mean that in an ego-filled way. But just go play. If anybody here doesn't think you can still win, you're crazy, you're nuts'...I can remember watching MLB Network when they made the playoffs and jumped on the field and went crazy. I remember how proud I was of everybody I had touched."

The following season Hurdle joined the 2010 Texas Rangers as their hitting coach. It was perfect—he would mentor their slugger Josh Hamilton, who also battled addiction issues. Well, Hamilton won the MVP, and the Rangers won the pennant. In April of 2010, the Rangers were in Boston to face the Red Sox. Hurdle was at Fenway Park when he got a call from longtime Major League Baseball manager and coach Marcell Lachemann.

McGregor had died unexpectedly. He was 47. "I went out to the monster, man," Hurdle said of Fenway's Green Monster. "I cried for a half hour, bawled. I went inside [where they have the hand-operated scoreboard]. I was the only one in there. Nobody came in, nobody walked in."

Of course, McGregor and Hurdle had arrived at Fenway Park in 2007 as National League Champions. This was where Hurdle managed his first World Series game. Meanwhile, the Rockies were in Washington. I was driving back into D.C. from suburban Virginia; Mark Strittmatter (the Rockies catching coach) and I were visiting a friend from Rockies Fantasy Camp. That's when I got the call about McGregor dying. I must have said, "No fucking way," six times. I couldn't believe it. He died suddenly in the middle of the night in the same Salt Lake City Hotel where, on a previous ski trip, we had stayed. He was there, working to continue to expand the Rockies brand in Utah. McGregor had a rare virus in a heart muscle. He'd been in good shape when he passed away in a Utah hotel room. Hurdle flew back to Colorado to speak at the funeral. "He was the first believer of the success of the Rockies," said Hurdle, who became the Pirates manager, leading Pittsburgh to the playoffs in 2013 for the first time since 1992. "He was the first true believer."

• • •

It worked because Jim Tracy worked. The 2009 Rockies season was saved by the grace of Trace, Genuine Jim, this caring new manager who was truly saddened when he got the job—because it meant his friend no longer had it. Tracy and his wife had talked prior to spring training in 2009 about this. He told her over and over that he dreaded having to possibly replace Clint Hurdle. As soon as I hear Tracy's voice, I smile. He cracks me up. He is an entertaining, warm baseball original. But the Rockies hired Tracy to be bench coach because of his managerial experience. He'd been with the Los Angeles Dodgers back when Todd Helton would torch his team and he'd also been the manager of the Pittsburgh Pirates. After Hurdle was fired, Tracy took a long while until he actually took over the managerial office in the Rockies clubhouse. "I worked out of the coach's room. I wouldn't go into Clint's office. I wouldn't do it," said Tracy, who took over as manager on May 29, 2009.

It was a bonkers run for Tracy and the Rockies, who finished a National League best 74–42 and made the playoffs. "Anything could've happened to what ended up being 74–42. It's the same team!" Tracy said in his ever-excited vernacular and voice, which was seemingly preordained for a baseball manager. "It's the same team that went 18–28 with the exception of Joe Beimel, Rafael Betancourt at the trade deadline with Jason Giambi in September. Giambi threw some special shit out there from September 2009 to much of 2010, what a bench piece that was to have! But it was the same guys. It came down to an at-bat, catch, and pitch. Ryan Spilborghs' 14th-inning grand slam against the Giants. Then Albert Pujols doubled up on a catch in short right field by Clint Barmes. And then a pitch thrown by Joel Peralta in Milwaukee, I'll never forget that game.

"Those three scenarios right there are game-changers from the standpoint that, I'm not saying we would've finished poorly, but—to get the most wins in a single season in the history of the franchise—I don't think we would be talking about that. We would not be. I know for a fact we would not be. I'll never forget Joel Peralta in Milwaukee. We got bases loaded, and there's a 3–2 count on JJ Hardy, and we got one out."

The game was June 10, and Tracy's Rockies had already won six straight games. Bottom seven. The Milwaukee Brewers were up with two on and two outs, trailing 4–2. Full count to Hardy. "Everyone in the ballpark knows he has to throw it over the plate, right?" Tracy said. "So, I lean back and sit in the dugout at Miller Park and say to my bench coach, 'Hey, when he knocks the shit out of this fastball here, I hope someone's standing in a good spot to be able to catch it.' Little did I know Joel Peralta—and kudos to him—was going to have the balls to throw a 3–2 split finger with two on! And JJ Hardy's bowels locked up so badly, he couldn't have swung for a week, I mean when this guy saw that thing come out of his hand, he thought for sure he was getting a heater right down the cock to take a free swing at… and Peralta dumps that split finger on him that completely paralyzed him! Then Peralta turns around and gets Ryan Braun to get a little ground ball to short, and we're out of the inning. I'm like *Oh my God!* I mean the balls that it took. Well, there's our man again, catcher Yorvit Torrealba. How about the nut sack to say, 'Hey, you know what, split finger? Throw it over the plate.' Yorvit, he was a presence! And the group of guys that threw to him, they knew it! They knew he was, and there's another guy like you said, one of the all-timers. I mean, I'm sorry. There's certain situations that I don't know if we would've made it all the way through in the manner in which we did in 2009."

• • •

James Edwin Tracy was one of those baseball men who seemingly has a story for every day he has been in baseball. Trace is as intelligent as he is compelling, and no one tells a better story in the game. Tiny (Mike Pontarelli) and I still regularly break into our "Jim Tracy voice" and crack each other up. He made impacts wherever he went—playing for the Cubs in Chicago or the Whales in Yokohama, or managing the hot-shot Los Angeles Dodgers or even the minor league Peoria Chiefs. That summer in 1988 Tracy became a key character in the book, *The Boys Who Would Be Cubs* by Joseph Bosco.

He managed the Rockies from 2009 to 2012, leaving permanent impressions, producing two winning seasons, and one unforgettable turnaround. "Jim Tracy, much like Carlos Gonzalez, is a guy that you just want to be around," trainer Scott Gehret said. "Because if you're around him, you're smiling, and there's a pretty good chance you laugh. He just kind of exudes this unconditional love on people where you know that he cares. He's one of those guys that if he meets your parents, he's gonna remember their name. He might only meet them once. Lord knows how many people Jim Tracy knows in this world, but if he runs into my parents, he's gonna say, 'Hello, Mr. and Mrs. Gehret, how are you doing today?' Or, 'Hello Peter and Grace.' He's that kind of guy. He was a very special man.

"Talking about managers, I enjoy watching managers manage. When you're watching 162 games, I know the signs, I like the games, I like the chess match. Jim Tracy was great at it. Not saying the rest weren't, but he was really a good strategist in my opinion. Here's an example. I remember it was a day game one time, and it was the seventh inning," Gehret said of a game against the Atlanta Braves. "We had a right-hander that was pitching. The Braves' pitcher's spot was coming up. Our pitcher started looking at his hand and shaking his hand. There was a pinch hitter coming up. Tracy says, 'Scottie, let's go check on him.' The umpire comes out when a trainer goes out to make sure that it's not a official visit because they can't exchange any strategic information. So anyways, our pitcher is struggling with whatever. We go out there, and I look, and, yeah, this guy's got a huge blister on his finger. He can't pitch. I'm like, 'Trace, he can't pitch with this.' He looks at the home-plate umpire and he said, 'Have they announced that lefty as his pinch hitter yet?' He said, 'No,' so the guy's not in the game yet. He looks at our guy and said, 'Can you throw one pitch? One warm-up pitch?' He asked if I was cool with it, and I had no idea where he was going with it, but I said, 'Sure.' The guy throws his one warm-up pitch. And Tracy says, 'Look, get on the mound and stand here. I'll be right back.' I don't know what the fuck's going on here. We're walking off the mound, guy's got the ball. They announce the guy, 'Now entering the game, left-handed hitter, blah blah blah.' Jim Tracy almost turns right back around and grabbed the ball. Back in the dugout, I go, 'That's what you were fucking doing!' He goes, 'Yeah, I needed to burn the left-handed hitter.' So Tracy brought the lefty in, and Atlanta took the lefty hitter out and burned the hitter. That's the game within the game! I'm like, 'You're pretty fucking smart.' He said, 'Yeah, this isn't my first game managing.'"

One of my favorite memories in Rockies history wasn't even in a regular-season game. And come to think of it, it involved the Rockies failing. But you'll see what I mean. Tracy had three sons who all played in the minors. Tracy was Clint Hurdle's bench coach in 2009, and the Rockies were playing the Texas Rangers in a spring training game in Arizona. "As a matter of fact, Mrs. T. made that road trip," Tracy said of his wife, Debbie, "just in case he got in the game."

Tracy's son is Chad Tracy, but not the Chad Tracy who played nine seasons primarily with the Arizona Diamondbacks. Jim's son, Chad, never made it to the bigs, but in spring of '09, he was 23 and heading into a pivotal year as a Double A player in the Rangers organization. "And here he comes in the fifth and he's coming in to play first base, and I'm sitting there going 'Oh shit,'" Tracy recalled. "It was a proud moment for me. I had those dark Oakleys on, and we could've had a storm with black clouds, and I think I would've still left them on. I just didn't want anyone to see what was going on behind those glasses.

"In the seventh, the Rangers had runners on second and third with two outs, and David Murphy was the guy coming up, and at the time Clint had no idea it was my son waiting on deck. He says to me, 'Hey, Trace, I believe we'll walk Murphy here.' And between you and me that was fine and dandy, but I can tell you that in 11 years of managing in the big leagues I never intentionally walked one guy in spring training. So anyway, he said, 'We'll walk Murphy, and pitch to ol' number 76 over there. I said, 'Okay, that's fine.' We send Murphy on his way, and Chad goes up there, and Jhoulys Chacin gets two strikes on him pretty quick. And here comes the sliders and the 12–6 breaking balls. But Chad fouled off five to six pitches that could've definitely punched him out, he's hanging in there.

"Then Chacin tries to sneak a fastball by him, and I mean to tell you he knocked the shit out of it. He hit that ball to left-center field, and that kid's running around the bases, and I'm crying tears behind my sunglasses. And I can see Andruw Jones, a few guys are sticking their head out of the Rangers dugout and were giving me all kinds of shit! Clint turns to me and says 'Damn Trace, you would've thought they won the World Series. What's going on over there?' I go, 'Well, Clint, I may have something to do with that—that fellow that hit that grand slam, that's my middle son Chad.' That was a dandy."

• • •

One day, Walt Weiss struck out. It happens to even the best of them, notably against the guy on the hill this particular day. But as Weiss walked back to the dugout, he could feel a presence. He looked back at the mound; the pitcher was staring at him...and then spit. Well, Weiss waltzed to the clubhouse and called the other clubhouse. "I want to see him after the game," he said.

The clubbie was a little confused but dutifully planned to pass along the message. The opposing pitcher this day happened to be a particularly large and intimidating man, a guy accustomed to breaking the will of the opposition; Weiss is 6' tall and a buck 70. In the opposing clubhouse was a former Weiss teammate. After the game he heard about the phone call and found the pitcher. "I don't know if you're thinking about it. You can't," he told the nasty hurler. "Weiss will fucking kill you."

Yup, Weiss was such a bad ass, a mutual friend was looking out for the pitcher in the potential fight, not Weiss. And so, the pitcher got on the clubhouse phone and called up Weiss: "I'm sorry man, heat of the moment, shouldn't have done it."

Walter William Weiss, I've often said, had the unique ability to be the toughest guy in a room while also being the nicest guy in that room. He also possesses a great dry wit. A longtime slick-fielding shortstop and leader, he also became extremely accomplished in mixed martial arts in his spare time. "[Weiss] played the game hard, played the game smart. He's as tough a guy as you can possibly imagine, and that's the kind of thing we're trying to breed in here," Michael Cuddyer said in 2014. "We saw that as a unit last year. When things started going south after the All-Star break, he still believed in us, he never abandoned ship or started pointing fingers at the players, and that speaks a lot to the players. When you have a manager and a coaching staff like that, and players too, you can feed off each other."

Born six days after the John F. Kennedy assassination, Weiss became something of a New York state baseball legend and went on to star at the University of North Carolina. And while that era in Chapel Hill is remembered for Michael Jordan and James Worthy, consider that the first overall pick in the 1985 draft, as well as the 11th overall pick, were Tar Heels B.J. Surhoff and Weiss, who, by the way, both hailed from New York City suburbs.

Weiss became a spark plug on those late-1980s Oakland A's. He won the Rookie of the Year in 1988 and the World Series in 1989. (He hit three homers all season, but, sure enough, hit a homer in the '89 Fall Classic.) Before he was the larger-than-life "Tulo," he was just a boy named Troy. And his California family would drive over to watch the A's, the true Bay Area giants. And while young Troy Tulowitzki soaked up the aura of Mark McGwire and Jose Canseco, sluggers' sluggers, "I always had a liking for shortstops," Tulo shared in 2014. "So I watched Walt Weiss growing up a lot, so there's no doubt that I watched plenty of his games. It's kind of cool that I'm playing under him."

In 1995 Weiss' playing experience helped guide his Rockies teammates into their first postseason play. And Weiss hoped to relive the glory days (or lone glory year) as the Rockies skipper. He was hired for the 2013 season and remained at the helm until 2016. He was an unexpected candidate for the job. For quite a while, Weiss didn't even consider himself a candidate for the job. But this was in an era when teams were taking chances on 40-something former leaders to manage… without managerial experience or even big league coaching experience. There was Mike Matheny in St. Louis and Robin Ventura on the South Side of Chicago. And, in Denver, they vetted the tough, old shortstop who would've even fought the pitcher who stared at him and spit. "When I first got the call [from Dan O'Dowd], I was definitely caught off-guard," recalled Weiss, who'd been coaching Regis Jesuit High School and helping out with youth baseball in the area. "It was the last thing on my mind. I'd stepped away for four years. And while I had visions of getting back in at some point, I hadn't thought in that way. I had to think for a minute and I don't think I told Terri [his wife] right away. I waited a day or something. See, I'd got this phone call. And I never used to say who it was from, but it was from Dan. He started it with, 'My son Jack is looking for a youth team. You know some people out there, the Slammers guys. You think you could help out?' I said, 'Yeah, man, I'll get him hooked up.' Then you know Dan. All of a sudden, he goes zero to 60. 'You want to manage [the Rockies]?' I'm like, 'What?' I said, 'Dan, I'm sitting here at Chick-Fil-A for this team fund-raiser.'

"'This is your job, man, this is your job.' I'm like, 'What are you talking about, Dan?' 'This is your job. You were groomed for this job. It's perfect for you.' And I'd had a lot of history with the organization, obviously, and I think that's what he meant. It was out of the blue.

"It might have been a week at the most. I made a call to Bill Geivett because Bill was the acting GM on the major league side...He was around when I was a special assistant on the minor league side. I'd see him occasionally but never went in depth. So I had to call him. I'm sure that was a weird phone call for him. But Dan's like, 'You need to call him. That's the first step you need to take.' I called Geivo and said, 'I wouldn't mind throwing my hat in the ring here.' And he said, 'Okay... let me talk to some people, and I'll get back to you,' type of thing. [He] calls me a day or two later and he lived by me and said, 'I want you to come over to my house, and we're going to talk.' So I went down to his basement and his office he had down there. I was there three-and-a-half hours. I could tell I piqued his interest because we were just talking philosophy, and this is the first time we'd had any conversation in depth besides, 'Hey, how's it going?' in passing. At the end of the night, he goes, 'This is real interesting, Walt. I want to do this again.'

"So a week or two later, same thing, but this time I was there like four, four-and-a-half hours. When I left, I felt like I'd made a good impression. I was just being me. I didn't know where it was going to go. He called me back and said, 'You're one of the three candidates left. The last step is you need to go in and you need to have an interview with Dan and [owner] Dick Monfort.' This was suit and tie and going into the office. I spent the whole day with them. Looking back, it was like 15 hours of interviews. They vetted me pretty good. It wasn't like they just plucked me out of the high school coaching ranks and put me in... It took a week, and I told my wife and said, 'I didn't get it. I would have heard by now. We'll just carry on.' But then I got the call from Tiny, the clubhouse manager. 'Hey, I know you're on the shortlist. I'm getting jersey numbers for the shortlist. What number would you like?' I'm like, 'Tiny, you know what number I want? I'm 22.' 'Okay, okay. I had to call to [be sure].' That was the first inkling that I got it. Sure enough, I think that day, I got the call.'"

One of the first calls Weiss wanted to make was to the legendary Tony La Russa, the Hall of Famer who managed Weiss in Oakland. "But he called me before I called him," Weiss said. "He's like, 'I'm in New York. I have to fly home to Oakland tomorrow, but I'm changing my flight. I'm flying to Denver, and we're going to spend a day together.' This is the day after I was named manager. He flies to Denver, we spend an afternoon together, and he spills his guts to me about what's important as a manager. [He] cut the learning curve in half for me in three or four hours that day. From that point on, he was always a phone call away. If I didn't call within a week, he'd call me. 'Why aren't you calling me?' Anytime I had a tough situation, 'Tony, what do you think?' He was gold for me."

• • •

Before Reed Saunders, there was Alan Roach, this fellow bellower. Both men are famous around Denver for their particularly deep voices. Roach is recognizable everywhere from sporting events to commercials to the terminal-connecting train at Denver International Airport ("Hooooooold on please!")

In 1998 at Coors Field, Roach had the honors of being the public-address announcer at the All-Star Game. Talk about a constellation of stars. It was the summer of Mark McGwire and Sammy Sosa. On the career list of baseball's home run leaders, eight of the top 15 were on 1998 All-Star rosters. And Roach had the honors of announcing: "Batting seventh, from your Colorado Rockies, center fielder, Laaaaarry Waaaaaalker!" (Walker played center because Tony Gwynn was in right and Barry Bonds was in left.)

But after Walker, there was another similarly loud cheer—for an Atlanta Brave. It was Walt Weiss, the Rockies fan favorite from their first playoff team three years prior. And at 34, Weiss was the oldest player to ever be voted to start his first All-Star Game. And many of the fans knew Weiss' amazing backstory. Earlier that season his son, Brody, contracted E. coli at an Atlanta water park. Brody was three and was one of three children who developed Hemolytic-uremic syndrome. It had the possibility of being fatal. Weiss had flown home to Atlanta to be with Brody and the family. Ultimately, Brody persevered, but his family hesitated on flying him commercially to Denver for the All-Star Game. But the Rockies owner at the time, Jerry McMorris, heard the story and sent his own private plane to Atlanta to pick up the Weiss family and cater to Brody's needs.

So, as Roach announced: "Batting eighth, from the Atlanta Braves, shortstop, Walt Weiss!" the cameras cut to Terri Weiss in the stands. Her smile glistened. And in her lap was the clapping Brody. Terri pointed to the big screen in the stadium, and when Brody realized they were on there, his smile illuminated millions of living rooms in America.

In 2013 Weiss had coached Brody's high school team in Denver. Next thing he knew, Weiss was up for the Rockies managerial job, asking to explain his coaching philosophy to Bill Geivett, the Rockies executive. "I want you to put your philosophy on paper," Geivett asked. "What's important to you?"

"Tough and smart," Weiss shared with me. "That was the foundation we had. I said I wanted the team to play tougher than everybody. I wanted to play smarter than everybody. That can be foundational. The other stuff will come, but that's got to be in place for the culture. I still have those papers. I broke down offensively what was my philosophy and defensively what was my pitching philosophy, what the culture should look like. I spent a lot of time on that. It's funny. When he told me to do that, I'd never done anything like that before and I loved it. It was the first time I had ever poured out my soul about the game on paper. It was easy. I remember in the first hour, I had pages already."

Weiss was an eternal sponge who had played for Hall of Fame managers, Tony La Russa and Bobby Cox, as well as the beloved Don Baylor in Denver. "A lot of what I wrote was just about, and this isn't revolutionary or anything, but it was important to create a culture of respect and trust down the chain of command," Weiss said. "There was a lot of that in my paper. The culture was at the top of my list because at the end of the day it's about leadership. The X's and O's, you're baseball guys, you're going to figure that out. Speed of the game, you figure it out. We've been figuring it out our whole lives. You figure out the speed of the game and adjust. The culture, I think that's where managers earn their keep. Because once players are out on the field, it's up to them. But creating an environment where players don't want to let you down, don't want to disappoint you, where they do trust you, they do respect you because you talk to them in a certain way that creates respect, that's Leadership 101. I really focused on the cultural part of it and the environment I was going to try to create."

He sure as hell tried. Weiss oversaw three players winning batting titles and Troy Tulowitzki in his prime and helped develop what would become an All-Star left side of the infield. But he didn't have pitching. It was—and forever is—so hard to pitch at altitude. Pitchers can't command pitches. And batted balls seem to sail farther than they should. In 2012, Jim Tracy's final season, Dan O'Dowd and Bill Geivett even tried to benefit from a four-man rotation, limiting his starters to 75 pitches, hoping to avoid going through batting orders a third time.

Weiss suffered through much consternation, some from Rockies Nation, as he tried to find ways to win, ways to motivate. "It got postal a couple times on our club," Weiss said. "When it got to the times where it felt I had to babysit grown men is when I would lose it. I typically had a pretty long fuse, and that's one of the things that would set me off. I had a couple pretty legendary team meetings. The one I had my first year, I scared myself. It was bad. Nolan probably would have been there. There's some guys who would have been there in 2013. Tony [La Russa] lost it on occasion, but usually not in the dugout, showing players up. That wasn't my style and was never going to be my style. I did my tough love behind closed doors. That meeting I had in 2013, I felt I might have been losing the club. It was my first year as a manager, I had a GM in the clubhouse with me and I thought that I might have been losing credibility. And there were some things going on that I didn't like culturally. It was against everything I was trying to implement, and I could smell it. It got to a tipping point and I went crazy. But it had to happen. In my eyes it had to happen. I felt that was a big day for me as a manager. I was a little embarrassed afterward for the way I acted. But looking back on it now with big picture perspective, it had to happen. They needed to see that side of me and needed to know how much I cared about what I was doing. But I was embarrassed. I walked into my office afterward going, 'What the hell is wrong with you?'"

But it made a difference in the club. "Oh yeah, absolutely," Weiss said. "And look, I get it. From a player's perspective, who's running the show here? Is it the guy upstairs, is he running the show? I walked into a very difficult situation. I had built credibility as a player, I hadn't as a manager yet. So it was like, 'What is this?' They don't trust him because they have a guy down here looking over his shoulder. So I felt like I started to lose credibility with the club. I had to earn that like a player has to everything else, but because of the circumstances, I felt that the deck is kind of stacked against me. I could feel it slipping away. I could smell it. I think that was a big day for me."

The moments that make a man sometimes take a man. Young Nolan Arenado, a future star, hit a comebacker to the mound. So, he started peeling off early to the dugout. But the pitcher kicked it around a little bit, threw it in the dirt. "And by that time," Weiss said, "Nolan had started to run again, but he's out as he's lunging for the bag. I had to have that tough conversation with him. I pulled him in the middle of the game, which is embarrassing for a player. But he talks about how that was impactful in his career. Tony La Russa, he talked about how you have to get to shape and mold players before that third year because that's when they start making a lot of money and their values are pretty much set in stone. It was important for me to hear that from him, and that's why I took a Nolan Arenado out of a game and had those conversations with the young players."

When Arenado spotted Weiss in 2018, he scurried over and gave him a meaningful hug.

Weiss had a similar conversation with Carlos Gonzalez in spring training of 2014 and told him that he needed him to run everything out full go to set the proper example for the young players. "[I] was so fired up when I saw him ground out last night, but I saw he was out by half a step," Weiss said of the hustle. "My heart was going. I loved it. He's got a dynamic personality. He went through some tough times. CarGo had some struggles when I was there, and there were tough conversations there. He was always so professional when we had those conversations and he was always accountable. He'd always hit third or fourth, and then I called him in and said, 'I'm going to move you to the six spot in the order.' He was struggling and kept him there for a little while, and then one day you could smell him starting to come out of it and he came into my office and said, 'Skip, I'm ready man. I'm ready to move back up.' I said, 'You're ready, huh? All right, I trust you. I'm going to put you back there.' And then he took off. But that's that give and take, that trust that you have to have with your players. But I love him as a person. He's one of those guys that everybody likes, everybody pulls for because of who he is."

Weiss moved on after 2016, his fourth season. It was a tough go for a good guy. In 2018 he was hired as a coach for the Atlanta Braves, so their All-Star and Gold Glove outfielder Ender Inciarte called a fellow Venezuelan. "He said, 'We've got Walt. What was it like when he was with the Rockies?'" CarGo said. "I was like, 'I'll tell you what. When you have a manager like him, you really like the manager you have and you wish he could be your manager for a long time.' He's just one of the awesome persons where you wish him the best…I felt kind of bad when he was our manager because he didn't have the talent. He didn't have the pitching we do now [in 2017 and 2018]. We had a great offense, but we didn't have what it takes to win in this division…People might forget about his time here because it wasn't too pretty, but he's part of the process. He's part of this group here. He pretty much taught us the right way to play the game. He'd give you responsibility. He'd set goals in your head. You've got to do this, you've got to do this. Then some guys would take it the wrong way and think he's trying to be hard on me. But if you do what he was telling you to do, you'd end up being a pretty good player. At the end of the year, I'd have to thank this guy because he was teaching me the right way, the way I was supposed to do it. There's a lot of guys in this clubhouse from when he was here as a manager and became good players because of him."

Trainer Scott Gehret had a front-row seat to the managerial styles of several skippers. And of Weiss, he said what that spitting opposing pitcher already had learned. "If you said, 'Who in this league do you not want to fight?' The answer was Walt Weiss," Gehret said. "Walt Weiss is a man's man. And he would treat every man in the clubhouse with respect. That's his thing. Whether it's me, you, his star player, or the

Always a good quote, manager Bud Black speaks to reporters before a game in June of 2018.

person that's vacuuming the clubhouse when he's leaving at midnight. He's gonna treat you all the same."

• • •

Harry Ralston Black was the ideal man to be the ideal manager with ideal ideals and even the ideal nickname: Bud. "He doesn't get too high or too low, but he's fiery and he cares," Nolan Arenado said. "He's always checking up on me and he's a good man...I like Buddy, same guy every day. That's something I love about a coach. Walt was a great guy, and I like Walt too. Buddy brings energy, and he's just the same guy every day."

Even as a teenager in a timber town in Washington, Buddy was just buddies with everyone, even though he was the star athlete. His childhood friend Kirc Roland told *The Denver Post*: "Buddy is just one of those big-hearted people. The stoners, the jocks, the nerds, the kids taking special education, they all loved Buddy Black."

It's reminiscent of when Ed Rooney's secretary describes the popularity of Ferris Bueller, whom they all thought was a righteous dude.

Black became the Rockies manager for the 2017 season, and the Rockies returned to the postseason for the first time since Jim Tracy's team in 2009. He was an ideal hire for so many reasons. He's got a pitching pedigree, he's managed successfully in the division before, he's a baseball thinker and a baseball man. I love being around him. He energizes each day. He has a great vibe to him. Jeff Bridich hit a home run when he hired Black. Privately, I would call Rockies public relations director Warren Miller—a former San Diego Padres employee and a longtime friend of Black's—and ask him how it was looking. I hoped that as Bridich went through his process, Black would end up being his hire.

Sure enough, one of the people in Black's past was Dan O'Dowd. They were close during their Cleveland Indians days in the 1990s when O'Dowd was a rising executive and Black a retiring pitcher. "Entering 1995, two teams were coming after me, the Giants and the Indians," Black said, "and I decided to go back to Cleveland. I had a great relationship with John Hart. Dan was there at the time."

The 1995 Indians. My goodness. One of those teams that ranks as the greatest teams to never win a championship. The season started late because of the strike, so they only played 144 games. And the Indians went 100–44! That's a .694 winning percentage. The 1998 New York Yankees, a baseball benchmark team, had a .704 winning percentage (114–48). And for these Indians, Albert Belle hit 50 homers with 52 doubles in the 144-game season. Black, meanwhile, had a 6.85 ERA and turned 38 on June 30th. "Right after the All-Star break, Mark Wiley gave me a call," Black said of his pitching coach, who now works for the

Rockies in pitching development. "'Hey, Buddy, John and I need to talk to ya.' Called me at 9:30 in the morning, that doesn't really happen. 'Hey Bud, we're gonna let you go.' I was mentally sort of done and physically. My elbow started hurting late. It had bothered me the last couple of years so I think I was really close to being done. [After time off in July,] I called the Indians, and they said, 'Come on back, and we'll start your post-playing career.' I jumped in right away. I didn't take the one year off, the two years off. I went right in, which was probably the best thing I ever did. So John said, 'Hey Bud, I want you to go to Triple A Buffalo. I want you to write up a few reports on our pitchers. Go down to Single A Kinston. There's a kid down there name Colon, I want you to watch him pitch.'"

The kid was Bartolo Colon…though it's hard to ever think of him as a kid. He went 13–3 as a 22-year-old that summer. Colon would make his debut with the Indians in 1997, later win a Cy Young, pitch on four All-Star teams…and was still in the bigs at 45 in 2018. For perspective, Colon made his big league debut on April 4, 1997. Just two weeks later, Peter Lambert was born. Lambert was the Rockies' second-round pick in 2015 and a Triple A pitching prospect in 2018, and Lambert's lifespan thus far had been the length of Colon's big league career!

But back to Black. He was helping out the Indians organization in 1995 and in September did some advanced scouting and work with the current Indians team. "In the middle of September, I was in Cleveland, and there was a left-handed pitcher throwing against the Tribe that night," Black said. "[Coach] Charlie Manuel said, 'You wanna throw BP?' 'Well, fuck yeah, I'll throw BP.' So I threw BP to like Albert, Eddie Murray, Manny Ramirez, whatever, and they go, 'Oh fuck, you throw good. Come tomorrow.' So here I was, I'm throwing BP to these guys in late September and I was their teammate a month and a half ago and now I'm like a coach already. I was sitting in on coaches' meetings, dressing in uniform and I had known all these guys, Buddy Bell,

Hargrove, Wiley. Everyone was cool. So I was with the team through the playoffs and World Series. So, that was sort of the building block of front office and coaching, those next couple of months. That next spring training, I went to Winter Haven, and my role…I was one of the first special assistants to the GM that was an ex-player, got paid $15,000 in '96 to sort of rove around our system."

Black became an Indians minor league pitching coach and was hired by the Los Angeles Angels of Anaheim in 2000 to be their big league pitching coach. He joined what became one of the most storied staffs in history, considering manager Mike Scioscia and the gang won the 2002 World Series, and the staff had three other future MLB managers—Joe Maddon (of the Tampa Bay Rays and Chicago Cubs), Ron Roenicke (Milwaukee Brewers), and Black (the 2010 National League Manager of the Year).

In some respects Black has been like a baseball *Forrest Gump*, always there for history in the making. He was college teammates with a young phenom named Tony Gwynn. He was the starting pitcher for the Kansas City Royals in the George Brett "pine tar game." He was on the 1985 World Series champions, which won, in part, thanks to the infamous Don Denkinger call at first base. He was teammates on the San Francisco Giants with Barry Bonds. And he was the losing manager to the Rockies in, yep, Game 163.

He had a successful career, won a lot of games, tasted great team success, and learned much about himself as a man in the process. "As a young player in Kansas City, I'd snap," he shared, "glove thrown down in the tunnel, get removed from a game, rip my locker up. And then as I got older, that sort of leaves you. I remember in Kansas City, I think this might have been my rookie year, bad game, got removed early, was coming into the dugout, and there's this fan who hammered me from about the time I got to the foul line to the time I reached the first base dugout, and I heard him, looked up, saw him, just getting after me big

Drew's Diary

July 7, 2018:
Colorado Rockies at Seattle Mariners

It's a great matchup on the bump with Kyle Freeland and James Paxton, one of the best in the American League. Paxton, a Canadian native, earlier in the year had no-hit the Toronto Blue Jays and was sitting at 8-2. It didn't look good when the Rockies had the bases loaded in the third inning and none out with the top of the order coming up but did not score. They would take a 1-0 lead in the fourth, however, on a leadoff single by Ian Desmond, a stolen base, and a Carlos Gonzalez bullet to center. Freeland would allow one run in five innings, a solo shot by underrated Jean Segura. Paxton dominated the first five in the Rockies lineup, who would go a collective 1-for-22 on the day. But when a club is in a good place, it finds new heroes each day. In the seventh inning with runners at first and third, Noel Cuevas tried a safety squeeze on the first pitch he saw from Paxton, and the ball went foul. The next pitch is a slider over the plate, which he hit off the metal barrier above the Rockies bullpen for a three-run, game-altering homer. Colorado went on to win 5-1, its fifth in a row and eighth in their last nine. Bud Black fielded numerous questions after the game but finally told the gathered media: "I'm surprised no one's asked yet about Noel Cuevas' homer, and you should." It was classic Buddy, scolding in an affable way but more importantly wanting to give credit to a young player for providing the biggest swing of the day.

time. And I was pissed, just gave it up. I went upstairs in the clubhouse and I'm thinking I'm gonna call ticket sales, I'm gonna figure out whose season ticket that is. And I was just about to call and said to the clubbie,

'Hey man, who's in charge of season tickets?' And I was gonna go to the phone and then I go, *What are you doing?*"

Managing himself made him a better manager decades later. Understanding players, understanding emotions, understanding passion, these are qualities that make Black an elite manager of men. "I don't think there's truly a baseball philosophy," Black shared. "It sort of depends on your personality, it depends on your team. There's some fundamental things whether you believe in the bunt, whether you believe in the hit and run or stolen base, you believe in the strikeout, all those things are important. I think management or leadership is truly how you handle people in any role, in any capacity. So as it relates to that in my role is three primary things. On the philosophical side, I feel like I'm a teacher, leader, and motivator. So every day that I go to the park, those three things are at the front of my mind. It's trying to know different personalities and how to get to them. That's always a challenge and to know that certain players need more attention than others, certain players need different messages than others. Eventually, there's an instinctual vibe that you feel good or bad."

CHAPTER 8

GENERAL MANAGERS

Charlie Manuel is in the Philadelphia Sports Hall of Fame. Not just Philadelphia Phillies Hall of Fame—we're talking the whole city of Philadelphia. Manuel managed against the Rockies in the 2007 National League Division Series. In 2008 he guided the Phillies to the World Series championship. In 2009 his club defeated the Rockies in the NLDS, won the National League Championship Series and advanced to the World Series, losing to A-Rod and the New York Yankees.

In his career Manuel literally won a thousand games. His record was 1,000–826, and he could've been Colorado's. "And Charlie Manuel," Dan O'Dowd said, "is who I should have hired as my first manager... Charlie and I had numerous conversations about altitude and how it played, things of that nature. And that is ultimately who I should have hired as my first manager. Not derogatory toward Buddy [Bell]...I don't know why I did that. And Charlie went on to have an incredible managerial career. But Charlie and I were as close as I was with Buddy. [The relationships] were no different."

But after the 1999 season, the new Rockies general manager, O'Dowd, chose a different Cleveland Indians coach to manage Colorado. Bell, a former Detroit Tigers manager and big league All-Star, was hired on October 21, 1999. The Indians promoted Manuel to be their manager on November 1. O'Dowd fired Bell in the midst of the 2002 season and promoted Clint Hurdle. But the Rockies didn't make the playoffs until 2007. O'Dowd admitted that certain decisions— including some he wasn't allowed to make—slowed the building of a Rockies winner. "What people don't realize is that when I interviewed for the job with Jerry [McMorris] back in 1999, I laid out a complete vision for the franchise based on my assessments," said O'Dowd, who had been in the Indians' front office. "We had very few prospects. We had Matty Holliday. Choo Freeman [a 1998 first rounder], we always questioned if he could really hit. Jamey Wright, had major concerns about his delivery and if he was ever going to be a consistent strike thrower, heavy sink. John Thomson. Had a few pieces, but in reality it was a dearth of prospects. So I laid out a vision, where we needed to kind of start over. And so I got the job, I thought based upon that vision. I wasn't in the job for very long to see that Jerry McMorris didn't want any part of [a rebuild]. Very logical reasons, I just wish I would have known all of those reasons because I had other opportunities with Milwaukee and Seattle. I had three job offers at the same time. But if I had been allowed to do what I wanted to do, all the trades that I made, the 'Dealin' Dan era' would have been players that would have played in High A or Double A, not the bigs. But Jerry was real concerned. It was a newer franchise. Attendance models, they had come off a really bad season. I mean, when you are new in the history of the franchise, that is very understandable. But if I had known that up front, I would have gone in a different direction only because I knew what I was good at. And I knew I was good at scouting and developing. And I knew what we did in Cleveland and I knew how to duplicate that again somewhere else, which then would have given me more of a time to get my arms around it, to really understand the dynamics of altitude, but Jerry wanted to, not win right away, but be competitive right away...And we did that first year in 2000. We went out and went 82–80. It was a speed team. Jeffrey Hammonds [.335], Tom Goodwin [39 stolen bases], Jeff Cirillo [115 RBIs after he was acquired in a trade involving Wright]. I mean, we were a fun team to watch. But I knew it wasn't sustainable."

One night at dinner during the 2017 Winter Meetings, O'Dowd said: "I had the best deal of all that nobody knows about. I had a deal set up [in the 2000 season]. It was Pedro Astacio and Jose Jimenez. You ready for these three names? And Jerry McMorris turned it down. It was with the Toronto Blue Jays. "Chris Carpenter, Kelvim Escobar, and Vernon Wells—all three."

All three were 25 or under at the time, and Carpenter went on to win a Cy Young and become enshrined in the St. Louis Cardinals Hall of Fame. Escobar was a starter who, after 2000, had a 3.76 ERA. He even closed one year and tallied 38 saves. And Wells, well, he was a three-time All-Star (and three-time Gold Glove winner in the outfield) who hit 270 career homers.

At the time of the potential trade, Astacio was 31. The previous year he won 17 games. And though his ERA was 5.27 in 2000, his road ERA was 4.05. So why did O'Dowd's boss turn it down? "He looked at it as a rebuild," O'Dowd said. "Pedro was in the prime of his career. Pedro was really good for us. 'You can't trade him; he is our ace. We need to win now.' So I used this line. I used it with Jerry: 'You can deny reality all you want. Eventually, you cannot avoid the consequences of denying reality.' I used that line over and over and over. And I can remember [another executive] literally threw his papers up in the air in his room [when the owner turned it down]. Carpenter might have not turned out like [a Cy Young winner] in our place. But remember Escobar, how big he was? And Vernon Wells. Think about it—he would have been a younger reincarnation of Ellis Burks in our ballpark. He would have hit 50 home runs in our place. That is the deal nobody knows about. That was turned down. That would have changed the course of my history there. That would have been the best deal in the history of the franchise."

In 2003, for example, Toronto's Wells had 33 homers, 49 doubles, and hit .317 with 117 RBIs. Imagine Wells at Coors? "And then a year later I had to trade [Astacio] anyway because he broke down," O'Dowd said, "for Scott Elarton."

That trade was in July of 2001. In four starts for Colorado, Elarton struggled and then missed all of 2002 due to shoulder surgery. He was released during the 2004 season. In 22 starts for the Rockies, Elarton had a 7.60 ERA. He was who Colorado got for Astacio—instead of a haul of Carpenter, Escobar, and Wells.

So just where were the Rockies going around the turn-of-the-century? "In my Cleveland days," O'Dowd recalled, "one thing Hank

Peters taught me was: 'You can't do both, Dan. You can't rebuild and win at the same time.' And how he explained it to me, it's not even like it had anything to do with money. It's when your scouts are out watching players. They can't watch two plays. It is a confusing message every day. Are you acquiring this player to win now? Or are you acquiring this player to win down the road? You have to get everybody on the same page again in the organization, you have to have one train of thought. So you become really good at that one train of thought because you're doing it over, and over, and over again. The good-to-great concept. And then we overachieved [in 2000 at 82–80], and it was a fun year. And Todd Helton [.372, 42 homers] was, oh my gosh, different than any other kind of player I have been around…His hit ability was different than any other player I'd been around in my life, just amazing. And that is when the fatal decision was to sign Hampton and Neagle, and I never felt good about that from the inception of that just because one I never felt like I had a good enough feel for where we were as an organization. And I knew we never had the depth to support anything that could happen from an injury standpoint."

Mike Hampton and Denny Neagle. In Denver they're often said in the same sentence, sometimes as just a single entity— "Hamptonandneagle." It was hoped that this pitching prowess could save the Rockies similar to "Grayandbutler" as Jon Gray and Eddie Butler rapidly moved up the ranks in the early-to-mid 2010s.

In October of 2000, the New York Mets faced the New York Yankees in the World Series. After Game 1 the Mets' Hampton and the Yankees' Neagle both arrived to Trump International Hotel and Tower in Manhattan. Per an article in *The New York Times*, it turned out both guys lived there. "We got on the elevator together, and I said, 'Hey, good luck tomorrow,'" Neagle said at the time. "Next thing you know we're reaching for the same button. It turns out we were like four doors down from each other."

Later in that World Series, which the Yankees won, Hampton joked to Neagle that they should sign a package deal as free agents. Sure enough, both signed with the same team and the most unlikely of teams. Neagle signed a five-year, $51 million contract with Colorado, and Hampton signed for eight years and $121 million. Both would pitch in the pinball machine that was Coors Field pre-humidor. Hampton's contract was historic in team history. But the dude was good before signing. In the three seasons from 1998 to 2000, Hampton was 48–21 with a 3.12 ERA.

And in his first couple months with the Rockies, he was that pitcher, toting a 2.98 ERA after a June 10 win. Colorado's Hampton even made the 2001 All-Star team. Many people forget that. But from the June 16 start until the end of the year, his ERA was 7.37. He began to change his mechanics to induce more sink on his two-seamer. "Jerry wanted to sign a guy, and Hampton, his age, ground-ball rates [checked boxes]. The only checklist he didn't check off was walks per nine. They were too high," O'Dowd said, "which you know for me, I would have learned more about as my years went on there because in Cleveland we weren't exactly scared of walks per nine if we had a guy who had heavy ground-ball rates and a good strikeout per nine ratio. We had a good bullpen and a dynamic offense. It turns out years later I really understood walks in that ballpark are like death...

"And then he woke up and lost the sinker. He lost the sinker and went into a complete freak-out mode. He lost his confidence, didn't know how to compete. Overnight he said, 'I lost my sinker, so I am gonna become a four-seamer.' And then for me it was a spiraling downhill because we wrote a check that we couldn't afford to write. And then it was all I could do creativity-wise to dig ourselves out of that mess—and unfortunately it cost me credibility within the market that I never recovered from. And it cost me the most favorite player I could say I may have ever had with the Rockies in Juan Pierre because the only way I could move the contract was to attach an asset to the contract. It wasn't even that Juan was this superstar player. He just was everything you wanted from a player."

Indeed O'Dowd traded Pierre, who Helton said was one of the best teammates he ever had in Colorado. The trade was Hampton and Pierre in November of 2002 for Preston Wilson, Charles Johnson, Pablo Ozuna, and Vic Darensbourg. The following year, Pierre would hit .305, steal 65 bases, and win the 2003 World Series with the Florida Marlins.

Of course, O'Dowd and the Rockies put it all together in 2007 with all those big names and big bats that stuffed the box scores. But it was a series of smaller moves regarding pitchers that helped the Rockies get to the World Series. O'Dowd masterfully moved pieces that season, creatively bolstering the bullpen and handing out starts to guys who couldn't yet rent a car.

He called up 23-year-old Ubaldo Jimenez (15 starts, 4.28 ERA) and 21-year-old Franklin Morales (eight starts, 3.43 ERA). "It wasn't that we felt that they were ready," O'Dowd admitted, pointing out that Rodrigo Lopez (14 starts, 4.42 ERA) got hurt. "We knew that their stuff would play, but it was the consistency and being able to literally throw strikes. But when we started losing guys, we just had to [bring them up]. We had no other option. I mean, our system wasn't developed to that point because we had some drafts with Matt Harrington [seventh overall pick who didn't sign] and some other things that we didn't do a good job with, and so we didn't have that depth of pitching prospects, which we eventually accumulated later in my tenure there. So it was a choice that I decisively made. It probably hurt Frankie in some ways long term. But overall at the end of the day, he was going to end up in the bullpen as it turns out anyway. But they did a great job for us—without a doubt. We forgot Taylor Buchholz [2.70 ERA in 33 relief appearances] in that bullpen too…Because of the depth of our bullpen, we really did what Terry Francona was able to do in the 2016 World Series with Cleveland, we really did in 2007, but the whole month of September and the whole month of October, it was just not talked about a lot. But we really truly were the originator of that [type of] bullpen. We used the bullpen, our greatest weapon. And Clint did a masterful job. I remember one game we started Denny Bautista. Remember him?"

On September 12, 2007, the plan was to start Bautista, who had a 19.06 ERA in seven relief appearances (yes, you read that stat correctly), but the plan was that he would be on a 40-pitch leash. "Clint and I had this hilarious conversation," O'Dowd recalled, "which was: 'I don't think we will get much, but whatever we get, be thankful! And then get him out.' And he did exactly that. And every strike he threw was like, 'Okay, he got a strike!'"

Bautista was a cousin of Pedro Martinez, but the similarities stopped there. In 131 career games, he finished with a -1 WAR (wins above replacement). But on this September day, he pitched two scoreless innings—yep, the starter went just two innings—and the Rockies went on to win. That game was particularly bizarre. In the top of the first at Philadelphia, Holliday lined into a triple play. And in the bottom of the first, Bautista loaded the bases with no outs...and got out of it without allowing a run.

The bullpen stacking worked. "The beauty of that was," O'Dowd said, "I sensed that the position players felt like, 'Hey, guys, if we [get] a lead by the fifth or sixth inning—because the way this bullpen is going—we can win this game.' So that team was really confident in our bullpen, and you know what is funny? You can really never duplicate that kind of pen again because Jeremy Affeldt—we were on awhile—and he was a failed starter. Our group felt that moving him to the bullpen would just [do wonders]. Eliminating his number of pitches and simplifying everything that he did because the one thing that we knew about him was his durability. The guy could throw every day. And he competed. He found his future in Colorado. He made his living after Colorado because he found a home in the bullpen and then went on to have an incredible career with the Giants. But each guy was a unique guy. Matt Herges was a starter but kind of failed as a starter and bounced around and then he figured out his weapon of that circle change. And that circle change was a hard circle change, that he would change speeds with, that he would put action on, that it was almost unhittable."

Indeed the 2007 Rockies bullpen had a miniscule 1.30 WHIP (walks and hits per innings pitched), which ranked third best in the National League. And only five NL teams had a better bullpen ERA than Colorado's 3.85. For some perspective, the following year's pen was ninth with 4.13 and in 2009, a playoff season, it was 13th at 4.53. Even in the wild-card year of 2017, the bullpen's ERA was 4.40 ninth in the NL.

But much of the 2007 bullpen's success was thanks to the catcher, the oft-heralded Yorvit Torrealba. O'Dowd had coveted him for years but hoped during 2005 that Torrealba would actually play poorly. "When you got a good feeling on a guy, you hope he doesn't perform well because not only are you going to get him, but then you get him for a lower cost acquisition because he hasn't performed well," said O'Dowd, who traded Marcos Carvajal for him in December of 2005. "That was one of the better acquisitions that our group had. We were on him for a long time and we did a good job of scouting him and getting to know him, hoping he didn't play well in Seattle, which he didn't.

"I thought the one guy that got overlooked more than anything in that run was Torrealba because he was the edge man. I don't think back then I really understood or appreciated the value of his skillset during that stage of my career. I realized it later in my career, but looking back at it, he was phenomenal behind the plate. His game calling, his receiving, his emotional connection to the pitcher. He got big hit after big hit. He is the one guy who got in a fight that year. If you remember in Pittsburgh, he is just that kind of guy. He had an emotional energy that transcended the whole ballclub. In some ways he was our heartbeat from behind the plate because he brought it every game—every game. But it was a really good group of guys. I mean, the pitching staff wasn't dominant. Clint and Bob Apodaca did a really great job. And they pieced it together. But I'll tell you, our bullpen was good."

• • •

I wish that my sons, as they got older and grew into young men, would've had the chance to interact with Keli McGregor. Everyone McGregor touched was better for it. Of course, Clint Hurdle spoke glowingly about how McGregor taught him to be a better man. And so did Dan O'Dowd. "He helped shape my life," he said. "And I was older than Keli. So, that is how powerful he was. Keli didn't walk on water, etc. But he was damn close to it for me.

"He was just totally authentic. He didn't have a phony bone in his body. He never had an agenda, he always looked out for what was best for people. And he always found out what was best for people. And he saw that within me when others didn't."

It was McGregor in September of 2007, who told O'Dowd to "buckle up" because he saw the Rockies' magical ride coming. And he had great instincts prior to the 2002 season. "Both Keli and I had a strong feeling that Clint was the perfect person for our job [to replace manager Buddy Bell]," O'Dowd said. "Unbelievably intelligent, high level of energy, we just knew we were going to go through some tough times. As Keli said, 'We are going to row the boat back to shore' because we got over our skis so bad that we were drowning. I mean, we were drowning. We were in trouble as a franchise, and Clint would be the right person to get us through that. So I was totally at peace with that decision, and Clint was really ostracized on that staff. I mean it was Buddy and the staff—and then Clint was over here. He wasn't even a part of the staff. So I couldn't promote any of those other guys because

Everyone who had the chance to interact with Rockies president Keli McGregor was better for it. He was a great man.

they were so connected to Buddy. In every way shape or form, we just felt like Clint was the right guy."

Monfort, McGregor, O'Dowd, and Hurdle. Rocktober wouldn't have happened without that quartet. "For me Keli was just an authentic human being," O'Dowd said, "taught me how to be a Christian man. Where I thought I was one, I wasn't. He showed me that road map…He helped me grow up."

While chatting with me, O'Dowd was sitting next to his son, Chris O'Dowd, who was a high schooler during 2007. "I have never seen you respect someone so much," Chris said.

When McGregor died unexpectedly in April of 2010, Chris was playing college baseball for Dartmouth. Dan had gone up there to watch some games and was flying back to Denver. When the plane landed, Dan turned on his phone, "and I started crying on the plane," Dan said. "And the flight attendant came over to me and asked if everything was alright. And I said, 'I just lost someone really close to me.' I called my wife [Jackie], and she was crying, I mean, really crying. [I] got in the car, drove home, picked her up, went and picked Lexie up at school. And we drove to the McGregor home. [Lori] was upstairs, and I walked through the door, and it was like—well, it was awful—I can't even talk about it."

• • •

Jeff Bridich grew up in Milwaukee. A baseball and football standout in high school, he played catcher in college at Harvard. He loved the game—and wanted to live the game. "I was taking a lot of grief from friends that were all going into banking and consulting and had their eyes on six-figure salaries," said Bridich, the studious son of a high school coach, Rick, a fellow Harvard grad. "And I just wasn't built that way. I wasn't wired that way. I had no interest in something like investment banking. Could I have done it? Sure. But I had no interest in it, which I think helped ultimately because it wasn't like I had one eye over here and the other eye over there. I was just committed to doing something and seeing if I liked it. It's pretty obvious that I've lived a baseball life and that I love the game. Let's see if this path might fit for me. I remember my late grandfather said to me while I was in college, 'You're going to have a great education. Just make sure you research everything that might be available to you with that education.' So I think that was part of the thing for me—let's see what this whole professional baseball thing is about."

His journey took him to the Major League Baseball offices in New York and then in 2004 to the Colorado Rockies, where the thinker would tinker with new ways to approach scouting and player development. Not unlike the prospects he oversaw, Bridich himself was a Rockies prospect. He rose through the ranks, eventually becoming the Rockies' farm director, the job that oversees the development of all the minor league players. And in October of 2014, when Dan O'Dowd left the Rockies, Bridich became the general manager. He was 37. Three Octobers later, the Rockies were in the playoffs.

• • •

At his spring training locker in 2015, the Rockies' prized possession showed off his prized possession. "I kind of have that cowboy look," said Jon Gray, 23 at the time, holding up his pair of brandy-colored Justin full quill ostrich boots, which sell online for $539. "This is the kind of toe you want. You want a walking heel. And I prefer ostrich because they're so comfortable. It'll be a little bit expensive, but it'll last you forever."

These were the Jon Gray of boots—an investment in country strong durability. The only difference, I suppose, were these boots were made for walkin', while Gray was made for strikeouts. The Oklahoma kid knew he was the future of the franchise—and potentially the new look of a franchise finally relying on its pitching instead of just surviving with its pitching. "They know I can pitch, or I wouldn't be here," Gray said that day, four months before what would be his big league debut. "But I want to show them that I'm more mature and responsible now, so I want to show them that I can come to another level."

As senior director of player development starting in December of 2011, Jeff Bridich prided himself on growing the arms on the farm. Naturally, this carried into his new role as general manager in the fall of '14. With first-round picks Colorado had nabbed pitchers Gray (2013), Kyle Freeland (2014), Mike Nikorak (2015), Riley Pint (2016), Robert Tyler (also 2016), and Ryan Rolison (2018).

The goal was to create a culture of confident pitchers, many of them power pitchers, and have them ready to erase fears and embrace Coors Field. "Even though we've got lots of people who are a part of our decision-making process—it's expertise on top of expertise on top of expertise—those decisions ultimately still are under the GM's guise," Bridich said. "These are all decision-making avenues—scouting, development, analytics, information management, research, and in these jobs we're all paid for how our brains work and how well they work together. We're not paid for what we did 10 years ago or what's on the back of a baseball card. We're paid for how well we work through these problems and these processes together to come to good decisions year after year...Some of the success has to do with [me] being involved in the organization for 11 years prior to having this job. I think some of the familiarity with the organization for a decade really helped. If I had gone to a different organization in this role, first time through, it might have been a little bit different in terms of feeling that need to micromanage or control every little thing. I feel very fortunate and lucky to have had a lot of that understanding of people, of process, of the why prior to having the job."

In 2017, the year it came together for the Rockies, the rotation featured the likes of Gray (age 25), Freeland (24), Tyler Anderson (27), and Antonio Senzatela (22), all of whom were originally drafted or signed by the Rockies. Tyler Chatwood (27) had been in the Rockies system since 2011, and German Márquez (22) was acquired by Bridich himself in one of his most intriguing deals.

In the January before the 2016 season, Colorado knew Corey Dickerson could rake but couldn't remain healthy. Bridich had nabbed Gerardo Parra from the free-agent market and also had Carlos Gonzalez and Charlie Blackmon in the outfield (in addition to rising prospects such as David Dahl). So Bridich dealt Dickerson and minor leaguer Kevin Padlo to the Tampa Bay Rays. In return Bridich got two key contributors to winning Rockies baseball. There was relief pitcher Jake McGee, who saved 15 games in 2016 and had a sturdy 3.61 ERA out of the pen in the playoff season of 2017. And the minor leaguer Marquez, who has possible No. 1 stuff. The Rockies had been enamored by Marquez since they first saw him as a 16-year-old. They were unable to sign both Marquez and Antonio Senzatela that year, but their fondness for the Venezuelan righty never wavered. In 2017 Marquez finished fifth in the Rookie of the Year voting and he is growing into a front-of-the-rotation starter in 2018. "At the end of the trade," Bridich said, "that was a pretty lengthy process. We kind of kept talking a little bit and talked about how it was interesting that we were both reviewing our own internal processes and that we don't do that more often.

"There's almost a sense of fear in trading a prospect for a prospect. You don't see those kind of deals a lot. I can't tell you exactly why, but at the time, it made a lot of sense for us. We were in need of more pitching prospects, and Tampa was ripe with those kinds of guys and they were looking to add offense. You look at it, and Tampa is one of these organizations that's known for developing pitching talent. Here with the Rockies, we tend to pick out offensive talent and develop strong hitters. So why not utilize each other for our respective strengths to find some common ground? If we had just kind of been categorically opposed to that, then we would have missed out on some quality guys we're really excited about. You have to be open-minded. You have your ideals and your core beliefs, but if you're so stuck on those things all the time, that's not how this human business works. You have to be malleable...If you're somebody who takes this job, or any job like it in any company, if you're not prepared to make tough choices and have to be okay with those tough choices, then don't take the job. Some tough choices are really going to work out well, and some of them won't. Or some of them are going to be clear and easy, and some of them are going to be a bit messy. I think that there was that element, particularly with the Tulo situation."

Yes, it was Bridich who traded Troy Tulowitzki. The Toronto Blue Jays first contacted Bridich about a trade at the 2014 Winter Meetings. But it wasn't until July of 2015—another long summer filled with Groundhog Days of big offense but offensive pitching—that Bridich decided to rid the club of Tulo's massive contract and get some young arms in return.

It was poignantly fitting. The Rockies lost Tulo's final game on a walk-off homer after the bullpen blew multiple leads. Colorado was at Wrigley Field that night, and it was Chicago Cubs rookie Kris Bryant who homered into the bleachers. Bryant had been the second overall pick in the draft two years prior. Colorado used the third pick on Gray.

In the Wrigley Field visiting clubhouse, the beige door remained shut, as the fate of the Rockies unfolded behind it. Still in uniform, Tulowitzki had entered the manager's office after the game. He remained in there as he became a Blue Jay. Manager Walt Weiss was in tears while delivering the news. Tulo got Dick Monfort on the phone. In the deal with Toronto, Bridich had nabbed two of their better pitching arms, including Jeff Hoffman, the power righty who was the ninth overall pick in 2014. They also had to take Jose Reyes and his contract. Reyes was a Rockie briefly, but he was released the next spring after his arrest for domestic abuse.

In 2015, as well as the following season, the talented Tulowitzki helped lead the Jays to the American League Championship Series. But from that point on, the big money shortstop battled numerous injuries. Hoffman made some good starts in the 2017 season for the big club but also some tough ones. But the deal was done, and the Bridich era was going in full. "There were people who didn't really understand why we were doing it or what the goal was," Bridich said. "Or they said, 'Oh it's just the Rockies being the Rockies,' and that's just what comes with the territory. In terms of trying to divorce yourself from [the emotional] side of a trade, I would say that you shouldn't divorce yourself from that. I think you can try to distance yourself, but you want to know the good and the bad, the messy about all of these guys. If you try to divorce yourself from that, you're probably making a less informed or a shallow type of decision. If you are doing that, if you're okay with that—making emotional, quick twitch moves, lacking of thoughts and conversations— you're probably not going to be long for the job. So we try not to divorce ourselves from it.

"I think I'm personally blessed with a capacity to not really care what is said about me all that much. I don't really buy into the whole media evaluation. The reality is—and this is going to sound petty and bad—if you just objectively look at the people who are evaluating us every day, you know they've never come close to doing this job and all the work that goes into it. And most of them, probably 99 percent of them, they've never even led anything in their lives. They've worked for themselves. They've been self-interested beat writers who have worked for themselves and they have a job to do every day. I had the good fortune of seeing that for a long time before taking this job. So I knew not to put a whole lot of time and energy into what they think about me. It'd be like if I went to a hospital every day and wrote a blog about the job done by one of the surgeons and the things he screwed up. That's crazy. I know nothing about brain surgery, nor have I ever even worked on the path to become a brain surgeon. That's what goes on in this industry and other sports industries."

Back at Coors Field from the road trip, everything was happening at once. Tulo was gone. Reyes was at shortstop. And Gray had been called up. He'd make his major league debut the next day. "It's ironic that the face of the franchise has moved on, and we have one of our young kids we've been anticipating making his debut right afterward," Weiss said before the game. "I guess there's some irony there…Our team is ever evolving over the course of a season, and this is just part of it."

Over breakfast at a downtown L.A. hotel, the day of a 2018 game against the Dodgers, Bridich shared with me one of the cooler insights I've heard about the general manager job. "There has to be," he said, "a certain amount of fearlessness."

Fearlessness. It was such a fascinating way to describe his mind-set. And then he began to explain a moment when he showed it most—the controversial signing of Ian Desmond. "This was discussed when we took these jobs, that we were going to have an open and honest process internally, and there had to be an element of fearlessness," he said. "If we were committed to a set of core beliefs—athleticism being one and pitching being another—and you're scared to take chances and make some decisions, you're not going to get much done."

Bridich needed a first baseman…so he signed a former shortstop and outfielder to play it. Desmond had been a two-time All-Star most recently in the 2016 season with the Texas Rangers. He was revered for his leadership, toughness, and team-first attitude, which he displayed by changing positions with Texas. So in December of 2016, Bridich signed Desmond, 31, to a five-year, $70-million deal. The deal was discussed on Twitter and talk radio shows for months.

Desmond battled injuries for the first time in his career that 2017 season and hit .274 with 15 steals in 95 games. And in the ninth inning of the wild-card game—one of the higher-leverage situations of his career—Desmond singled and scored on a Carlos Gonzalez hit. That made the game 11–8, bringing up Nolan Arenado (with Trevor Story on-deck). Alas, Arenado grounded out, and Arizona won.

Desmond was more impactful the next year, though he battled consistency in 2018. Though his batting average was low, he had produced a number of huge, game-changing hits that season. "There's a small portion of validation," Bridich said. "But I'd say a bigger portion is that there's some pleasure and relief in that a guy is doing what we believed that he could do. Watching a guy like Ian Desmond

July 11, 2018:
Arizona Diamondbacks at Colorado Rockies

The best way to break a nine-game home losing streak to the Arizona Diamondbacks? Throw out a 19 spot! The Rockies score a season-high 19 runs on 19 hits. Paul Goldschmidt hit a first-inning homer off German Marquez, and I'm thinking, *Here we go again.* But Colorado scores five in the first off of Shelby Miller, including Ian Desmond hitting a 472-foot, three-run homer—the longest at Coors Field this year. The Rockies add four in the second and three in the third. In the fourth they score six, as Carlos Gonzalez hits a three-run shot for his second homer of the night. With two outs in the fourth, Arizona turns to Daniel Descalso to pitch. It's the earliest a position player has entered a game on the mound since Sal Bando in 1979. He would go two-and-a-third innings, and Alex Avila pitched the final two. CarGo drove in six, and Desmond drove in five. For the first time in club history, three players scored at least four times—CarGo, Charlie Blackmon, and DJ LeMahieu. It's, however, not a club record for runs. That number is 20. They needed a laugher and got one and then some. It's a fun broadcast when you're on the right side of it.

become more comfortable at first base and his ability to hit the ball and drive in runs, that is a window into the thought process. When you make a decision and you make a commitment and a guy pays off, that gives you a window into some of the thought process that went on in wanting to go with him versus other guys who were out there… Is it nice to see it at some level that a guy still has it in him and you believed in him? Yeah."

On the other side of the infield, Bridich replaced Tulowitzki with Story, who has blossomed into an All-Star shortstop in his own right. Colorado drafted him in 2011 out of high school, and he thrived in Bridich's farm system, slugging .514 in 2015, the year Tulo was traded. Manager Walt Weiss strategically batted Story second on the big club to make sure the kid was protected in the lineup, and Story became a national story with his dingers and his dynamic play at shortstop. "It helped having been the farm director and having an understanding of the players that were coming up in our system, having an understanding of the trials and the tribulations and all of the progress that had been made," Bridich said. "If I had gone elsewhere and had zero knowledge, it would have been very different. It helped just having that feeling of knowing that Trevor Story had a chance. We didn't know how it was going to go once he hit the major league level, but he had a chance to become a bona-fide everyday MLB shortstop. We knew that because of the years working with him from the time he was drafted and on up, knowing we were willing to take that chance and knowing the kid and his work ethic and the issues he had. It helped us to be willing to say, 'Okay, we're going to take a shot here.'

"We didn't know it was going to work out [so fluidly from Troy to Trevor], but being comfortable making an educated guess or an educated assessment of how that person might play out helped us make that move... You have to have checks and balances as part of your process. For instance, all of our professional scouting we have going on, we make sure that we get multiple looks on our own system from our own internal scouts. We've done a nice job there where they can pretty much say what they see, and their feet are not held to any kind of fire. The research and development process that we're continuing to grow, looking at our guys from a pure statistical/analytical standpoint, that's part of that, too. Probably, the most important part of that is paying attention to the small details about these guys and their careers. I think you have to challenge yourselves to understand that these guys are human beings. They are not robots and they're not baseball players that just roll off assembly lines and get thrown on the field for the game. They're human beings and they're going to have human foibles and human issues just like the rest of us normal people. You have to honor that. You have to be okay with imperfect players being part of the future, just like you have to be okay with imperfect things that happen to these individual players in your decision making."

Perhaps the decision that'll be most connected to Bridich is his hiring of Bud Black. And the relationship between the general manager and the field manager? "It's critical," Bridich shared, as he began to offer a glimpse into the emotions of the Rockies' front-office dynamic. "We choose to be a hands-on front office. It's not hands-on to the point of some of the other stories you've heard around the league. But we are hands-on, and there's a lot of different facets to that. One is that we choose to be inclusionary in terms of the decision-making that needs to go on...Whether that's free agents or trades or putting guys on the roster to protect them from the Rule 5, Buddy and some of our major league coaches are most often involved to some degree in those sorts of decisions, and that's by design. We choose to do that in order to help us make the best decisions possible.

"Another facet is that there has to be a mutual respect for the job. That would be my job, that would be Dick's job, that would be Buddy's job, and what each of them takes. So if there's mutual respect for the challenges of each of those jobs and the difficulties that lie in those jobs and the scrutiny and the effects of that, then I think there's a real chance to have good working relationships. There has to be the ability for human beings in these jobs to look at each other and have difficult and uncomfortable conversations. Sometimes, those conversations go really well and are well-timed and lack high emotion. Sometimes it's the opposite because we're all competitive and emotional. But the absence of those types of conversations just kind of leads you down a path of ignoring problems or creating other problems on top of that."

CHAPTER 9

DICK MONFORT

Born on third base, some of these sports owners try to force phony personas, the way a batter tries to force the issue with his lead-off hit to the gap…and finds himself thrown out at third. You've seen these guys, who wear a designer suit to an event but place a ballcap on their heads. Their idea of mingling with fans is waving from afar—behind the safety of a partition or security guard.

And so, one of the cooler things about the Rockies is that owner Dick Monfort sits with the fans on almost a nightly basis. Yep, he's just down there in his regular seats behind the Rockies dugout. Monfort is just like you; he's got the same emotional investment in the Rockies. He just has a little more financial investment in them.

He takes great pride in interacting with the Rockies fanbase. "Lately, especially this year, I think that I get a lot more compliments this year and last year than I've gotten in the past," he said in 2018. "We have great, passionate fans, and I want to be a genuine person. I want them to know I'm a fan just like them. I get upset just like them. I think I've created a lot of friends; I go up and down the concourse a lot partly because I'm old and have to use the restroom, but partly because I'm nervous and I talk to a lot of people, and that's fun. That makes me feel good. It makes me feel good that people will reach out to me and say, 'Hey!' Or 'I like this; I don't like that.' I want to be accessible. I want to be just like them. I want them to know that I'm not that much different than they are. I'm cheering on our team just like they are."

That's because, really, Monfort was just a fan in the state of Colorado, when his life changed forever. "Way back when Denver got the franchise, three guys from Ohio were going to be the general partners," said Monfort, who turned 64 in 2018. "Jerry McMorris was in charge of raising what I think was 70 million of limited partner shares. Jerry knew my dad well and he asked my dad if he'd be interested, and he wasn't. So, Jerry said, 'Do you mind if I ask your sons?' And my dad said,

'That's fine. I don't think you need to waste a lot of time with Dick, but Charlie might have an interest.'"

How Dick Monfort got into the Rockies mix is an amazing twist in sports history. "So, Charlie got involved. And of course, then the Ohio guys sort of got in trouble," Dick said. "And then in '95, Jerry reached out to my dad, and his trucking company was having some troubles. He needed a loan, and so my dad called me and said, 'Would you meet with Jerry and go over this?' So that's how I got involved. We lent him some money. His stock was his security, and so I got involved and I retired— or left Conagra in '95—and so it was about '96 when I got involved with the Rockies...After Hampton and Neagle and the fact that we've gotten ourselves in a financial mess was where I figured out I couldn't be passive anymore. Somebody was gonna have to get involved and get this thing cleaned up...

"And there were a lot of issues especially with the baseball and the business side. I mean, everybody's pointing figures at everybody. It just wasn't a good situation. So, I think the other thing was that Keli [McGregor] and Dan [O'Dowd] came to me and said, 'Hey, our culture sucks. We need to tie things back together. We need to get on the same page.' I think that I had a financial background and led a family business that was pretty well-knit was another reason why I got more involved."

When McGregor passed away in 2010, Dick said he had three choices. He could promote someone from within to run the Rockies, which was daunting, or hire someone from the outside. "But Keli had built such a great culture that I just didn't think there was anybody on the outside that wouldn't screw it up," Dick said. So the third option was to mesh his ownership role with a team president role. "I started getting involved," he said, "and I had no freakin' idea how much I had to do."

But Dick grew into the role and made the prominent hire of Jeff Bridich to run baseball operations after the 2014 season. Dick is fiercely loyal to his employees and purple-clad fans. He gushes over how many employees—recognized in Year No. 25 of the franchise—have been with the Rockies since the beginning. As far as a percentage of revenue, he said the Rockies payroll would probably be in the top five almost every year. They're not afraid to spend, even on relief pitching, as seen in the winter after 2017. He takes pride in the fact that the franchise has grown families of fans, and his own family of fans will run the Rockies for decades to come. In a private chat with me, he opened up about his goal to mirror the best days of the O'Malley family, which grew baseball in a new region of the country in their own right, when they moved the Dodgers to Los Angeles in 1958.

In reference to his sons, Walker and Sterling, Dick Monfort said: "The fact that they love baseball is great, and we did this 30-year lease on the stadium, and it's because I plan on my family running this for many years—and making it better. It's the anxiety every day to win the game. Even when you don't have a good record, you still want to win the game. And so that's a little troublesome, but there's a lot of fun for Walker and Sterling. There will be a lot of fun in this thing, and they're going to be a lot more prepared than I was to do a good job…

"I truly believe—and I hope it happens when I'm around—the Rockies will become a Cubs, a Red Sox, a Dodgers, a Yankees. I mean, they are gonna be. This community already loves the team, but it's going to grow more and more and it's going to be the 'in' thing to be a Rockies fan and to go to Coors Field. We'll keep spending money on it and making it the best place to go. So, I truly believe this is something that we'll all be proud of for a long time."

Dick likes to joke that the Rockies spring training facility went from "the outhouse to the penthouse." They now have the benchmark for spring facilities, as well as a first-class Dominican Academy, and Coors Field, of course, is considered a gem of the National League. "If you're building a new park, you're coming to Coors Field to see how we do it," Dick said. "I bet [Atlanta Braves chairman] Terry McGuirk called me

Rockies owner Dick Monfort (with the glasses) confers with former general manager Dan O'Dowd in 2010, but he also spends a lot of time mingling with fans.

100 times to ask me different questions for their new stadium. We're in a good place, and I'm proud of where we're heading.

The Rockies are breaking ground in the fall of 2018 on a multi-purpose series of buildings just to the west of the park. "The new standards you go around—Atlanta, St. Louis, Texas, Chicago—the new model is building around the park," Monfort said, as he began to share details of his plans, which he hopes to have completed by January or February of 2021. "Enhance the experience of the game. It's another way to create more revenue. In our case that revenue goes to the stadium district. I've been to St. Louis, I've been to Atlanta, I've been to Chicago, I've toured what they've done. What we wanted to do was create an area next to the ballpark, which before the games was more family-oriented. Like I told somebody, the restaurants will be where you take a date, not where you find a date. We're going to have some condos. We're going to have an office building. We're going to have a hotel. And inside the hotel, we're going to have a Hall of Fame and we're going to try to create a Hall of Fame that is unlike any Hall of Fame anywhere. We're going to have more video, more virtual reality, more games, more fun stuff for kids…We can do smaller concerts, we can do pregame stuff. We can do stuff in the offseason. The plaza is actually going to have an area where people can actually sit and watch the concerts, or watch a volleyball game being played in the plaza, or watch their kids on an ice skating rink we may have there in the winter."

For those of us who've been in this town for a while, it's amazing to see the renaissance that Coors Field inspired in lower downtown. I often remark to my colleagues from out of town how special Lodo is, and they will concur, adding that Denver is among their favorite stops in baseball. I love our city. And much of its vibrancy is tied to what the Rockies have created as the centerpiece of Lodo.

CHAPTER 10

THE GOLDEN THONG AND OTHER STORIES

Perfectly, the news was listed in *The Denver Post* under: ROCKIES BRIEFS. "Jason Giambi didn't just pack his bat for his arrival in Denver," read the newspaper note from September 2, 2009. "He also brought along his famous golden thong."

This magical undergarment first came into the slugger's life with the Oakland A's. He'd once explained that he never got tan lines because he'd wear a thong when he sat out in the sun. So the sports apparel company Toolshed gave him a complimentary golden thong, which represented powers unbeknownst to even the makers. On the New York Yankees, Derek Jeter, Johnny Damon, and Bernie Williams borrowed it. "It's never not gotten a hit," Giambi said. "'But it is an act of desperation, a last resort.'"

With the Rockies, Giambi would sometimes place the thong in a guy's locker, granting him slump-busting powers for the day. Other times, if a guy had the gall, he'd ask the grown man to borrow his thong. The graying slugger was 38 when he first put on the purple pinstripes. And his infusion into the 2009 team was immediate and impactful. In 31 plate appearances for the playoff-bound squad, he had a .452 on-base percentage with two home runs. "When we got Giambi," Ryan Spilborghs said, "our group of guys thought we were getting Giambi from the early 2000s, the New York-media Giambi. But then you get Big G and realize he wears the same pair of jeans and the same shirt and backpack and he shows up like an hour before the game, and he's the nicest guy you ever met. And he had these strange things that he did. He had these big weighted softballs and he was always doing this thing with his fingers. And he used this tired old blue elbow guard. And he had the golden thong. When we heard we got him, Tulo and I had a locker right beside each other, and we moved over to create a space for Giambi. We were so fired up to get Giambi. And we had this idea of the Giambi we were going to get, and it was the opposite. But he brought real good baseball IQ to a level that we had never experienced before, talking about pitch sequences and picking up small aspects of a pitcher, whether he's giving away a pitch…He loved the game so much. He was a really good student of the game, and watching him take a pinch-hit at-bat was a treat."

His first Rockies homer was huge. Sure, yes, he'd hit over 400 in his career when he came into our world, but in September of 2009, the Rockies were in a playoff hunt. It was top of the ninth at Arizona, and Colorado had a 7–4 lead over the Diamondbacks. Well, pinch-hitter Giambi hit a three-run homer, giving Colorado a cushion comfortable for even someone wearing a thong.

He played parts of four seasons for the Rockies. His on-base percentage was .375, and he hit 22 homers in 420 at-bats. Every time he'd come up late in a ballgame, I would say: "*Here* comes the big man." You know, it just felt right. That's what a pinch hitter should look like— big arms, strong dude strutting up there, maybe a couple tats on his arm. He's the type of guy where it looks like he's trying to do one thing—hit a ball 500 feet. I loved when he came up. And he was a special favorite of Dick Monfort's. He had that presence in the clubhouse. And it was just cool, a former MVP in our presence. "Frankly, he was like a player/ manager," trainer Scott Gehret said. "Guys were just around him all of the time. He's a baseball nut. He loves to talk about baseball, he loves the history of baseball, he'll talk hitting until forever. And that's what I think drew guys like Tulo, Seth Smith, and Ian Stewart toward him. He'll talk hitting all day. He'll talk about A-Rod's hitting, our hitting, the other team's hitting. He had more knowledge than anybody I've ever been around."

Toward the end of spring training in 2012, a young minor leaguer in big league camp was struggling. Giambi had come to the batting cages to hit, but instead "just came in my cage and fed me off the tee and was telling me little things to work on," Nolan Arenado shared. "Then he went back outside and didn't even hit. He just helped me out and went back in. It was really cool. It was one of the greatest things ever, something I'll remember the rest of my life."

We had one player, who was like-minded with Giambi in one way. After 11 seasons with the Minnesota Twins, utility man Denny Hocking joined the 2004 Rockies. On a flight one night, Hocking decided to give one of our flight attendants a little break. I hear him come by our seats and quietly and politely ask: "Dessert?" I look up from my magazine, and there is Hocking holding a tray of an assortment of cookies...and wearing only a thong. I suppose it was the original Rockies thong. Fourteen years later, it's an image I'm still trying to erase from my mind.

• • •

In this baseball ecosystem, there is often an indoctrination of the new kids—from rookies to clubbies. In 2011 a 20-year-old from Colorado named Cody Wise got a cool gig as a field guard. He's one of those guys in helmets who sits in foul territory right by the stands. "You get to be on the field during the game, watch batting practice every day, have interaction with the players," Wise explained. "It was a pretty cool thing. And I grew up in Colorado, about one-and-a-half hours from Denver, watching Rockies baseball on TV, and now you're on the field, up close and personal. My first homestand, they were playing the Dodgers. The night before, I had worked the game and stayed late. I was one of the last people to leave. I shut everything down. The next day, I come in for my morning meeting before the day game, and my head supervisor says, 'Do you know where the batter's box key is?' And I'm like, 'What?' And he says: 'Yeah, it wasn't put back last night after you left, and you were the last one to leave, right? Did you put it back?'

"At this point, I'm new on the job. I don't want to screw up. So on the inside, I'm stressing and freaking out that I did something wrong. So he says: 'Maybe it's out in the bullpen. That's where you were, right? Ask the bullpen catcher. Maybe he picked it up.' So I'm walking into the outfield by myself, just thinking, *What did you do with this key?* I get out there and I ask the guy. He says: 'You know, I haven't seen it either. Ask the bullpen coach.' So I go and ask him, and he hasn't seen it. 'I don't know what to tell ya.'

"I go back to my supervisor. I tell him I have no idea where the batter's box key is, and they didn't know either. So my supervisor suggests I ask the equipment manager for the Rockies. I go into the clubhouse, and, sure enough, there's the equipment manager. He hadn't seen the key, and I get sent around to four to five people to the point where I'm in the Rockies' indoor batting cage. The player, Chris Nelson, was taking batting practice, and I'm with one of the clubhouse attendants, who says, 'Guys, by chance have you seen the batter's box key?' And Nelson is like: 'Nah, man. *You lost it?* How are we supposed to hit out there?'

"Now I'm just freaking out. So they said to go ask Jim Tracy—the manager. I come into the dugout, and he's finishing his pregame media availability. He's wrapping it up with reporters, and I walk up in my field guard-attire purple collared shirt, tucked in, khaki pants. And I just go: 'Jim, do you have any idea where the batter's box key is? They told me to ask you.' And he just gives me the biggest smile and says, 'Son, you just got fucking played.' Everyone lost it, and I caught on. It's an ongoing joke in Major League Baseball. The rule is if someone asks you for the batter's box key, you always deny and send them to somebody else. You know how it is as a kid on the job: for the first couple weeks, you just want to do everything right. I'll definitely hold onto that story forever."

• • •

The hardest working Rockie I've ever seen was Juan Pierre. At spring training in his early years, he would arrive to the ballpark before the sun came up. Before actual team workouts, Pierre had a private workout with first-base coach Dallas Williams. Often times, they worked solely on the art of bunting. Manager Buddy Bell was impressed but also worried about burnout. So when Bell scheduled a spring training day off for the team, Bell told Pierre: "If I hear you came to the complex, I will fine you!"

For his career Pierre hit .295 in 14 seasons, stealing 614 bases. In his two-plus seasons with Colorado from 2001 to 2003, Pierre hit .308 with exactly 100 stolen bases.

Once a Rockies hitting coach, Duane Espy worked with the San Diego Padres and Tony Gwynn in the early 2000s. Gwynn was diligent about his routine; he'd hit off the tee every home game with Espy. So it struck Espy one day when Gwynn asked to postpone his workout. "See that kid over there," Gwynn said. "He wants to pick my brain about hitting."

Espy told Gwynn that he'd be available whenever Gwynn wanted to hit that day. "That's okay," Gwynn said. "This kid is special. I have a good feeling about him."

Two hours later, Espy headed back to the field, and Gwynn was still talking with Juan Pierre.

• • •

Curtis Leskanic, the righty reliever, was wonderfully wacky. His cousin was Katrina from Katrina and the Waves, who sang "Walking On Sunshine." Originally drafted by the Cleveland Indians, Leskanic was an original Rockie. He pitched for the club from 1993 to 1999 and was teammates with Jerry Dipoto, a fellow reliever with a fascinating personality. Dipoto became a forward-thinking general manager with the Seattle Mariners. Prior to embarking on a front-office opportunity, he almost became one of my partners on Rockies telecasts. He would have excelled in that role just as he has used his intellect and innovative thinking for success as a GM.

They were both drafted by Cleveland in 1989 and were Colorado teammates from 1997 to 1999. In July of 2018, I visited Dipoto in Seattle. All I had to say was eight words: "Give me a couple of Curtis

Known for being delightfully eccentric, Rockies relief pitcher Curtis Leskanic throws during an extra-innings game in 1999.

Leskanic stories." And he took me on a wild journey into Leskanic's warped world.

"The first time I met Curtis," Dipoto said, "we were rookies with Cleveland in A ball. I walked into the Best Western Hotel, which is where we stayed in Tucson. The very first day of our first spring training, I walk into the hotel room. I don't know who it's going to be. I throw my bag on the bed and I looked, and someone else has already clearly been in the room. The bed's ruffled, there's a bag on the bed, there's a drawer left open. I go to take a leak. I walk into the bathroom. And as soon as I walk into the bathroom, I find Curtis in the midst of a full-blown bubble bath. He pops up buck naked and he's got a razor, shaving his body in this bubble bath. I remember thinking, *What the hell is this?* He extends a soapy paw and says, 'Hey, Curtis Leskanic, from Pittsburgh.' So I shake his hand and introduce myself, and he immediately throws his leg over the side of the tub and starts shaving again. I asked him what he was doing, and he said, 'I'm getting aerodynamic, bro, I'm getting aerodynamic.' That was before he was a genuine cuckoo. It was always how he was wired.

"Those years in Colorado, we pitched a lot. Curtis, when he could go into the games, he had a routine. He'd go over to the fountain and wet his head and he had that long hair. Then he'd start whipping his hair around like he was Bo Derek or something. Then he would go up and methodically get ready, throwing his iron ball before throwing his pitches. It seemingly took him forever to go in and get ready for a game. He would throw, six, eight games in a row. The appearances were just starting to pile up. We would have to sing a song to Curtis. I'll backtrack. For the years Curtis played with Walt Weiss, whenever he went into a game, he would run in and throw his eight warm-up pitches and then he would come back off the back end of the mound, and Walt would run in and put his glove over his mouth. They weren't conversing on anything going on in the game; Walt would sing him a song so that Curtis would get into his rhythm. You could see Curtis would start getting going, and then he'd get up on the mound and throw. He had to get his balance and his rhythm. After Walt went to the Braves, Curtis would come over to the cage before he went in, and we'd sing him the songs. He'd give us a genre of music. He'd say, 'Give me something peppy.' One day he was walking over, he'd kind of been run into the ground and he goes, 'How about a little Bruce Springsteen, "Dead Man Walking"? So we start singing the song, and the umpires are waiting for him to come into the game, and he's just hanging on the right-field fence, listening to us sing the song.

"We were playing the Seattle Mariners, and this is interleague in 1999. This was the high-powered Mariners team. Curtis comes in to pitch in one of those bizarre Coors Field games, where 20 runs are going on the board, and it's raining, then hailing, then it's sunny. [Colorado would end up winning 16–11]. The game starts and stops and has a long delay. The game was official, and it was a blowout. We were ahead. We come out of this long delay, and Curtis is pitching, and because we're well ahead, our skipper tells him to go ahead and hit. I'll never forget this. Rafael Carmona is pitching, and he throws Curtis a hanging slider. Curtis is not a prolific offense player by any stretch, but he just unloads on a ball and hits a 457-foot home run to left field. As soon as he hits it, it's like he's had this plan his entire life. He hits the home run, he immediately drops the bat and does the Shucky Ducky like Dante [Bichette]. Then he pops out and takes the big loop toward the dugout. As he gets over there, he starts tugging on the shirt like Ricky Henderson. Each step that he takes, he's doing something from a different famous player. He goes flap down, Jeffrey Leonard. Over a third he's stutter-stepping like Albert Belle. Then at home plate, he stops and does the Sammy Sosa kiss the sky. The whole time the Mariners guys are watching him like, *What the hell is this guy doing?* We're thinking, *Oh man, this next guy is definitely getting drilled.* It was the only home run of his career, I think, but it was magnificent. After that we called him 'Magnum' because of the length of the home run, he enjoyed that.

"There are so many Curtis stories. He'd come up with some of the quirkiest things. There was one day we went on a road trip, and we did not play well. It was kind of rough on the record, and we had been in it and now we weren't. We always knew we could come home and get healthy and we really needed one of those brighten-it-up, keep-things-light moments. Curtis was ordinarily the last guy into the clubhouse. If stretch was at 4:00, he'd show up at 3:57. Curtis is a big Pittsburgh

Steelers fan and always had a Steelers helmet in his locker. So we come in for this homestand after a really tough road trip, and he knows we need the pick-me-up. So he and Mark Wilbert, who was at that point our strength and conditioning coach, dragged one of the Woodway treadmills down from the training room into the main clubhouse. They moved all of the couches and made room for it in the middle. They get the treadmill up and running, and Curtis grabs his Steelers helmet and some running shoes and starts running. He's not wearing anything else. It's just the Steelers helmet and the running shoes. Immediately, you walk in and you just start howling. What is this guy doing? I'll give him credit: he had to be gassed because he kept running until every single guy came in that room and had a chance to see it and break down laughing. It got everybody loose, and we wound up having a great homestand and got back into the swing of things. He had a knack for cutting through the barriers. Everybody, whether you were Latin American, African American, domestic white guy, Curtis crossed over to everyone. He was as good a teammate and as fun to be around as anybody I've ever played with."

Recalled the longtime Rockies trainer Keith Dugger: "On day games, I would come very early…Well, I get into a day game one morning and I could hear the Swim-X going, which is our therapy pool. The lights are off, and I'm like, 'What in the heck is going on?' I go in there. It's about 7:30. Curtis Leskanic is naked on a boogie board, tied to a rope, boogie boarding in my Swim-X pool. He was a character."

• • •

The Godfather is two hours and 58 minutes. *The Godfather Part II* is three hours and 22 minutes. Combined, that makes for six hours and 20 minutes, which is just four minutes longer than the Rockies-Padres game on April 17, 2008.

And the game was scoreless until the 14th inning! Jeff Francis and Jake Peavy, the two aces, started the game. Colorado scored in the top of the 14th, San Diego countered in the bottom, and neither team scored again until the 22nd. That's when Troy Tulowitzki's double put the Rockies up 2–1. During his 15-game stint as a Rockie, Kip Wells' most memorable game was that night. He pitched a scoreless 19th, 20th, 21st, and 22nd to get the road win.

Some of the players, who had already played and were removed in the game "started doing rally shots," trainer Scott Gehret said, "and they did 10 innings worth of rally shots. We had some hammered guys by the time the game was over. I remember doing the high-five lines; it smelled like a brewing company. So that was funny."

Some crazy numbers from the box score: Willy Taveras went 3-for-10, the only player to tally 10 at-bats. The opposing leadoff hitter, Brian Giles, went 1-for-9 on the night. In the 22 innings, only three total errors were committed. Brad Hawpe did go 0-for-7, but his bases-loaded walk in the 14th drove in the game's first run.

After scoring two runs in 22 total innings, the Rockies traveled to Houston, landing during morning rush-hour traffic. I will never forget it. People are driving to work, and we haven't been to bed yet. It reminded me of landing the next morning in Philadelphia after Game 163 in 2007. I thought, *We are going to get smoked tonight.* In the first inning that night against the Houston Astros, the Rockies scored six runs (and won the game 11–5). We won the next night also. Go figure.

• • •

Catcher Michael McKenry, who'd appropriately wear a T-Shirt in the Colorado clubhouse with "The Great Hambino" from *The Sandlot*, had 862 plate appearances…and no triples. And then on June 6, 2015, McKenry scurried into third for his first MLB triple. "The umpire actually said something to me," the Rockies catcher recalled at the time of the first-inning triple. "I got on third, and he said, 'Ah, that's not going to count. It's going to rain in a minute.'"

In a weird way, that might have made for a better story—a man plays a full major league career, and the only triple he hits doesn't actually count…because the game was canceled.

Instead, it got even weirder. After the 862 plate appearances without a triple, McKenry hit three triples in his next 18 plate appearances. They avoided rain, so the June 6 triple ended up counting, and then McKenry hit two more in the next 17 trips to the plate.

Asked if he could somehow explain how triples machine Honus Wagner was suddenly reincarnated in the form of a 5'10", 205-pound catcher, Rockies manager Walt Weiss said: "I can't because his legs are really short, and it almost seems physically impossible for his legs to run 270 feet. But he does have sneaky speed. All kidding aside, he does run pretty well for a guy built like he is."

• • •

Dante Bichette hit 40 home runs in 1995, Colorado's first playoff year. And from 1993 to 1999, he averaged 29 homers and 118 RBIs annually for the Rockies with a .316 batting average. "He was one of the most unusual personalities in the history of the game…One day, he was committed to selling out for power, the next he was committed to flattening out and hitting to right-center," teammate Jerry Dipoto said. "It changed every day. My favorite Dante story was we're in spring training 1998, and Dante has been at the top of the offensive food chain in the National League for a number of years now. When he first came to the big leagues, he had a cannon of an arm. We're sitting in our lockers; his was next to mine. I loved to play long toss, did it every single day, and the pitchers would rotate doing it with me because none of them wanted to do it with me every day. Dante said to me, 'I gotta get my arm strength back. I don't want to take the criticism anymore. I want to shut them all up about that. I'm committed to getting my arm back. I'm going to long toss with you every day. We're going to go out there, we're going to do it, don't let me tell you no. If I tell you no, just grab me and drag me out there.'

"So we go out there the first day, it goes really well. It's great. Don Baylor is beside himself with glee over this. We finish up and go in, and I said we'll get after it tomorrow. He reminds me, 'Don't let me tell you no.' The next day I come back and I get ready, and he said 'No way, I'm not going.' We start arguing back and forth. He says he needs to recover. And I remind him of what he told me and grabbed him by the shirt and pulled him off the chair. He gets up and he looks at me stone-faced and says, 'Walk away or I will kill you.' That was the end of his efforts to regain his arm strength."

CHAPTER 11

INSIDE THE CLUBHOUSE

One day in the trainer's room, Scott Gehret took a jab at Todd Helton. So Helton literally took a jab at Gehret. "He didn't like what I said and hit me as hard as he could on my left shoulder," recalled Gehret, one of the Rockies' trainers. "It hurt, it hurt bad. But he went and got three hits and the next day he hit me again three times because he got three hits. Then he got four hits. He came in the next day and hit me four times. As much as I want him to get a hit, I didn't want him to get a hit the next day because—you can ask Doogie—my arm was black and blue! The next night he got only one hit, so he only hit me once."

It was painful but playful. Helton, like most players, looked at the trainers as part of the team, part of the fraternity. When Gehret was in his first year, the multi-millionaire Helton quietly gave him all of his per diem money on Rockies road trips. One time, Helton called Gehret's hotel room to confirm he was there. Next thing Gehret knew, two custom suit makers arrived at his room.

Helton's relationship with Gehret epitomized an aspect of baseball seldom seen—the constant interaction between players and the in-house staff. I've always felt that if you wanted the pulse of a team—not what the players tell the manager or the media—hang out in the trainer's room. That's their comfort zone, a clubhouse within the clubhouse. "You develop very, very close relationships with these guys—sometimes closer than family because we're with them eight months in a row, 12 hours a day," Gehret said. "We travel with them, we live with them, we love them, we hate them, we want to kill them, we want to hug them. It is a family, it's a traveling fraternity. They know that they can talk to us, and it's not going to go anywhere."

How often are you amateur psychologist? "Every day," Gehret asserted. "It's anything from not feeling good about their performance, to interpersonal relationships within the clubhouse, to worrying about their career, to worrying about, 'If I fail, what do I do about money?' To 'I'm having problems with my girlfriend; I don't know what to do.' You name it. They talked to us. If things get outside the realms of our scope, then we have professional people that could help, but as far as an amateur level, we deal with stuff everyday that's way outside the realm of baseball. One of the reasons is because you have great relationships with coaches, but your relationship with them is performance-based. Unless you really, really have a special relationship like Clint and Todd did, usually they're not going to go to a coach. They're going to talk to us."

Gehret is officially the assistant athletic trainer, while Keith Dugger—the aforementioned "Doogie"—is the head athletic trainer. Doogie has been in baseball for more than three decades and he's remembered by fans as the trainer helping up Matt Holliday, following Holliday's headfirst slide to win Game 163. Dugger is forever in the frame of one of the Rockies' greatest images. Both are tremendous at what they do and admired throughout the league for their well-deserved reputation. They are two of my favorite people to BS with during the season.

In the aforementioned image, Dugger looks enraged. "People ask, 'Why did you look so angry?'" Dugger said. "I wasn't angry. I was just trying to clear people away so I could hear him and understand what he was saying back to me. I think when Spilly and all those guys were trying to shake him a little bit, you could just see in his eyes that he wasn't ready for that. He didn't need that stimuli right there. The best thing for me when I cleared him was he said he had no head pain, no neck pain, no headache. 'Let's get you up and inside the clubhouse so we can clean you up and examine you a little bit.'

"I didn't get to celebrate right there, and everyone's going crazy. So I get in the training room, shut the door, and I scream at Dan O'Dowd and Keli McGregor. I'm a very even-keeled guy, but when I take control of things and people aren't listening to me, I don't give a shit who you are. I told everyone to get the f--- out, shut the door, and let me examine him. Let me get the doctor in, and then I can give you all an update.'

It was me just kind of taking control of the situation. Then once I felt comfortable, docs had cleared him, and we cleaned him up. He was acting more normal, then we went and celebrated."

Doogie and Scottie have a great reputation. "They're the best two trainers I've ever had," said Josh Fogg, "The Dragon Slayer" who pitched for four different big league teams. "When I got to Denver, even in that first spring training, I had some minor nicks and stuff here and there. I was worried about going in there. I'm trying to make this team as a non-40-man, free agent, came off a horrible year. I'm scared to death to walk in the training room to tell them I'm [playing through pain]. I go in there—I had tweaked my groin early on—I went and said, 'Hey, just so you know, I'm throwing my bullpen session later. I'm making my next start, but my groin hurts.' They're like, 'Listen, you don't have to come in here and do that. We're going to do everything we can to let you pitch. We're the opposite of 'hold you back.'

"I knew at that point forward that they were both on my side, and that's kind of the biggest thing. Can't be a narc, No. 1. You can't be going to the manager saying, 'Oh, this guy's arm is really bothering him. You can't pitch him.' If you want the ball, you should get the ball. They're also the psychiatrist of the team besides the actual team psychiatrist, which some teams employ now. But those are the guys you're worried to talk to because they might tell someone. If you had an issue with something off the field, on the field, the coach, [the trainers] always had good advice because they've probably dealt with it before."

Mike Pontarelli, the Coors Field staple nicknamed "Tiny," is the clubhouse manager, along with his assistant, Tyler Sanders. Pontarelli is a Denver baseball lifer. As a kid "Tiny" worked for the minor league Denver Zephyrs and then the Rockies and he has seen it all and had the wildest of requests, including, one might recall, Troy Tulowitzki's lobster for Game 163.

Prior to managing the home clubhouse, Tiny was the visiting clubhouse manager or "clubbie." "There are certain things all the way down to what kind of soap and shampoo a player uses," Tiny said over a meal one night at Don and Charlie's, the longtime spring training dinner spot for numerous people who work in baseball. "With the Dodgers, as classy of an organization as it is, they had their own sets of [food] rules. They were doing what everyone else wasn't doing. So I had two sets of food. If the Dodgers were coming in twice in the same month, I would get Tupperware and repack everything for them.

"There's a lot of custom clothing. Every year Majestic comes in, and everyone has to have the exact cut. Jayson Werth is one guy that stands out and he had very specific Nationals needs, and I would get an email from his agent, and it would give me instructions on how to prepare everything, and that's a lot of time for just one person. Denard Span is another one. He had food shipped in when he came with the Giants. These two guys couldn't be nicer people; they just had two very specific needs. Matt Williams when he was with Washington, he had a very specific soap that he would use. There was certain beers the Giants could and couldn't drink. It was very tailored to each team that would come in. The traveling secretary would give me a laundry list of stuff and bullet points that could not be missed.

"There are all sorts of odd requests. We try to keep things within reason. The word 'enablers' comes to mind because you want people to be somewhat independent outside. There was a young guy on the Rockies shortly after I accepted the full-time job in the clubhouse. This is a guy that had two years of service time, and his wife was high-maintenance. The team was coming back from the road, and this is before I traveled full time. He wants me to go buy groceries for his family—and load them into the fridge. I was thinking, *I don't have time, and this isn't what I signed up for*. But I did it. Because the way I looked at, we sucked it up and did it, and it kept the guy happy. As the clubbie you learn these little tricks. It might not sound fun, it might sound demeaning, but to be totally honest with you, just keep the guys happy within reason."

One time when Tiny was a young assistant, he accompanied the team to New York for a Mets trip on his own dime. He wanted to see the Big Apple for the first time. To save money he stayed in broadcaster George Frazier's room at the Grand Hyatt on 42nd Street. I promised Tiny I would take him out to dinner in Little Italy after the Mets-Rockies game. Dinner after games in New York are always particularly late since it takes about a half-hour via subway to get back into Manhattan. So we have a great meal in Little Italy, share a bottle of wine, and head back to the team hotel. At this point, it's now about two in the morning.

Tiny quietly opened the door to Frazier's room…and there in a chair is Frazier, wearing only boxers and dress socks. He has his feet kicked up. There is a cloud of smoke surrounding him as he takes a drag on a cigarette. It's like he was a dad staying up to wait for his kid to get home. "What are y'all doing?" He asked with a sly grin in that Oklahoma accent of his, as if there was nothing peculiar about what *he* was doing. It was hilarious, and that image is unfortunately burned on my brain.

• • •

The clubbies and trainers agree: the craziest dudes on any team any particular year are the relief pitchers. "They have a different language," Keith Dugger said.

"And I think the closers in general are probably the craziest," Scott Gehret said. "It's like a field goal kicker. If they blow a save, they feel like they cost their team the whole game. They're nuts and they have to be. Because if you give up a game, you know how it is when you get walked off. It's gut-wrenching. But you have to turn around and you've got 22 hours to get over it. The good ones—Brian Fuentes, Manny Corpas, and Huston Street—had the ability to do that, but they were nuts. They were in their own world.

"Now Fuentes, in general, isn't nuts. He was just a product of the position he was in. Was he nuts? No, he has a very dry, somewhat sick sense of humor. He wasn't as crazy as Huston. Huston was crazy. Huston was a slave to his routine. It was minute to minute for 24 hours a day, much like Todd's, much like any successful baseball player. Huston had a sleeveless fleece that he'd never wash that smelled like a sewer. If that thing went missing, he was dysfunctional. He would chase Tiny around or one of the assistants until they found it. If he didn't get it on, he was not right. Anything that gets them out of their routine, they were a mess. The closer and usually your eighth-inning guy will hang around [the clubhouse] until the seventh inning and then go out. It's amazing to watch them. Because if it's Huston or if it's Greg Holland, if it's 8:30 and they don't have to work for another hour, Huston might be playing chess online with some 16-year-old in Binghamton, New York. But then when it's time to go, he flips a switch and he goes. Same thing with Greg Holland, he'll do a crossword puzzle until 9:00, but come 9:55, he wants the ball. Their ability to disassociate themselves from the reality of their importance to the game up until they go in is amazing. That bullpen door opens, and they come running out and they just flip a switch. They go into a whole new universe."

One of the zaniest characters to ever play for the Rockies was reliever Joe Beimel, who had the distinction of being the only No. 97 in major league history. (The pitcher chose that number because it was the year his son was born.) When Beimel played for the Los Angeles Dodgers, he became sort of a cult hero. In fan voting he beat out numerous Dodgers stars to have a bobblehead night at Dodger Stadium.

With the Rockies he often had longer bushy hair and a beard, too. Beimel's entrance song at Coors Field was Johnny Cash's version of "God's Gonna Cut You Down." "Joe Beimel stands out in my mind. He was kind of a rock star-kind of guy," Mike Pontarelli said. "He wore sunglasses inside—no joke. He was all inked up. He wore a robe and he was like the fifth Beatle. He comes around and he would say, 'I'm letting my tea steep.' It's not every day you hear in the clubhouse about someone's tea is steeping."

• • •

Occasionally, you could walk into the Rockies' clubhouse or trainer's room, and there was Peyton Manning. During his Denver Broncos days, the legendary quarterback spent a bunch of time there. Manning was teammates at Tennessee with Todd Helton, and Keith Dugger had helped with Manning's rehab in Denver. So you'd walk downstairs, and there was Manning just hanging out with Scott Gehret.

Now, there's an old story about Vince Lombardi. He'd tell his team, "Only three things in life matter: God, family, and the Green Bay Packers." For Gehret there are five: God, family, the Colorado Rockies, the Colorado State Rams, and his fantasy football team. And I cannot guarantee the order either. Virtually every major league team has a fantasy football league. It's not uncommon to see players wearing NFL jerseys in the clubhouse on autumn Sundays. Draft night in late August is one of the most anticipated events on the calendar for the club. "The week of the [2013] fantasy draft, Peyton came into the office," Gehret said. "I shut the door. 'I need to talk to you about fantasy.' He said, 'I don't know shit about fantasy.' I said, 'I need a sleeper pick, Peyton. Who are you going to throw it to?' 'Julius Thomas.' And I said, 'Stop messing with me. Everyone knows [Pro Bowl receiver] Demaryius Thomas.' And he said, 'No, I said *Julius* Thomas.'"

Entering the 2013 season, Julius Thomas had been a seldom-used tight end with only one career catch. Many Broncos fans didn't even know the former Portland State football and basketball player was still on the Broncos (or ever was, for that matter). On his way out the door, Manning also said: "You might want to think about drafting me, too."

"I took Julius in the 16th round. There wasn't even a sticker for him," Gehret said. "The whole league laughed at me. And in the first game,

Manning threw seven touchdowns against Baltimore, two to Julius Thomas [who also had 110 receiving yards]. The next day, guys came up to me: 'He fucking told you, didn't he?' And I won the league, boat-raced everyone."

The Broncos went to the Super Bowl that year, and Julius Thomas had 12 touchdown catches. "Now, the week before the Cowboys game, Manning came in to me with a fantasy question. 'Do I get points if I run one in?' I explained the scoring, and he said, 'Watch the game on Sunday.'"

Sure enough, Manning, who ran slightly slower than Helton legging out a triple, scored a rushing touchdown on a naked bootleg. He came in on Tuesday that week, the Broncos' off day and said, "How did you like that? Enjoy it. It's never happening again!"

One time Manning texted a group message inviting everyone to Broncos training camp. He included: "And bring Scottie, so he can scout." Gehret has a screenshot of that text blown up and framed.

• • •

The late Don Baylor was a man's man, as I like to say. A former American League MVP, Baylor was the first manager of the Colorado Rockies. He managed from 1993 to 1998 and then served as Colorado's hitting coach from 2009 to 2010. They called him "Groove." He played in the majors for nearly two decades, hit 338 homers, and was hit by 267 pitches, leading the league in beanballs eight times. "He is one of the finest human beings I ever met," Scott Gehret said. "I love that guy. He's another guy that was as tough a man that you'll ever want to see. He got sick one time in the dugout—and it was no secret he had a chronic illness that ultimately cost him his life—but it was an illness that affected your body's ability to fight off infection. He was as sick as you could be on a getaway day and he was in the dugout. I was watching the whole time, just waiting for him to collapse and I remember telling him, 'Hey Groove, let's go up [to the trainer's room].' He was like, 'No,

Everyone, especially the training staff, knew how tough Don Baylor was. A real man's man, he managed the Rockies and then became their hitting coach.

Scottie, we're not going up.' At the end of the game, he kind of made his way to the training room. We got Dr. Schreiber involved, who said, 'Listen, this guy cannot get on the airplane.' We forced him to go to the emergency room, and he spent three days there with pneumonia. This guy was gonna get on an airplane and go work! That's the kind of guy he was."

Baylor would often take the clubbies or trainers to dinner, and Baylor was always paying. When Baylor wasn't retained as hitting coach, he called Gehret just to thank him for being a friend. "When he was the hitting coach, like most hitting guys, he has a disdain for certain umpires when they're screwing his hitters," Gehret recalled. "Angel Hernandez is behind home plate. Angel was missing call after call in Don's opinion. I had met Angel. I had walked him back to the hotel after a game in St. Louis. I loved Angel; Angel is a good guy. Don? Don does not like Angel. So it was early in the game. Angel's missing calls, screws up a lot of them. Angel takes a foul tip off his face mask and he's stunned. He's like a boxer that got hit, he's a little wobbly on his feet. I get up and go to check on him. On my way up the stairs, I feel a hand latch through my belt and it's holding me back, literally holding me back. I turn around, and it's Groove. Groove said, 'Stay right here.' And I said, 'Groove, the guy might have a concussion. I have to go look.' Groove said, 'I don't give a shit. He'll probably umpire better if he has a concussion.'

"I said, 'Groove, there are people watching this on TV.' I'm not going to have a discussion with Groove while Angel is not steady on his feet. I'm like, 'Groove, get off me!' I'm slapping at his hand, and that big son of a bitch will not let go of me! I can't shake him. I'm like, 'Groove, I have to go. Let go of me.' He said, 'All right, well I hope that cocksucker has a concussion.'

"I get out there and I'm like, 'Angel, you all right?' He said, 'Yeah, I'm all right.' I said, 'Sorry I'm a little late getting out here. Groove grabbed onto me, and I couldn't get out of his grasp.' He said, 'Yeah, Groove and I go back a long way. Is he mad at me today?' I said, 'Yeah, he's not real happy with you at this point, but let's not worry now. How's your head?' He said, 'Don't worry about my head, just give me a second. Did Groove call me a cocksucker?' I said, 'As a matter of fact, he did.' He said, 'Yeah, when he's mad at me, that's usually what he calls me.'"

• • •

Mike Pontarelli's childhood was spent in a baseball clubhouse and now he runs one for a living. Like all of the other behind-the-scenes guys, he works obscene hours. They spend their lives serving others so those others can get all the glory. And that's exactly what motivates these guys—to be part of a team even if they don't play baseball. They're in the game for the right reasons, and when that happens, something special can result. "The game takes you in with open arms," Tiny said. "People in this game can smell disingenuous personalities…Even today [during 2018], I was sitting in Buddy's office, and the media started to come in, and he said stay in here. So, everyone gets their camera set up, and he goes: 'Tiny, ask the first question.' And I'm cool as a cucumber. It's my mecca. I'm comfortable. This is coming off a night game, so I ask him how hard the turnaround for the players is when you play a day game after a night game. And he goes, 'It's not as hard for the players as it is for the clubbies.' That's the manager patting the clubbies on their back."

"It's a brotherhood," Keith Dugger said. "It's a bond and it's very special. Even when these guys get out of the game, I'm still in contact with players from 30 years ago, which is pretty cool when you see it. These guys are starting to have kids come around. Example: Eric Young Jr. played for the Rockies, and there's Tony Gwynn's son. Now, if I get a third-generation player, that's when it's time to shut it down."

As Dugger continued to share some stories, it turned out one of his best stories was eerily similar to Scott Gehret's story. Perhaps it's fitting. Todd Helton truly left his mark on both Gehret and Dugger. "So we got in this one rut," Dugger said of 2005. "Well every day, I'd tape his wrists, and he'd poke me in the stomach hard. With his right hand, [he'd] poke me right underneath there. And he'd bruise the shit out of me. It was hard! Then I'd tape his right wrist and when I was done I'd slap him across the face. He'd go with the left one and poke the crap out of me. I'd get done with that one and slap him on the other side of his face. We did that every day he had a hit. Well, holy shit, how long was his hitting streak? I don't even remember how long it was, but it got so bad that when I took my shirt off, my wife was like, 'What's wrong with your stomach?' I had a complete circle of dot bruises that looked like somebody had taken markers. That's how bad the bruises were. It got so bad that I had been slapping Todd's face on the right side, and his cheek was getting swollen and his eye was starting to swell. This went on for weeks, and we were both worn out, but we couldn't stop. Same routine every day. Same exact time, same tape, same corner I'd have to go to, same table we'd stretch him out on after he got dressed the same way, put his socks on or whatever else. Finally, he doesn't get a hit. And the two of us are so worn out that we're like, *thank God*. I was sore as shit for weeks!"

CHAPTER 12
INSIDE THE BOOTH

It's one of my favorite calls ever—this confluence of exuberance and disbelief on August 24, 2009. In the bottom of the 14th inning, the Rockies were batting, trailing 4–2. The bases were loaded with one out. "Ryan, 1-for-6," I said on the call when, all of a sudden, "in the air, deep right-center field, way back...Rockies win! Grand slam, Ryan Spilborghs—*You gotta be kidding me!* He's sprinting around the bases! Wow! Wow!...Those who have stayed—and those who have stayed up—have been duly rewarded."

And there was manager Jim Tracy, who had one arm pointing to the sky while falling into his bench coach in delirium. "This to me was a testament to what he represented throughout his entire career as a major league player," Tracy told me. "He fucking crushed one. He was so excited to get this at-bat, I'm telling you from the body language I'm observing. When he got to third and fired that fucking helmet the way he did and was going full speed running into that home-plate area, I never got out of the dugout. I was sitting there crying, I had never been happier for one of my players that had played with me in the big leagues than I was for that guy at that moment. I'll never forget that moment for as long as I live."

Now one of my broadcast partners, Spilly is one of the great characters of his generation, a truly funny, self-deprecating guy. He was one of the live wires in the clubhouse. And he's one of those guys when you're watching him, and you think, *This guy's going to be on television.* But would it be baseball broadcasts or *Saturday Night Live?* Spilly even hosted a seldom-seen online series called "Spill the Beans," in which he took on the Zach Galifianakis role from "Between Two Ferns," asking his guests—Rockies teammates—peculiar and inane questions, thriving on awkwardness. They're worth a YouTube search.

As a color man on the broadcasts, he's the great foil to my straight guy. And he works his tail off. He does exhaustive research. He's really into analytics. "It's a cool job, and there's a responsibility that I never fully realized. Baseball is 135 years of storytelling," said Spilborghs, whose final game in the big leagues was on September 5, 2011, his 32nd birthday. "I love quoting Vin Scully: 'A player's career is just a mere moment of time between an All-Star Game and an Old Timer's Game.' I've been here in the booth for five years and I've watched careers already come and go. As a broadcaster I've lasted two major league player lifetimes and I'm just starting. That part to me, you respect that if you stay within your lane and are wise about it and do your work, you can be in this game for a long time…Where it really hits me in the face is when I walk the concourse. The power of your word and description—you're a member of someone's family. 'You know my wife Martha, right?' It's like we're in the household every night. They feel like they know you… You help try to grow a generation of baseball fans. And that aspect to me, I think about more than most. I realize that our day and age is Twitter, 30-second bytes. How do I best give enough information in our medium? I can tell you a story about a four-seamer. I can tell you about park adjustment as an advanced metric. I can try to make you laugh. Only in baseball's medium do you have this range. And that's why people love watching baseball. The broadcasters are given freedom to play to your imagination, to entertain you."

Spilly's shenanigans have become legendary around Denver. He has fun whether it's in the booth or as a sideline reporter. At "Bark In The Park," Spilly's out there during the game—interviewing dogs. There was a Great Dane, which literally weighs 200 pounds. And he said, "Is this a Chihuahua? I'm with Tammy from Aurora, and she's got her Chihuahua with her."

Occasionally, he'd do his report from the most remote seat in the ballpark. He was doing that, and the Rockies rallied. So during the next homestand when the Rockies were down late, I said, "Spilly, dude, start climbing stairs, man!"

"All right, I'm off," he said. We checked back on him next inning, and he said, "We've got a problem." His rally seat was being occupied by a girl on a date. So Spilly's like: "I'll work it out." And a few pitches later, Spilly's sitting on her lap! "I have to sit in this seat, I'm sorry! It's good karma for us!"

When we were playing the San Francisco Giants late in the season, he literally went into the hand-operated scoreboard in right field. He stuck his head out of one of the rectangles that should have a number in it and did his sideline report. I said, "Spilly, we need the Cubs to win today. Give 'em a 6!" And he starts grabbing a 6 and putting it up on the scoreboard. Next thing you know, he's peeking out of one of the open spaces and razzing Hunter Pence, the Giants' right fielder, who is like 35 feet in front of him. He asked him, "Hunter, you want a slice of pizza?"

In July of 2018, the Rockies acquired Seunghwan Oh from the Toronto Blue Jays. So that meant the Rockies also got Eugene Koo, Oh's Korean translator, who became sort of a cult figure in St. Louis, when Oh played with the Cardinals. Koo goes essentially everywhere Oh goes except for the pitching mound and the bathroom.

In Oh's first game with Colorado, Spilly was the sideline reporter. So Spilly spoke about Eugene Koo and his role with Oh, a former closer. Spilly got tongue-tied for a moment, accidentally referring to Oh as the "most savingest" pitcher from South Korea. Well, by the time he wiggled his way through that description with that sly smile on his face, I couldn't resist. I asked him, "Spilly, have you considered asking Eugene to be your interpreter, too?"

In the booth Spilly is often a mascot magnet. He survived a popcorn avalanche from the Phillie Phanatic and even an awkward flirting session with Cincinnati's Rosie The Red and her oversized mascot head. I asked him, "Do you two want to get a room?"

Spilly is famous in Denver for his playfulness and self-deprecation, but he was a damn fine ballplayer and he personified perseverance. "In

Ian Desmond douses my broadcast partner and a true character, Ryan Spilborghs, with water after an extra-innings victory against the San Francisco Giants in 2018. (USA TODAY Sports Images)

2009 I lost my mom in February," he said. "I'm a newlywed. I never fully processed my mom passing away. My melancholy wasn't processed properly. I began the season a starting outfielder. I'm playing every day, and then you lose the job—to Carlos Gonzalez...I'd been in a dark place. I was Superman 3. I was Evil Superman...So when you see me running around the bases after the grand slam, that wasn't strictly a baseball moment. It was an unleashing. That was more cathartic, me releasing."

• • •

At the first game I ever broadcast with George Frazier, we were stationed on a picnic bench behind home plate. Years before Frazier and I did the Rockies broadcasts, we were first paired up for a 1988 college baseball game—Wichita State at Creighton—in the early days of Prime Sports. There was no press box—just a 25-year-old me and a recently retired big league pitcher, calling a college game on live television from a picnic table in Nebraska. "We were about a foot behind the umpire," Frazier recalled. "If he called it a strike, and we said it was outside, he could hear us."

Frazier began doing Rockies telecasts in 1997, and I started in 2002. We were together until he retired in 2015. In the grand tradition of the game, he is a true character. He pitched for 10 seasons primarily with the New York Yankees and Chicago Cubs. Renowned for his spitball, he famously said: "I don't put any foreign substances on the baseball. Everything I use is from the good old U.S.A." He took great pride in his craft, but he loved to have fun. In the booth he was the same way. You think of Dizzy Dean butchering the language but with this charm you can't fake.

Frazier had a story for every situation, though some of the stories he would tell—well, they just can't be entirely true. But he's such a warm person, a caring teammate, a giving guy, and hell, they were so damn funny that we couldn't care less if they were embellished a bit.

He was like your crazy uncle. There were times he would yell at umpires from our broadcast booth with his booming voice. We're 200 feet away, and he's yelling at Bruce Froemming: "Hey Grumpy!" And next thing you know, Froemming is looking around and spots Frazier. He asked fans to send him the wackiest hats they could find, and in the booth he'd wear a buffalo hat or one that lit up like a Christmas tree. During the 22-inning affair against the San Diego Padres, I said on air that I was starving, so Frazier announced mid-inning that he would valiantly procure us some food. He was gone for multiple innings! At some point—God knows what inning, maybe the 16th—he came back and had a slice and a half of pizza. I'm like, "That's what you could come up with? You've been gone a half an hour!" He passionately declared, "There's no food left in the ballpark. It's gone. Every pizza, every hot dog, every hamburger, everything's been sold, it's gone. This is what we got!"

"I laugh about this one," said Frazier, who was 63 in 2018. "We were in L.A. doing the game, and Jeff Schinker said: 'Hey, I'm going to go get Kid Rock and Pamela Anderson to come to the booth.' I was like 'Seriously?' And he was like, 'Yeah!' And to be honest with you, I didn't know who Kid Rock was. No idea. So they walk to the booth, and Pamela Anderson's two kids sit in my lap, and Pamela Anderson is standing right behind me and she leaned forward constantly while I'm trying to do a broadcast. Kid Rock is on the headset, and the two [boys] are sitting in my lap. Well, at break they asked me, 'What's that screen to the right?' And I said, 'Well, do you ever watch football games and see guys draw X's and O's on the screen?' And they said, 'Yeah!' So I said, 'Take your finger and draw an X.' So they drew an X, and I said to hit the right bottom button so it disappears, and the producer said we're coming back in 10 seconds. So about that time, they shoot us in the booth coming back from break. Both boys had circled Pamela Anderson's breasts behind my head. So I punched the right bottom button and said, 'Kill the telestrator!' The producer was laughing so hard, and I don't know if he got it killed. And Pamela, I thought she was going to fall over laughing. Kid Rock was laughing his head off. But it wasn't funny if you're in my shoes because the Rockies fans at home don't understand and think I'm the one that drew it. So that was pretty bad.

"Now, fast forward two weeks later when we're in Atlanta, Georgia. So I've gone from Kid Rock, Pamela Anderson, two kids circling breasts on air to when they tell me President Carter is coming in the booth. *Oh really?* Well, I'm sitting there broadcasting and I get a tap on my shoulder, and there's three guys in suits behind me showing me a golden badge. So I'm like 'What the hell? What did I do?' And they go, 'We're with the Secret Service. President Carter will be up shortly. I was like,

'Really?' So President Carter comes up a few minutes later and he was on air for a minute and a half. So I went from Pamela Anderson to President Carter in two weeks. I asked President Carter what he did for fun and he said, 'Well, Rosalynn and I will go to the donut shop and order donuts with the Secret Service sitting outside, and I'll go out the back, get in the truck with my buddy to go quail hunting, and give Rosalynn my phone. They can't find me, and it drives them crazy. And me and my buddy are off laughing while we're quail hunting while they're searching for me, and Rosalynn is laughing and saying, 'I don't know where he went. He went out the back door!' You never knew who was going to walk in our booth. I think we had a lot of laughs."

Frazier talks faster than he pitched. His stories are stunning and head-spinning. The one that's requested most often is about the Cook County Courthouse. He pitched for the Cubs from 1984 to 1986, and his close friend in Chicago was a defense attorney. Frazier swore that sometimes for kicks his buddy would let him be his "co-counsel." So Frazier would put on a suit and play lawyer. And this was Chicago, not Podunk Iowa during Single A. So as Frazier tells the story, "We were at the Cook County Courthouse. They've got burglars on the first floor, drug dealers on the second floor, murderers on the third floor." Apparently, this is a drug trial of some sort. So Frazier's buddy said, "George, the eyewitness is on the stand. You know all the details of this case. You go cross-examine him!"

And Frazier got up there and said: "So you tell me that you saw this drug transaction on Fifth and Elm, and you were standing where?" And he goes, "I was on Fourth and Elm."

"Well, we went out and measured that, and it's approximately 237 feet away. And I notice you're wearing glasses. What's your vision?" And he said, "20/400." And Frazier responded, "Well, with vision 20/400 from 237 feet, there's no way you could've clearly identified anybody in any transaction." Right when he says that, the judge slammed his gavel down and said, "Case dismissed!" I die laughing at that one, thinking to myself, *did the jury not have a say in this trial? Did they just change U.S. legal procedure?* My good friend John Reynolds, our longtime booth director in Los Angeles, told Matt Vasgersian the rough details of that story. Every time I see Vasgersian, he asks me to retell it to whoever is around.

On the phone with Frazier in 2018, he shared that another time he was at that courthouse "and this dude walks in for a bail hearing and goes: 'Yo, Frazier with the Cubs! I watched you pitch yesterday!'"

Some of Frazier's best stories came from his time playing winter ball in the Dominican Republic. "The old Pirates player Rennie Stennett had twisted his ankle all the way around backward and he says, 'I want you to go with me on my off day tomorrow,'" Frazier said. "So I say, 'Where are we going?' He says, 'Aw, don't worry about it, I just need you to ride with me.' So we ride through a crossing gate, and he says we're in Haiti. And I go, 'Haiti? What are we doing here?' So we take off up into the mountains. I say, 'Hey, Rennie, where are we going? I don't like this.' He goes, 'Don't worry about it. Everything's going to be fine.' We pull up in the mountains, and there's smoke and there's more smoke, and I don't know if you want to call it a tepee or what, but this dude comes out of that tent with horns on the side of his hat, smoke flying. He was a voodoo doctor. I stayed in the car. I was not leaving the car. He went in there and got it fixed and played better. A voodoo doctor! I said, 'What am I doing with a voodoo doctor in Haiti? Are you kidding me?' I wasn't about to go anywhere near that place."

For all the stories and tomfoolery, Frazier was on those broadcasts because he could talk baseball with the Rockies fans in a way that felt comforting. He took pride in growing smart baseball fans in Colorado, developing their thinking with his explanations of the game he loved, always with a little "Oklahoma-ese" mixed in.

His final broadcast was more emotional for him than he thought it was going to be. We did a whole George Frazier week. We had guys like Vin Scully wishing him farewell. And then we had a party at our house, and our crew put a huge video together. He brought his whole family, and it was pretty emotional but pitch perfect. On the video longtime Cincinnati Reds broadcaster Marty Brennaman said: "You've been stealing money for how long as a broadcaster? You were stealing as a pitcher, too!" People come up to me often and ask about Frazier, and they wonder if I still talk with him. He remains a close and loyal friend, and I talk to him once or twice a week. If I ever need a laugh or some entertainment on a long drive, I call him up.

• • •

Color commentator Jeff Huson and I have become so close that we finish each other's sentences. From Day One, the overwhelming sentiment you get from Huey is that he is genuinely nice. I know he was a caring teammate as a player and is exactly that as a broadcast teammate. I cannot tell you how many times we giggle off the air about something that just occurred or something we both thought of—and thankfully didn't say on the air. There have been many instances where we can't look at each other for a few minutes, so as not to make the other one lose it. It's like two 10-year-olds up there.

And he just has the best life story. You think about how meticulously baseball is scouted and how players are earmarked for greatness at such a young age. And then there's the story of Huson, who played 12 years in the big leagues but didn't even have a college baseball scholarship offer out of high school. He was from Arizona and planned on attending U of A as a regular student. "And the last thing my dad says to me before I leave is: 'I just want you to think about this. I don't want you to look back in 10 years and regret you didn't try to play baseball.' So I drive four hours, I get to the U of A, I've got my check in hand, and I was basically walking up the steps to go pay my tuition,"

Huey said. "And I can hear my dad. I walked back down the steps, got in the car—and this was obviously pre-cell phones—drove back the four hours, handed my dad the check, and said I was going to try to walk-on at a junior college."

Huson went to Glendale Community College, and it came down to him and another ballplayer for the last spot on the team. Well, he made the team. By his second year, he was a Junior College All-American. He's now in the Glendale Hall of Fame. He drew interest from Lamar (down in south Texas), as well as Wyoming, where he proceeded to have a terrific two-year career as a shortstop. He was told there was a good chance he'd get drafted. When he didn't, he looked for a chance to play just a little more. So for his final summer after senior year, Huson was on a semipro team out of Beatrice, Nebraska. "My last chance to play," Huson said, succinctly.

The team advanced to the National Baseball Congress World Series in Kansas. A scout spotted Huson there. It was Montreal Expos scout Bob Oldis, an old catcher from the 1960 World Series-winning Pittsburgh Pirates. Oldis offered Huson $1,500 and a plane ticket to spring training. Three years later—September 22, 1988—the kid, who almost didn't even attempt to play college baseball, made his major league debut. He played in the bigs until the year 2000.

He and his wife, Wendy, also a Wyoming graduate, have three kids. All three were college athletes and are terrific people. He has become a close confidant on many of those family-related topics. We both share a deep love for the game, and some of our greatest thrills have been working with our kids on the game.

There are so many times that he or I say exactly what the other one was about to say. We will pull the headsets off in the commercial break and say, "I was just about to go there." One of my favorite things to tease him about is his ability to devour desserts. It's impressive. Ice cream, cake, cookies, chocolate eclairs, it doesn't matter. Yet he never gains a pound. He's still at the same weight he played at nearly 20 years ago. I call him the fattest skinny guy I've ever met. I think he picks his road games based on which team provides the best dessert in the media dining room. It would take one of his kid's weddings to miss the ice cream in Philadelphia!

• • •

As a Rockies broadcaster, the question that fans ask me the most is: "What happens in a typical day at your job?" While my boys do homework at night, allegedly, I do homework in the morning. I'll read a 10-page-plus email sent from the Stats Inc. research department, as well as articles by the beat writers covering both teams and a personal email of Rockies facts from our in-house researcher, Dan Hyatt. You have to become an instant expert about the opposing team. Numbers help tell the story of where an individual or team is currently situated. Then there are human interest stories. These anecdotes add flavor and background. The tempo and pace of a baseball game lends itself more than any other major sport to storytelling.

The "open" to each broadcast is like the first song at a concert. It's a powerful tone-setter. We have passionate discussions during the day about the topics with which to open a broadcast—and how the truck will enhance the open with video, graphics, and sound bites. For example, before a game in August of 2018, I got a call from our producer, Alison Vigil. The Rockies had recently blown numerous late games. "We need to devote the whole first segment to what's transpired with the bullpen and specifically Wade Davis," I said. "If we don't, the fans, who religiously turn us on and listen intently, will think we are ducking what is on every fans' mind." Vigil concurred. She and our other producer, Tavis Strand, have just a brilliant touch. They understand how to tell the story—and our responsibility to tell the proper stories—and enhance it with video and graphics. They are passionate, dedicated, and exceptionally well-organized, which helps in navigating the craziness of live television.

They were both hired by our former executive producer, Ken Miller, who now runs the entire on-air operation at Altitude. He and I grew up in the business together. We both played baseball into college and met initially in 1987 when I moved down from Aspen. Our love for playing sports and covering it made us become close rather quickly. In fact, back in our mid-20s before marriage and kids, Miller and I would travel around the globe together—from Thailand to Bali to the south of France. We've been a ton of places together with stories that make us roll even when retold for the umpteenth time. Miller is a tremendous director of live sports as well. In addition to having a keen eye for talent, he gave Charissa Thompson, Alanna Rizzo, Ryan Spilborghs, and Jenny Cavnar their first big breaks, though Cavnar had established herself in San Diego. He remains, among many good friends, my closest in the business.

Our immediate crew consists of Strand and Vigil, who share producing duties. (Strand handles about two-thirds of the games.) Our two directors, Fox and Erica Ferraro, share duties too, with Fox handling roughly two-thirds. Javy Prieto is our lead tape operator, which means, among many duties, he is a master editor. Susan Strand (Tavis' wife) and I have worked together since she was a teenager working for her late father in the production truck. She is our graphics coordinator and the absolute best of anyone I've worked with in over 30 years of doing this.

Charlie Felix is our regular traveling handheld cameraman and responsible for shooting numerous pregame and postgame interviews and feature stories on players. He is a tireless worker. And we have countless camera operators, audio folks, and technicians who do a marvelous job night after night. I have said this many times—and it is not in the least bit gratuitous—we have many of the finest and most talented folks working in Denver.

Our current on-air team with Cavnar and Cory Sullivan is a fun, dedicated group who enjoy needling one another to no end. Cavnar came home to Colorado from San Diego and is superb at anchoring our pregame and postgame shows. She grew up in a baseball household as her dad, Steve, captured a couple of prep baseball state titles (at Smoky Hill High and Regis Jesuit High). Sullivan has made a smooth transition from the field to the studio. Sullivan is sharp and competitive and will bet you on anything—from the golf course to the name of the drummer in Maroon Five.

As for gameday prep, I typically get to the park three-and-a-half hours before first pitch (unless I'm stealing a few innings of one of my boys' games and arrive later with the blessing of Strand or Vigil). Each day is about acquiring information, anecdotes, and emotions. The first place I head: the clubhouse to catch a couple of players. From there I head to the dugout to listen to manager Bud Black answer questions from the media. My partner and I that night will often chat with him privately to ask about other topics, which may or may not be suitable for the broadcast. As fans know, one of the vital aspects to a game is bullpen availability. We'll privately ask him who's available, and he'll share info—some usable and some that's not for public consumption. The reason we ask about the bullpen privately is to ensure no one from the visiting media happens to hear it and accidentally passes that onto the opponent. If your closer or top set-up man is down, that info in the other dugout puts you at a competitive disadvantage. Even if it's an unlikely scenario, asking those questions in private is appreciated by Black, as it was with Walt Weiss, Jim Tracy, and Clint Hurdle before him.

The next thing I do is perhaps the most useful and important of all my pregame rituals—I hang around the batting cage. There I observe, make small talk, or ask a couple specific questions to players and coaches. It may be a scouting report from coaches Duane Espy or Jeff Salazar on that night's opposition pitcher—and how they want to attack him—or asking Nolan Arenado about how well he knows a certain player on the other team from Southern California. I'll hang around for the opposing team's BP, too. Again, it's all about gathering information and cultivating relationships. Sometimes, you get some really interesting new info that make for good copy on the air. Sometimes, it's just watching the interactions with players. Sometimes, it pays dividends down the road because you've developed a relationship. When the Rockies signed Ian Desmond in the winter prior to 2017, he came over after his press conference and gave me a hug before sitting down for an interview. Not that we were long-lost buddies, but he and I had talked numerous times through the years around the cage. I had a good feel for the kind of leader and stand-up guy the team had invested in. Baseball is a small fraternity. From just standing around the batting cage, it is amazing how many anecdotes I have passed along to the fans.

During the day and into the late afternoon, I'm in communication with my broadcast partners. Following the walk-off loss with Davis on the mound, I wanted their take on responding to gut-wrenching losses. Ryan Spilborghs and Jeff Huson don't fall back on the "that's just baseball" or "wash-it-off" cliched narratives. They have acknowledged in past situations that all losses are not created equal. They'll share insight to the postmortem of the clubhouse and the psychology of trying to bounce back.

One hour before game time, we'll have a graphics rehearsal in the booth. Wearing headsets in communication with the production truck, we'll lock down exactly what'll happen in the open of the broadcast, as well as all the statistical graphics, sponsored items, and sound bites that may hit the air. After that rehearsal we grab a bite to eat in the media dining room while going through both teams' official game notes. Additionally, somewhere in the lead up before first pitch, we will duck into the visitors' booth (or vice versa) and compare notes and updates with our announcer brethren from the other side. I actually enjoy the reading and the note taking and certainly the conversations with people as part of game preparation, but the greatest joy is actually sitting down and calling the game.

The second question I'm asked most often is: "What's it like to travel with the Rockies?"

If the Rockies have a trip after a home game, we'll leave after the game regardless of if it's a day or night game. So let's say it's a Sunday day game, I'll arrive at the stadium with my overly large suitcase (and sometimes golf clubs) and drop it off at the Coors Field loading dock.

After the game, the bus for the airport leaves one hour after the final out. Like many players, I will drive my own car to the airport, which isn't the main terminal at Denver International Airport. It's at Signature FBO, a smaller terminal for private planes. Once at Signature we walk right out, get wanded by TSA, and walk from the tarmac to our Boeing 757.

The traveling party includes the 25 players plus players on the disabled list who are going on the trip. There's Paul Egins, the director of major league operations, which is sometimes called "traveling secretary," such as when George Costanza had the gig for the New York Yankees on *Seinfeld*. Egins has been with the Rockies since the inception of the team. He handles and juggles travel and tickets and rooms for players, the players' families, and oddball requests. He is the best. Just don't call him when his alma mater, the Georgia Bulldogs, are playing football.

The manager, coaching staff, and sometimes front-office executives travel, too, along with two members of the media relations staff led by the incomparable Warren Miller; Julian Valentin, who is in charge of social media; Matt Dirksen, the team photographer; Kunio Nakatani, the team massage therapist; Gabe Bauer and Mike Jesperson, who lead the physical performance department; Tyler Hines, the club nutritionist; as well as Mike Pontarelli and often Tyler Sanders, who run the clubhouse.

Drew's Diary

June 19, 2018:
New York Mets at Colorado Rockies

A win! The Rockies prevail 10–8 in another game that should have been more comfortable. For the first time in eight years, Colorado goes back-to-back-to-back with Nolan Arenado, Trevor Story, and Ian Desmond. Carlos Gonzalez added an opposite-field shot in the fourth inning. Bryan Shaw gave up two in the seventh and needed Chris Rusin and Adam Ottavino to get the final two outs. Otto remains the lone steady hand as he got four outs. Wade Davis walked the leadoff man and ends up allowing two in the ninth but froze Michael Conforto to end it. There was an 80-minute rain delay at the outset, and we spent most of it sitting in the booth and conversing with Keith Hernandez. It was another reason I love being in the game. We talked hitting philosophy, his days in Triple A, his visiting Denver as a 19-year old, and hitting balls into the south stands in batting practice. Some of the best stories were about coming up with the St. Louis Cardinals and watching as the clubhouse was led by Bob Gibson and Lou Brock. "Brock was the good cop to Gibson's bad cop," he said. "I never would have made it without Brock. He taught me how to be a big leaguer. I was scared to death of Gibson. One time I was fixing a cut on my finger when Gibson walked in and said, 'What the fuck are you doing in here with a paper cut?' I grabbed a couple of BAND-AIDs and nearly ran to my locker. I didn't go in there the rest of the season!"

The television production team gets seven seats for two announcers, the pregame host/sideline reporter, producer, director, graphics coordinator, and sometimes our handheld photographer or lead tape operator will go. The rest of the road crew are local camera, audio, and other technicians who are hired locally in the cities we are traveling to. On the radio side, there are their two announcers, Jack Corrigan and Jerry Schemmel, and their engineer/producer Jesse Thomas.

Some teams have colorfully decorated planes, but ours is subtle and classy. There is just one purple line on the outside of the Rockies' plane. On the inside every headrest has a CR inscription, and all are first-class-sized seats. The teams' broadcast partners, PR, and front-office staff sit in the first section; the coaches sit in the second section; and the players themselves sit in the third section.

When you get on the plane, there are a couple areas with food available, including sliders and shrimp and egg rolls and fruit and vegetables. Then there's a menu with four entree choices. The first time my wife, Kristi, traveled with us on a wives trip, she said: "Don't ever tell me how hard this is!"

One of the neat things about working in the broadcast booth has been getting to know your colleagues with other teams. When we played the Los Angeles Dodgers, our booth naturally was next to Vin Scully's. To be able to have a relationship with Vin Scully was very cool, to say the least. He's the best there will ever be at doing this. His voice, his cadence, the poetry of his work.

A couple of anecdotes on Scully, who, as great a broadcaster as he was, is an even finer gentleman. My son, Jacob, was playing ball in Orange County, and the Rockies were in L.A. They always held an elevator for Scully after the game, so he could get to his car and driver and beat the traffic out of Dodger Stadium. I took the stairs and hurried to the parking lot. There was still time to take my rental car and catch some of Jacob's game. So I'm jogging through this area, pulling my rolling workbag, looking ridiculous, and I pass a car as I'm running through the lot. It pulls up, and the window goes down. It's

Scully in the back. "Drew," said the melodic famous voice. "Do you need a ride somewhere?"

Another time, we were at a game at Coors Field, one of those marathons with runs, pitching changes, and more runs. After this particularly long day, we each walked out of our respective booths at the same time by chance. "Drew," he asked in that beautiful voice, "do you ever play crisp, two-hour-and-20-minute games here?"

And I just had to laugh and say: "Not very frequently, Vin!"

• • •

Once, and only once, I got to work with the legendary broadcaster Milo Hamilton. He had a lifetime of famous calls, notably Hank Aaron's No. 715 for the Atlanta Braves' broadcast. Well, I was supposed to do a college basketball game with him in the late 1980s. It was Colorado State at Baylor.

I was flying from Denver to Dallas on the first flight out in the morning for an evening game. Well, the flight was canceled. The next one went out, and we were above Colorado Springs, and all of a sudden, we had to turn around and go back because of mechanical issues. So now I've had two flights that didn't go and I had to wait until a 2:00 PM flight, which landed at 5:00 PM. It was a 7:00 PM game. So I needed a rental car to get to Waco for the game at Baylor, which was 90 miles away—and it was rush hour. I got in the car, got through traffic, and now I was driving 90 miles an hour down I-35. And I'd never been to Waco in my life. And it's not like I had GPS or a cell phone. So I pulled off when I got near Waco and I asked the gas station attendant, "Do you know where Baylor is?" And she responded, "Baylor? No." It was some poor girl with half her teeth. So I pulled off again, and this next place gave me decent directions.

So I pulled in and had to find the loading dock where the TV trucks were. I got my briefcase and I was hustling, running with this briefcase like O.J. Simpson in that old Hertz commercial. And they said, "Are you Drew? Follow me!" So we hustled down there onto the court, and everybody was standing because the anthem was being played.

And there, standing on the far end of the court, waiting to do the TV intro, was the legendary Milo Hamilton. So I scurried across the court, parked myself next to him, and shook his hand. They finished 'Home of the brave,' and—boom—"Hello from Waco, Texas, I'm Milo Hamilton alongside Drew Goodman..."

• • •

On a ski trip during college, I remember spotting a TV station on Main Street in Aspen. KSPN-TV in the mid-1980s did a variety of ski and mountain lifestyle programming, high school football, and news. The small studio was in an old Victorian in Aspen and also would get stories from their Vail bureau. The news director called me back and showed genuine interest. He was coincidentally from New York, too. So on the day after Christmas 1985, about seven months after graduation, with my little Datsun packed to the gills, I began the drive to the Rockies.

To supplement my entry-level salary in a not-so-entry-level-salary town, I got a gig as a trainer at the prestigious Aspen Club. It provided me with three things: a few more bucks, a free place to work out, and a who's who of potential TV interview subjects. During those 19 months, I did long-form interviews with Martina Navratilova, Sugar Ray Leonard, Joe Morgan, O.J. Simpson, Chris Evert, Andy Mill, Reggie Jackson, and several others. On one particular afternoon, I recall seeing a guy on the lat pulldown machine. It was Arnold Schwarzenegger. Jane Fonda was a regular and once asked me for additional tricep exercises. I (sadly, but understandably) don't believe I ever got a mention on her '80s workout videos.

Navratilova made her home in Aspen and was an outstanding all-around athlete—in addition to being perhaps the greatest female tennis player of all time. She loved basketball and had a group of people with whom she played. As a member of that little group, I remember

Drew's Diary

September 3, 2018:
San Francisco Giants at Colorado Rockies

The Rockies return home in the airtight National League West just a half-game behind the Los Angeles Dodgers in second place and a half game ahead of the Arizona Diamondbacks. They open a 10-game homestand with three against the San Francisco Giants and Madison Bumgarner. The Rockies return struggling Tyler Anderson to the hill. Anderson has a 1-2-3, first inning with two strikeouts, and in the bottom of the first, the Rockies go off on the Giants ace like never before. Charlie Blackmon singles and DJ LeMahieu follows with a 437-foot home run to left-center. Nolan Arenado rips a double to the left-field corner. Trevor Story follows with a massive homer to dead center. After a fifth-inning, three-run homer by Story off of Madbum, it's 7-2 Colorado and looking like an easy victory.

Not so fast. The Giants chip away, and when Seunghwan Oh gives up two eighth-inning homers, the Giants suddenly and improbably take an 8-7 lead. In the bottom of the eighth, Ian Desmond singles, and Chris Iannetta hits a pinch-double off the wall in right. Noel Cuevas pinch hits versus Tony Watson, and the rookie rolls an 0-1 pitch up the middle to plate two, and the Rockies go back up 9-8. Wade Davis strikes out the side in the ninth inning, and the Rockies' win—coupled with losses by both the Dodgers and Diamondbacks—means Colorado is alone in first place as we go to sleep on September 3rd. This team is going to make everyone go on heart meds!

sitting next to her on the floor. I was gassed after a number of games, thinking if I told someone back home about this, no one would believe it. Following a couple of games guarding Jackson, another frequent visitor, I called my dad to tell him, "You'll never guess who I've been hooping with!"

In the summer of 1987, the station shut its doors, and the owner Joyce Hatton moved several of us to Denver in the pursuit of starting a Rocky Mountain Super Channel. She wanted to acquire the rights to the Denver Nuggets and use skiing and the mountain lifestyle as a backdrop. It was loosely modeled after TBS. Ultimately, the whole thing got entangled in litigation with some other partners at the time. But it did place me in Denver with United Cable and enabled me to get in on the ground floor of the area's first regional sports network, Prime Sports Network.

The ubiquitous Irv Brown was my partner broadcasting Colorado State University hoops. We traveled throughout the Western Athletic Conference for a number of years. Brown, as every longtime follower of sports talk radio in the region can attest, has more stories than most of us could provide in six lifetimes. He knew every coach and every official in the country and had T'd up half of them. Brown rarely called me by name; it was always "kid." He refereed six NCAA title games. He took guff from Bobby Knight and handed it right back while keeping his composure.

I've had the good fortune especially in the 1990s to work a number of sports, including track and field, gymnastics, indoor and beach volleyball, tennis, hockey, hot air ballooning, rodeo, and ride and tie, a sport I literally had never heard of until I got on site. It consists of a team of two people and one horse, and the race typically goes through a wooded, hilly region. The event I worked was in the San Gabriel Mountains outside of Los Angeles. It begins with one member of the team riding out on a trail while the partner sets out running. At some point the runner catches up to the horse, which has been tied to a tree. The original rider has taken off running while the initial runner jumps on the horse and takes off. This goes on back and forth until the required distance is covered.

In 1992 I was hired to work a few ACC football games for Jefferson Pilot sports. That gig led me to my first big break in the summer of 1993 when NBC hired me to be one of their play-by-play guys on their coverage of the NFL. At 30 I was the youngest guy at the network, though I thought I was going to get fired at halftime of my first game.

The Indianapolis Colts were hosting Dan Marino and the Miami Dolphins, and I was working with Dan Hampton, the recently retired Chicago Bears star. Toward the end of the first half, I had to read a promo for our studio halftime report from New York. It was sponsored by Domino's Pizza. I said, "Coming up at halftime join Jim [Lampley], O.J. [Simpson], Mike [Ditka], and Will [McDonough] on the Domino's Pizza Hut halftime report." Yeah, I accidentally added "Hut" when I spoke. It just kind of naturally rolled off my tongue. I immediately thought, *I'm done.* I just gave a mention to Pizza Hut, Domino's chief competitor!

Toward the end of the game, as Marino led the Dolphins down the field, the producer got in my ear to tell me to welcome the rest of the nation, as we were the last game still playing. I was pleased overall with my first taste of network TV, but the whole flight home, all I could think about was the Pizza Hut incident.

The next morning my phone rang around 8:00 AM. NBC's coordinating producer for the NFL, Tommy Roy, was on the other end. I braced myself for bad news. Instead, he said, "Great job, I thought it went well yesterday." I breathed again. Evidently no one—from the truck to the executives in New York—caught my mistake. I survived to work the following week.

CHAPTER 13

MY BASEBALL LIFE

I've always felt so privileged to do what I do. A number of times throughout the year, I'll be in the dugout and I pinch myself. This is so awesome. I love this. I love the game of baseball. I love the people who live baseball. And I love the art of broadcasting baseball. And I've always felt so fortunate to do what I do where I do it—in Colorado.

It's fitting that Colorado itself is shaped like a postcard. We live inside the front of a postcard with these glorious mountainous snapshots that are just our local playgrounds. I tell this to my kids on road trips so often that they know it's coming before I say it: "People come from around the globe to experience this, to see this, and it's in our backyard."

I love being outdoors. I love skiing. I love biking. I love running. I love barbecuing. I love how healthy it feels. Colorado fits me. It's funny, but when I first moved to Aspen, I initially didn't want to take the New York plates off of my car. I was ethnocentric, and everything was just a minor detour until I could get back to the Northeast. I still love New York; it is where I'm from. But my home, my life, and my peace are and will always be found in Colorado.

And Coors Field, our park, encapsulates all that's Colorado: the omnipresent green; the forestry behind the center-field wall; the sun setting over the mountains, visible from the first-base side; the expansive craft beers available; the Mexican cuisine options; the purple row of upper deck seats that signifies a mile high; the party deck in right, where Millennials mingle; the gargantuan, modern video board in left, uniquely shaped like a Colorado Rockie.

And our view from the broadcast booth is breathtaking—perfectly nestled between the decks of seats. And during the seventh-inning stretch, as the fans sing "Take Me Out To The Ballgame," we get to throw free bags of Cracker Jacks to them. (Alas, they still have to buy some peanuts.)

Drew's Diary

March 29, 2018:
Colorado Rockies at Arizona Diamondbacks

Opening Days are unique and special to baseball. There are first games of the season in all of the other sports naturally, but they are not the event that is baseball's Opening Day. Chase Field is naturally sold out and buzzing with anticipation. Bud Black is his laid-back and his amusing self during his pregame press get-together in the dugout. The storyline for the game beyond the Opening Day narrative is Jon Gray and how he will respond to his return to the place where he made his final start of 2017—the wild-card game in which he recorded just four outs and gave up four runs. He had been on a terrific two-month roll, heading into the playoffs but clearly was over-amped and did not handle his first postseason appearance. It's part of the learning process and evolution of a pitcher, especially someone who has the stuff and desire to be a true ace. Unfortunately, his opening inning closely resembled his first inning in October. After DJ LeMahieu hit a solo home run in the top of the first, Gray allowed three runs in the bottom of the first. He would last four innings in what ultimately was an 8–2 loss, snapping the Rockies' three-game Opening Day win streak.

My broadcast philosophy is I have the privilege of coming into people's living rooms. I don't take that for granted. Stylistically, I try to be an informed, pleasant accompaniment to the people watching their Rockies play. They're not tuning in to hear me; they're tuning in to see their team. I don't want to be overbearing, I don't want to be intrusive. I want to pass along a story or two, share some information, maybe deliver a funny line when it happens organically. It's just cool being part of the experience. Baseball is this journey, and they're with you for 162 mini-chapters. It lends itself to being anecdotal unlike any other sport.

I've done countless football and basketball games and enjoy those experiences immensely, but I cherish the nature of baseball, the lifestyle of baseball from its day-after-day calendar to its lack of a clock. In the press box at PNC park in Pittsburgh is a poster that has been on the wall since the doors opened. It's of kids from the 1930s, putting their hands on a bat to determine which team got last licks on the sandlot. The caption above it is from the great baseball author and observer Roger Angell: "Since baseball time is measured only in outs, all you have to do is succeed utterly; keep hitting, keep the rally alive, and you have defeated time. You remain forever young." I absolutely love that quote. I let it resonate.

I've been the Rockies' television play-by-play voice since 2002 and I've been an eyewitness to so many chapters of this young franchise's history and thus the chapters in this book. But I'll likely never see anything as cool as what my dad saw. He was there for the "Shot Heard 'Round The World."

Yep, how cool is that? October 3, 1951. He was in the right-field stands at New York's Polo Grounds. He was 16, working at the press gate, checking the press credentials of the writers as they made their way into the park. Then he got to stay and watch the New York Giants games.

When Bobby Thomson hit the homer and the Giants won the pennant, my dad jumped over the outfield wall and ran onto the field.

Fun fact: Rookie outfielder Willie Mays was on deck when Thomson hit the homer. That was my dad's guy. We all have a guy. One of my favorite aspects to Americana is this. You could be in a conversation with the richest person or the most famous celebrity, but if you ask him or her this question—"Who was your favorite player growing up?" the walls are down, and they're suddenly 10 again and your best friend, sharing stories about how a ballplayer just stirred something in them, made them giddy, and made them proud.

Also, incidentally, imagine Mays playing in Coors Field today, patrolling that vast outfield grass? When the Giants moved to San Francisco, it was my dad's first heartbreak in life. But in 1962 the New York Mets came along, and in 1963 I came along. He adopted the Mets, so I grew up rooting for the Mets and attending occasional games at Shea. One of my early recollections is being at a New York Mets-San Francisco Giants game. We were sitting there before the game, and they're doing the lineup. And after each announcement, I booed. I'm a kid, just being silly. And then: "Batting third, playing center field, Willie Mays." I started booing, and my dad grabs my arm. He said, "First of all, you should never boo a major leaguer because even the worst major leaguer is still a great ballplayer. Second, that guy is the greatest player who ever lived."

My dad taught me to appreciate the nobility of rare ability. And today from the broadcast booth of a big league team, I love that when a player gets called up, it is just really special to the manager, to the coaching staff, to the veteran guys, everyone. Because they get it. Because nobody knows how long you'll last. Their whole lives, since they were little kids, their dream was to play in the big leagues. The reality is 99.9999 percent of these kids don't get to live out the dream. I was one of those kids. Consider there have only been 19,000-plus major leaguers. That wouldn't even fill the lower bowl at Coors Field. They have been playing Major League Baseball since 1871. And here's this kid who will forever be in the baseball almanac. And I have the privilege of getting to call his at-bat? To be the narrator of his moment? What an honor.

The narrators of my childhood were Lindsey Nelson, Ralph Kiner, Bob Murphy, the broadcasters who did the Mets games. And there was this comfort. They let you in. They were Seavers behind the mic—pitch perfect.

My parents—Arthur and Marian—met in summer stock in the Catskills. Their shared passion was theater. My mom, who grew up in Brighton Beach in Brooklyn, was in the first graduating class of the High School of Performing Arts, of *Fame* fame (the 1980s hit TV show). She was a ballerina. And she danced professionally with the Canadian Ballet Company. Alas, I didn't get the dancing gene passed down, which was unfortunate since I grew up in the disco era. I could've used her rhythm.

I was born on Long Island, but then they built a house in Pound Ridge in northern Westchester, near the border of New York and Connecticut. Pound Ridge, New York, was home. It's where my parents taught me about having heart and caring with your heart.

I was enamored with ABC's *Wide World of Sports*, watching Frank Gifford or Bob Beattie reporting from the Hahnenkamm in Kitzbuhel, Austria, or some other exotic spot that's tough to spell. I recall getting out a tape recorder on many winter nights, writing out the New York Knicks and their opponent's lineup in a scorebook, turning down the sound on the TV, and doing my own broadcast. Other times, I would read stories from *Sports Illustrated* into the recorder, getting in the reps, even then.

And naturally, I loved to play sports, especially baseball and football. I knew I either wanted to be the one playing the games or the guy broadcasting the games. When I was 14, after my freshman football season at Fox Lane High School, my mom thought I had pink eye. She scheduled me for an eye doctor appointment in White Plains, about a 30-minute drive. My best friend was a kid named Dick Weiss, and he came along. My mom drove us back, and five minutes from home, a 16-year-old driver crossed the double yellow line. He was stoned. And he hit us head on. My mom died instantly.

I had a broken arm and some other stuff. The seatbelt saved my life. My best friend in the back wasn't in a seatbelt, and he went through the windshield. He lived, but he was in a body cast for about six months. He had two broken legs and other injuries. The other kid lived.

It was a Friday. November 25, 1977—the day after Thanksgiving.

The mind does things with trauma. I don't remember the moments leading up to it. I don't remember the impact. But I do have vague memories of sitting on the side of the road, and there are flashing lights, and I'm talking to a paramedic. I knew my arm was broken. And my buddy is screaming; his legs are broken. But I kept telling them: "Help my mom, help my mom!" Because she was still in the car. Later you realize the reason they're not doing anything is because she's already gone.

Somebody reached my dad at home by phone. They said, "There's been an accident, and your son is in the hospital, and he's okay." No mention of my mom. He had to drive to northern Westchester Hospital; he had to literally drive past the scene of the accident. So when he came up to the accident scene, he asked if there was a fatality. The cop said yes. When he arrived at the hospital, a doctor pulled him aside into a smaller side room. And before the doctor could say anything, my dad said: "My wife's dead, isn't she?"

My sister, Loren, is five years older than I am, and she was back in town from college for Thanksgiving. She was on a date that Friday night. When she finally got word and got to the hospital, it had become Saturday, her birthday. That morning my dad and sister came into my hospital room. And he said: "Mom didn't make it." I remember the words.

My sister eventually went back to college. It was just me and my dad. And every night, I would sit there at dinner, and my dad would have tears rolling down his face. He lost his partner, his best friend. I didn't want to cry in front of him because, right or wrong, I wanted to show strength. I was only 14.

As I did throughout my childhood, I devoted myself to playing sports—strong safety in football, catcher in baseball. I played baseball with a football mentality. What do I value the most? Toughness. Physical and mental toughness. I loved to hit people in football. I liked being involved, and as a catcher, you're involved with every pitch.

All these years later, I still gravitate to the players who epitomize toughness. That's why Colorado's DJ LeMahieu was easily one of my favorite players through the years. I value toughness in the highest regard—the mental and physical kind. Just ask my boys. I often say, I

Drew's Diary

April 6, 2018:
Atlanta Braves at Colorado Rockies

The Rockies' home opener is fit more for the Iditarod. After a one hour and one-minute delay, the first-pitch temperature amid snow flurries is 26, with a windchill factor of 19 degrees. Opening Day in baseball is like no other sport. It is a celebration of the dawning of a new season, a 50,000-fan raucous welcome mat for the returning stars, and, of course, the ushering in of the months of short sleeves and sunshine. German Marquez allows four in the first inning, and the Rockies fall 8–3 to the Atlanta Braves despite Carlos Gonzalez and Trevor Story hitting 440-plus foot home runs. The best line of the day comes prior to the game from Bud Black. Normally, his pregame press conference takes place in the dugout amid about eight to 10

Continued on next page

will take 25 guys at any level with a chip on their shoulder versus 25 "pretty" guys. LeMahieu is a chip-on-the-shoulder guy. He can find fuel from any slight, perceived or real, to ignite him. He has long tormented his former club, the Chicago Cubs, for choosing to go with Darwin Barney over him at second. LeMahieu is a vicious competitor without being outwardly emotional. In fact, LeMahieu is pretty quiet, but he'd probably be the guy most of his teammates would pick to go to battle with. And he's a winner. He won the batting title in 2016 (.348, while still hitting .303 on the road), two Gold Gloves, and a bunch of ballgames for the modern Rockies.

Continued from previous page

broadcasters and writers from various outlets. On Opening Day that group swells by about 15 to 20, and many will not make many more games the whole year. Because of the weather, the media scrum is moved into the new interview room, which resembles a shiny new classroom with work tables and a lectern in front. Black can't resist. He begins by joking, "Welcome to Econ 101, I will be handing out the syllabus in a couple of minutes."

It was perfect and had everyone sharing a good laugh. We thought it was humorous enough that we showed a clip of it in game on the broadcast. Our broadcast was uneventful—other than the challenge of attempting to stay somewhat warm. People ask, "Why don't you just close the windows on cold, inclement days?" The reason is two-fold. Your voice will bounce off the glass and not be as crisp going over the air, and I believe that with the window closed I am detached from the game. Thus, I have never in any sport done a game with the windows shut, no matter the weather. Our little oscillating heater on the floor provides a bit of warmth, but it took a couple of hours to thaw out when I got home.

I was proud of my high school baseball career. I was fortunate to win some awards, even MVP of the All-County Game, which featured several players who went on to play pro ball, and then I went upstate to Ithaca College to play ball and study communications. Ithaca recruited me to play both baseball and football. The school was a Division-III football and baseball power, but baseball, of course, was my first love. I made varsity baseball the fall of freshman year. Ithaca was the defending Division-III national champion. Eleven players from my era were drafted to play professionally. One of the team rules was no pick-up football.

Well, I was 18, it was my first fall away from football, and I couldn't resist. Sure enough, I broke my hand. That ended fall baseball and made for a very uncomfortable conversation with the head coach. In the spring I played on the junior varsity and did well, but ultimately I would fall out of favor during my sophomore year. I was at a crossroads. If I wanted to continue my baseball career, I would have to transfer. It was an extremely tough time for me in that I prioritized baseball at that time of my life. I knew I was at the right place from a career goals standpoint, but letting go of playing was excruciating.

I'd rubbed my coach the wrong way. It wasn't going to work in that particular baseball program. Looking back, I regret not having the courage to transfer to finish my college career. Of things I had control over, it was, to this day, the biggest regret of my life. It ate me up then, still eats at me today. But Ithaca was an ideal fit academically. I got to broadcast a community affair show and broadcast different sporting events, giving me a head start on my professional career. But you can only imagine how emotional it was to broadcast an Ithaca baseball game. In 1985 I got my first job in Aspen, Colorado. I haven't left the state since.

ACKNOWLEDGMENTS

This book could not have been completed without the diligent contributions from Tyler Kraft and Eli Lederman, as well as Bennett Durando, Edward Cameron Redler, Scott Mandziara, Kacen Bayless, and Mason Folz. Baseball-Reference.com, ESPN.com, *The Denver Post*, and *Sports Illustrated* were helpful references.

Thank you to Jeff Fedotin, Josh Williams, and all the other talented folks at Triumph Books. I sincerely appreciate their dedication and desire.

Thank you to the *St. Louis Post-Dispatch* sports editor, Roger Hensley. Thank you to Warren Miller and Jill Campbell.

And thank you to the Colorado Rockies—and to the fans of the Colorado Rockies.